Word Sorts and More

Solving Problems in the Teaching of Literacy

Cathy Collins Block, *Series Editor*

Word Sorts and More

Sound, Pattern, and Meaning Explorations K–3

KATHY GANSKE

THE GUILFORD PRESS
New York   London

A word is dead
When it is said,
Some say.

I say it just
Begins to live
That day.
—EMILY DICKINSON

■ ■ ■

© 2006 The Guilford Press
A Division of Guilford Publications, Inc.
72 Spring Street, New York, NY 10012
www.guilford.com

Printed in the United States of America

This book is printed on acid-free paper.

Last digit is print number: 9 8 7 6 5 4 3 2 1

Library of Congress Cataloging-in-Publication Data

Ganske, Kathy.
    Word sorts and more: Sound, pattern, and meaning explorations K–3 / Kathy
Ganske.
      p.   cm. — (Solving problems in the teaching of literacy)
    Includes bibliographical references and index.
    ISBN-13: 978-1-59385-050-0 (paper)
    ISBN-10: 1-59385-050-6 (paper)
    ISBN-13: 978-1-59385-309-9 (cloth)
    ISBN-10: 1-59385-309-2 (cloth)
    1. Reading (Kindergarten). 2. Reading (Primary). 3. Reading—Phonetic
method. 4. Word recognition. 5. English language—Orthography and spelling—
Study and teaching.   I. Title. II. Series.
    LB1181.2.G36 2006
    372.46′5—dc22

                         2005037027

About the Author

Kathy Ganske, PhD, is a professor in the Department of Reading at Rowan University in Glassboro, New Jersey, where she teaches graduate and undergraduate courses in literacy. She is a former classroom teacher of primary through upper-elementary grades. Kathy continues to be actively involved in classrooms through research and professional development work. She is the author of the best-selling *Word Journeys: Assessment-Guided Phonics, Spelling, and Vocabulary Instruction* (Guilford, 2000) and coauthor of the popular *Supporting Struggling Readers and Writers: Strategies for Classroom Intervention 3–6* (International Reading Association and Stenhouse, 2002).

Preface

This book is designed to help classroom teachers, tutors, reading specialists, and others who seek to improve children's understanding of how words work through categorization activities. It may be used to complement an existing phonics, spelling, reading, or writing program or serve as an adjunct to a resource such as my previously published book on word study, *Word Journeys: Assessment-Guided Phonics, Spelling, and Vocabulary Instruction* (Ganske, 2000). The latter includes research-based information for understanding and assessing students' word knowledge; practical and classroom-tested suggestions for engaging students in word studies, as well as tips for understanding various features of our English spelling system; and extensive word lists for use in activities and games.

Word Sorts and More: Sound, Pattern, and Meaning Explorations K–3 contains over 200 different word, picture, letter, and game-like sorts, spanning the emergent, letter name, and within word pattern spelling stages, with a few sorts that look ahead to the next stage: syllable juncture. More than 500 pictures have been incorporated into various sorts to aid the learning of emergent and novice readers and writers. Tips for using the sorts are offered, as well as a repertoire of basic activities to use with children at these stages of word knowledge, whether they are in the pre-K through third-grade range or are struggling readers and writers in the intermediate grades and beyond. *Word Sorts and More* is intended to save classroom teachers preparation time and energy; to enable them to help students develop their understanding of how our English spelling system works through hands-on, active learning; and to foster enjoyment and appreciation of our language.

Acknowledgments

I would like to thank the following people for their contributions: Diane M. Driessen, for the wonderful drawings that make the content of this book accessible and engaging for emergent and beginning readers and writers; Anthony Robb at Rowan University and Sandra Vázquez of St. Vrain Valley School District in Longmont, Colorado, for sharing their Spanish expertise; the many first graders who provided feedback on the drawings; the students and teachers who made title suggestions for the Literature Links; and the teachers featured in the Teacher to Teacher section, who generously shared their time and expertise.

I would also like to thank Chris Jennison, Senior Editor; Craig Thomas, Associate Editor; Anna Brackett, Editorial Project Manager; Paul Gordon, Art Director; and the rest of The Guilford Press staff for their insights and careful attention during the production process. Finally, many thanks to my husband, family, and friends, for the generous support and encouragement they have provided along the way.

Contents

List of Reproducible Pages

Appendix A

Appendix B

Appendix C

Appendix D

Appendix E

Part 1

Setting the Stage

The Context: What Is Word Study?

Though it is by no means a new term to describe the teaching and learning of how words work, use of the phrase *word study* has increased greatly over the past decade. It is an expression that has come to be used and described in different ways by different people. Because of the varied interpretations, I highlight those elements that I deem to be at the core of effective word study instruction and that form the basis for this teaching resource, as well as my earlier *Word Journeys* book (Ganske, 2000).

Frequently, word study connotes instruction that encompasses the areas of word identification (phonics, as well as the foundation-building work of phonological awareness), spelling, and vocabulary instruction. Such is the case with the word explorations described in this volume. However, because the "how" of teaching and learning can vary, I have created a mnemonic, THAT'S Word Study, to capture the essence of the word studies I describe in the pages of *Word Sorts and More*. The relevance of each of the key concepts is explained next.

> T = Thinking
> H = Humor
> A = Appropriate instruction
> T = Talk
> S = Systematic approach and some sorting

Thinking

Who would deny that memory plays a role in learning to read and write? However, effective word study instruction does not equal rote memorization. Estimates indicate that schoolchildren are exposed to nearly 90,000 different words in grades 3–9! If students are to be able to use more than a tiny fraction of these words, we must provide instruction that helps them to develop understandings about the sound, pattern, and meaning relationships of our language in ways that encourage them to generalize their understandings to other words so that word learning becomes efficient. This kind of instruction requires the students' active involvement and *thinking*. Knowledgeable teachers encourage these, realizing that even first graders can be "theory builders and hypothesis testers" (Ruddell & Unrau, 2004, p. 1463) of how words work.

When we plan activities that require students to carefully consider and conjecture about the ways words are alike and different, we also promote students' motivation. In the planning, it is important to reflect on just what the task entails and to ask, Is real thinking involved, or is this a task that students can complete with very little thought? Consider two scenarios.

Student A was asked to sort a set of word cards under the categories of "short" and "long *a*" and did so, as follows:

tag	bake
flap	shape
man	wade
jam	tame
had	whale
	late

All that the task really required was that the learner be able to visually separate out those words that end in *e* from those that do not. Because the task was primarily a visual one and did not oblige the student to connect the vowel sounds to the corresponding patterns, little thinking was involved. This reliance on the visual to the exclusion of sound can lead to problems. For instance, consider when the student needs to determine the spelling of a word during writing, and the relied-upon visual information is not available. Instead, it is the sounds that are accessible to the writer. Unfortunately for the student, because the task just described did not encourage association of the sounds with their patterns in memory, spelling of the word may difficult, if not impossible.

By contrast, consider Student B, who worked with the same set of words, but whose teacher approached the activity with concern that thinking be involved. To foster this, she did one or more of the following:

1. To encourage Student B to distinguish the two sounds, she first introduced the concepts of long and short *a* by using pictures for some or all of the words; then she asked students to pair up the words with their pictures to support a linking of the patterns and sounds.
2. She incorporated blind sorting (described later) into the activity routine so that at times the student had to consider the spelling of the words without the aid of visual cues.
3. She included in the sort one or two words with the same pattern but with an out-of-sync sound, such as *have* for the preceding sort, and then asked the student to consider sound and pattern as he sorted.

Including words such as *have* as "Oddballs" has the added benefit of reinforcing high-frequency words, as many of the most commonly used words sound different than their pattern suggests. Considering that 100 high-frequency words make up approximately 50% of all writing, their reinforcement is well worth attention. A second advantage of including Oddballs in a sort is the fact that their misplacement can alert teachers to students, like Student A, who are operating on "automatic pilot" and who, as a result, may later have difficulty transferring their understandings during writing or reading.

Humor

Word play, games, and other avenues for fostering appreciation of language provide opportunities for teachers to integrate humor into word-learning instruction. With the raising of standards and increases in classroom diversity, humor may be a more valuable attribute now than ever before. Although instruction needs to be deliberate and purposeful, a game-like quality can provide learners with pleasure and enhance their performance and learning (Krashen, 1994; Coles, 1998). Evidence for the importance of humor in the classroom can be found in recent investigations of the traits of most effective teachers, which reveal the use of humor among them (Block & Mangieri, 2003; McDermott & Rothenberg, 1999). In his work with second-language learners, Stephen Cary (2000) refers to the merits of a "Ha-Ha" factor for defusing learners' concerns and building their confidence and risk taking; the same view can be applied to struggling learners (Ganske, Monroe, & Strickland, 2003). We can easily find analogous situations in our own lives. For example, imagine being suddenly summoned to a meeting with a superior. Anxiety and a sense of distraction mount until the person begins the conversation with a joke or a short tale, relieving the tension and restoring our ability to concentrate.

Appropriate Instruction

Any observant teacher knows that students differ in their understandings of literacy. Many factors, including developmental, cultural, and language factors, can contribute to the diversity. Because word study is not a "one-size-fits-all" approach to instruction, we must come to understand students as learners and provide instruction that matches what they are ready to learn. In other words, we must teach to their *zone of proximal development* (Vygotsky, 1978). For word learning, observation and informal assessments such as the Developmental Spelling Analysis (DSA) provided in Chapter 2 of *Word Journeys* (Ganske, 2000) enable teachers to know which students are at which stage of spelling development and to identify those word features that children already understand (and thus do not need to be taught) and those that they are ready to learn, so that they may match instruction to the student. Without this, many children may not develop the necessary foundation on which to build increasingly complex understandings, because spelling knowledge advances from the one-to-one correspondences of letter–sound associations to increasingly more abstract pattern–sound relationships to, eventually, very complex interactions that involve sounds, patterns, and meanings. The sorting activities in *Word Sorts and More* primarily target those students who must learn to distinguish among units of sound and those who are ready to relate sounds to basic, as well as more complicated, patterns. Only a limited number of sorts in this volume introduce students to meaning-related issues (past-tense endings, plurals, and compound words). These higher level concerns will be the focus of the planned next volume, for more proficient readers and writers.

Talk

Making a conscious effort to integrate talk into word study through small-group and partner deliberations, collaborative learning opportunities, and one-to-one teacher/student "discovery discussions" (Block & Mangieri, 2003, p. 86) can yield double benefits. First, students are able to interact with others and to learn from them, which can increase motivation for an activity. Second, whether listener or participant, teachers are afforded opportunities to come to know their students better: how they approach word learning tasks, what confusions may be getting in the way of their learning, and which direction instruction needs to take next. The insights gained are sometimes surprising. For example, talk about a particular word may reveal that students are misconstruing its meaning, perhaps even confusing it with a word that has a similar pronunciation, such as *wait* for *wade* or *torn* for *thorn*. The Oddball category mentioned earlier opens the possibility for talk arising from dialect differences, as, for example, the talk that follows a child's placement of *then*, pronounced as *than*, in the Oddball, rather than the short *e*, category. Anecdotal notes are a wonderful way for teachers to keep a record of the understandings they acquire through talk.

Systematic Approach and Some Sorting

Systematic is another word that has been interpreted in various ways. Here I use the word to mean *preplanned, purposeful,* and that which *builds on what students already know.* It is not being equated with "lockstep." For example, just because a certain number of sorts are included for the teaching of a particular feature does not mean that all of them must be used every time the feature is taught. Teachers inform their instruction by assessing students' understandings with a dictated word inventory and by carefully heeding students' classroom performance. In addition, before choosing or rejecting a particular sort, they ask themselves these overarching questions: Do the children need this sort? Are they ready for this sort? Although the sorts and sequences used in this resource correspond to those laid out in the classroom-tested framework charts of *Word Journeys: Assessment-Guided Phonics, Spelling, and Vocabulary Instruction* (Ganske, 2000), they can easily be used without that text.

Let's also consider why *sorting* forms the basis for so many of the activities in *Word Sorts and More.* Categorizing is one of our most basic cognitive abilities, one that we use to develop concepts. Consider for a moment: We classify plants, animals, rocks, parts of speech, food groups, and so forth, and to help us determine category membership, we identify characteristics that distinguish one category from another. For example, *mammals* have hair, give birth, nurse their young, and are warm-blooded. We also note what it means to *not* be a mammal: Birds have feathers rather than hair, so birds are not mammals.

That we take the matter of categorization seriously can be seen in the way we also classify types of drivers' licenses, varieties of milk, difficulty levels of texts and ski slopes, laundry, fasteners such as nails and screws, dishes and utensils (even to the point of separating one type of knife or spoon from another), and the list goes on. So what else accounts for our fixation with sorting? We not only develop concepts through categorization, but we also organize the world around us. By arranging aspects of our everyday lives, we make retrieval of information and materials easier and thus more efficient. In a similar way, by categorizing words, students are able to be more effective in their word learning. English is a complex language, with borrowings from many other languages. When students compare and contrast word features, they notice similarities and differences within and across categories that help them, with teacher guidance, to form generalizations about how the words work. As previously noted, it is these generalizations that lend efficiency to word learning because they enable children to apply what they have discovered to the reading and writing of many other words.

A Basic Repertoire of Teaching Activities

What follows are descriptions of several activities that can be used with many of the materials in this resource to teach students about words. When these do not apply, other directions are provided. Additional activities and an expanded description of some of those in the basic repertoire may be found in *Word Journeys* (Ganske, 2000).

All Sorts of Sorts

Typically, a set of words is presented to students through a *closed sort.* This means that category key words or pictures provide a structure for the sort; the key words offer students clues as to how the words are grouped and what the chief characteristic of each category might be. Although teachers sometimes ask students to try their hand at sorting the words with just the key words as their guide, they usually provide direction and introduce the sort with guidance, such as through a *guided word walk* (Ganske, 2000). With this approach, teachers use modeling, demonstration, and some explicit telling, and they gradually release responsibility to students as the students become aware of how the categories work. After several weeks of completing word or picture sorts, children can often make accurate hypotheses about the characteristics of each category very quickly. They love the sense of accomplishment at having "figured it out." Sorting the remaining cards allows these children to confirm their hypotheses while providing less astute wordsmiths with further examples to clarify their understandings. Depending on the group of students, guided word walks can be carried out with greater or less teacher direction (see the examples with high, medium, and low levels of support that follow). It is good to keep in mind that too much telling will take away the challenges of exploring and thinking that add to motivation and that too little guidance may leave students confused and frustrated with the task. Keep a careful eye on students' reactions and their contributions to the talk that occurs during the initial sorting process; if they are responding correctly but with little enthusiasm, you are probably telling more than is needed. If they seem unclear about the task, you may need to be more explicit.

Once students are familiar with the sorting process, you can add excitement from time to time by asking them to decide how they think the words should be sorted before providing any key words or modeling. This type of *open sorting* is informative for you and engaging for the students, but due to its open nature, it can lead to widely different results than you may have expected. This can be problematic if you have particular categories in mind that you ultimately want the word cards sorted into. When open sorting is used, emphasize the importance of being able to articulate how the categories are alike and different. Also, as exceptions are introduced over time, help students to develop the idea that words (or pictures) that fit the characteristics of more than one category (or no category) should be set aside under the "?" label. Such words may be referred to by any number of names, from *Oddball* to *What's Up with That?* (See "Oddball Category Labels" in Appendix E for other name possibilities.)

Although each of the following guided word walks relies on words or pictures from a different stage of spelling knowledge, all three levels of teacher involvement can be applied to any of the sorts and thus to words at any spelling stage.

Guided Word Walk with a High Level of Support—Emergent Stage

A high level of support is evident in the teacher's identifying of each category at the start of the lesson and in the very explicit modeling and thinking aloud.

Focus: Alphabetic principle—Matching pictures with like beginning sounds to key pictures and their corresponding letter, *m* or *s*.

What is known: At least some understanding of the letter–sound relationship for one or both of the targeted consonants.

What is new: Contrasting the two consonants.

A guided word walk introduction to the sort shown in Figure 1, with much teacher support, would proceed something like this:

TEACHER: (*Places the* m *or* s *letter cards on the table in front of the children. Holds up the man picture.*) This is a picture of a man. *Mmman* begins with the /mmmm/ sound made by the letter *m*, so I'm going to put the *m* card next to man. (*Holds up the sock picture.*) And this is a

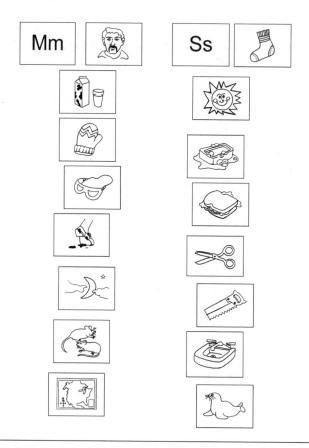

FIGURE 1. Guided word walk at the emergent stage with a high level of support.

picture of a sock. *Sssock* begins with the /ssss/ sound made by the letter *s*, so I'm going to put the *s* card next to the sock picture. Now I'm going to take the other pictures that I have today, and I'm going to put all of those that start with the /mmm/ sound like *man* under the picture of the man and the *m* card (*points to the cards*), and I'm going to put the ones that begin with the /sss/ sound like *sock* under that picture and the *s* (*points to the cards*). Keep your eyes right here, because I may need your help. (*Taking a picture, such as* milk) Here is a picture of milk. Let me see, *milk* begins with /mmm/, *mmmilk*, so I'm going to put this picture under mmman, because *milk* also starts with *m*. (*Taking another picture card*) This is a picture of the sun. *Sssun* begins with the same sound as *sssock*, so I'm going to put this picture under sock. *Sock . . . sun.* Both of these words begin with the letter *s*.

A similar process is used with the other picture cards. Sometimes two or three pictures that belong in the same category are presented one after the other, so the children don't incorrectly conclude that first a word is placed in one category and then the next word is placed in the other. After several words have been modeled, if students seem to be catching on, the teacher may ask the students to name the next picture and then invite a volunteer to place it under its category, reminding the child, if necessary, to name the picture and the key picture/letter, as it is placed. Errors are corrected immediately by saying something like "No, actually, *mmmask* goes under man, because it begins with the /mmm/ sound that the letter *m* makes, just like *mmman* does."

After the modeling and sorting, the teacher reviews each of the categories by asking students to join her in naming the key picture and its beginning letter and then each picture in the *m* category. Review of the *s* category is carried out in a similar fashion. With both categories, the teacher releases responsibility to the students to the greatest extent possible by fading her voice away.

If time allows, "Guess What Letter" may be used to engage students in a quick practice. The key pictures and their corresponding letters are placed in front of the children, and the remaining cards are gathered and shuffled. Showing the first card, the teacher asks, "Does this word start with *m* or *s*; does (*name the picture*) begin with the sound of *m* like *mmman*, or *s* like *sssock*?" Students respond by naming the letter or saying "*m* like *man*" with some children, the teacher may be able to distribute the cards among them and have them take turns placing a card and identifying its letter.

Guided Word Walk with a Moderate Level of Support—Letter Name Stage

In the following example, to provide a moderate level of support, the teacher models and demonstrates but does less explicit telling. Although students are asked to match their word to one of the key words, the teacher does not specifically point out that the words rhyme or that the rhyming part is spelled the same (*at*, *et*, or *ot*). The word identification/vocabulary component described is important for any guided word walk. It ensures that students recognize and understand the meanings of the words they are using so that they can focus their attention on the feature that is being taught rather than on deciphering words. It can also build students' vocabulary knowledge *and* inform your teaching. Any words or pictures that prove to be troublesome should just be omitted from the sort.

Focus: Differentiating words of different vowel word families: *at*, *et*, and *ot*.

What is known: Each of the word families has previously been studied but only in contrast with other word families containing the same vowel.

What is new: Examining families of words across different vowels. The rime (vowel and what follows) is consistent within a category but shifts across the categories, so that students begin to consider differences in vowels. An introduction to the sort shown in Figure 2, with a moderate level of teacher support, would proceed something like this:

TEACHER: Today we're going to revisit some of the rhyming words we've worked with before. But first, let's be sure you know all of the words and pictures we'll be using. (*Shows each of the cards to the students by panning it across the group and saying . . .*) Tell me all together: What's this word? [Or picture. Discuss any word meanings that may be unfamiliar to students or that could be confused with another word. For example . . .] Who can tell us what the word *trot* means?

STUDENT VOLUNTEER: A horse can trot.

TEACHER: Yes, a horse can trot. It's the way horses sometimes move when they're going quickly. People sometimes trot, too. For example, if you jogged around the playground, we could also say you *trotted* around the playground. Can someone show us what that would be like? (*Student demonstrates.*) Here's another word I want to be sure you understand. (*Holds up* vet.) This word is a short way of saying *veterinarian*. Who knows what a *vet* or *veterinarian* is?

STUDENT VOLUNTEER: It's kind of like a doctor, but it's for animals.

TEACHER: Good job! That's just what a vet is, and I like the way you told us without using the word *vet*. That helps me to really understand what that word means. (*A brief discussion of*

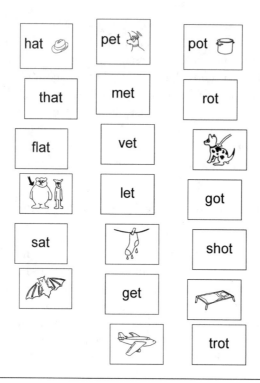

FIGURE 2. Guided word walk at the letter name stage with moderate support.

the children's experiences with vets follows.) This next picture may be confusing. (*Holds up the jet.*) Can anyone tell us what this picture is? Be careful, and look closely.

STUDENT VOLUNTEER: It's an airplane.

TEACHER: That's true; it is an airplane, but it's a special kind of airplane.

ANOTHER STUDENT VOLUNTEER: It's a jet. See this? (*Points to under the wing.*) That's how I know.

TEACHER: Yes, it's a jet. Can everyone say *jet*? [If confusion with this picture is anticipated, it could be compared with a plane picture.]

STUDENTS: Jet.

Identification of the words and pictures continues, with discussions of word meanings as necessary. Then the teacher introduces the sort.

TEACHER: (*Places the three key word/picture cards in front of the students. Pointing*) Our key words and their pictures today are: *hat, at, at; pet, et, et;* and *pot, ot, ot.* As we try to decide where to put each word, I want you to say the new word and listen carefully for a key word that matches its sound. Watch me first. (*Takes a card.*) Rot. . . . Rot/hat . . . rot/pet . . . rot/pot. I'm going to put *rot* under *pot.* (*Taking another card.*) That. . . . That/hat. . . . that/pet . . . that/pot. I'm going to put *that* with *hat.*

Modeling continues with *met* and as many additional words and/or pictures as are needed before students begin to understand how the sort works. As this happens, they become involved in placing the words under their appropriate category, remembering to say the name of the key words as they try to find the best category match. Incorrect matches are corrected immediately with something like, "No, remember, this word is *wet*, so it goes under *pet*." Before asking students to describe their thoughts about the categories, the teacher might ask them to read through each sorted column of words so that they can hear the repeated rime.

TEACHER: How are all of the words and pictures alike that we placed under *hat*?

STUDENT: They rhyme with *hat*.

TEACHER: That's an excellent observation. Do you notice anything else?

STUDENT: All of the words end in *at*. See: *at*, *at*, *at*.

TEACHER: Very good. That's another excellent observation. Now let me ask you: If all the words end in *at*, what about the pictures? For example, *fat*: How do you think *fat* is spelled?

STUDENT: (*Excitedly*) That's *at*, too, *f-a-t*.

STUDENT: And *bat* is *b-a-t*.

TEACHER: That's right. (*Summarizing*) So, all of the words under *hat* rhyme with *hat*, and they all end with *a-t*. Let's look at the "pet" category. What can you tell me about these words?

The talk continues with this and the final category. If time allows, students might play a game of Hold-It (see *Word Journeys*, Ganske [2000]), Chapter 3) to allow the teacher to check their understanding of the sort, or students might be asked to spell another word with one of the same rimes used in the lesson, for example, *brat* or *bet*.

Guided Word Walk with a Low Level of Support—Within Word Pattern Stage

Less support is evident in this sort, as the teacher models with some of the word cards and tells the children that they are categorizing by sound and pattern but does not explicitly identify anything about how the words are alike and different. As with the previous example, attention to developing vocabulary knowledge is incorporated.

Focus: Understanding pattern–sound differences among the following vowels: short *a*, long *a* spelled VC*e*, and *r*-controlled vowels with the *ar* pattern.

What is known: Short *a* and long *a* with VC*e*

What is new: R-controlled vowels and the *ar* pattern

The guided word walk introduction to this sort, which is shown in Figure 3, with low-level teacher support would proceed something like this:

TEACHER: Let's start by making sure you all know the words we're going to be working with this week.

The teacher shows students the cards, one at a time, by panning them across the group. Once everyone has seen a word, she asks the students to chorally identify the word, listening for the off-key note of someone who doesn't recognize it. When this occurs, she asks a student to identify the word and then tucks the card back in the stack to return to it again. She stops for two or three of

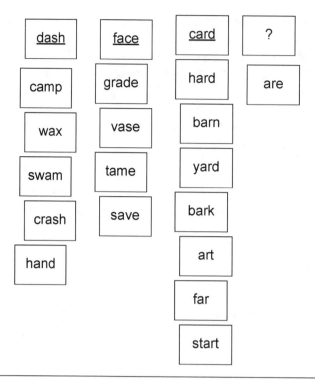

FIGURE 3. Guided word walk at the within word pattern stage with limited support.

the words to engage the students in talk about their meanings. Except for, possibly, *tame*, none of the words seems likely to cause confusion, so after verifying students' understanding of the word, she decides to expand their vocabulary knowledge by focusing the talk on words that have multiple meanings.

TEACHER: What can you tell me about *tame*? What does it mean?

STUDENT: Not wild.

TEACHER: That's right. *Tame* and *wild* are opposites, and they're words that are often used to describe animals. Can you think of a wild animal?

STUDENT: Lions are wild, and so are bears.

TEACHER: Yes, and what would be an example of a tame animal?

STUDENT: Cats and dogs are tame. . . .

STUDENT: (*Interrupting*) But sometimes they act wild. My cat runs around our house sometimes, and my mom says she's being wild and crazy.

TEACHER: When your cat or another animal acts tame, what's that like?

STUDENT: She's really gentle, and sits on my lap or rubs on my leg.

TEACHER: So tame means gentle and not wild. What about this word? (*Holds up* dash.)

STUDENTS: Dash.

TEACHER: Yes, tell me what it means.

STUDENT: The 100-yard dash.

TEACHER: Now can you tell me what that is without using the word *dash*? What is the 100-yard *dash*?

STUDENT: (*Thinking*) It's a race that you run really fast.

TEACHER: So if I dash off to the grocery store, I'm going really fast. Does anyone know any other meanings for *dash*?

STUDENT: When my grandmother eats scrambled eggs at our house, she always says, "I'll have a dash of hot pepper to go with them."

TEACHER: What do you think she means by that?

STUDENT: That stuff's really hot, so she means just a little.

TEACHER: That's right. When you eat French fries, do you want a dash of ketchup, or a lot?

STUDENT: A lot, because that ketchup's good, not hot.

TEACHER: You know a lot about *dash*. It can mean to run really fast, and it can mean a very small amount of something. Do you know any other meanings? (*Picks up the class read-aloud and points to a dash in the text.*) This is another meaning for *dash*. This punctuation mark is called a *dash*. Sometimes it's used in books to show a break, like here. The character has been interrupted, so the author put a dash to let the reader know that. *Dash* is a word I may want to put on *my* word wall,* to remind myself to look for ways to help you use that word. (*Continues asking students to identify the words, stopping to ask about the meanings of two more words:* bark *and* yard. *Then she begins the word walk.*)

Today we're going to be sorting by *sound and pattern*. So, remember, if a card belongs in a category, it will have the same sound and the same pattern as the key word. I've included a question mark in case any of our words doesn't fit in a category or in case any fit in more than one category. I've underlined the key words, so we can use the same key words in our work all week. They are *dash, face,* and *card.* Let's see . . . (*taking a card*) grade goes with *face,* so I'll put it here, and *camp* goes with . . . hmmm . . . camp/dash . . . camp/grade . . . no, that one's not right . . . . Camp/card . . . that's not right either. . . . camp/dash. *Camp* goes with *dash,* so I'm going to put it under that word.

As several children have raised their hands to try the next word, the modeling stops, and the teacher hands over a card to one of the volunteers. Students continue placing the cards. As the student with *are* begins to place the word under *card,* another student protests.

STUDENT: I disagree. *Are* sounds like *card,* but it has a different pattern. All the other words have *ar,* and *are* has an *e* on the end, just like *face,* but it doesn't sound like /ā/, so I think it's an Oddball.

ANOTHER STUDENT: Me, too. It's an Oddball.

STUDENT: Yeah, I think so, too; it's an Oddball.

The teacher continues to present words for the children to sort. After the last card is placed, she engages the students in the Think-Pair-Share strategy. First, she asks the students to think about the categories and how they are alike and different. Then, after a minute or two, she tells them to pair up with a partner and to tell the partner what they think and then listen while the

---

*A description of a Teacher Word Wall is included on page 13.

partner does likewise. The teacher allows about a minute for each partner to talk and then draws the group together by saying, "Now let's share your ideas with the group. How about the category headed with *dash*?" A discussion follows in which the students comment on each column of words. When necessary, the teacher adds to the conversation or clarifies thinking.

The session ends with students being asked to spell an alien word, such as *sar*, *vade*, *har*, and *fam*. As with these examples, the alien words are usually either real words that the children are just not familiar with yet or are syllables of longer real words, like *sarcasm*, *invade*, *harbor*, and *family*.

Blind Sorting

When this approach to categorizing is used, students make decisions about the placement of words without actually seeing the words. They are presented with the key words and point to the appropriate category (or write their response under the key word on a piece of paper, if the sort is also a writing sort), as a partner reads each word aloud. Once the category decision has been made, accuracy of the placement (and spelling of the word in the case of a written sort) is checked. When the task is completed, partners reverse their roles and begin again.

Speed Sorts

This type of sort is geared toward developing automaticity so that children can devote their mental energy to meaningful writing and reading, rather than to encoding and decoding words. The process is easy: Teachers provide students with repeated opportunities to practice sorting the week's words in order to acquire speed and accuracy. Challenges to "Beat the Teacher" or to improve a previous attempt keep learners motivated.

Word, Object, or Letter Hunts

To apply their understandings about words, teachers sometimes ask students to search for other examples with the same targeted features. This type of activity can be carried out in small-group, collaborative-group, partner, or in some cases whole-class formats. Emergent learners may search for examples of particular letters from cut-up magazines and newspapers. Emergent or letter name spellers may scavenge the classroom for objects whose names begin with particular consonants. Letter name and within word pattern spellers may search through text they have read or written for examples of other words with the targeted features.

Practice and Applying Activities

Additional practice can be provided through a variety of notebook activities, such as those described in Chapter 3 of *Word Journeys* (Ganske, 2000). For example, students might draw and label pictures with the features under study, write sentences for a few of the words and draw pictures and write labels for some of the others, or use letter tiles to make words and then record them. They might also carry out *word operations* to create new words by adding to the original, subtracting from it, or substituting one part for another. New words can also be generated through the use of analogy: "I know that *fit* is *f-i-t*, so *slit* must be *s-l-i-t*." Folder games and card games are further possibilities. Whatever the activities offered to students as options, once they have been introduced to a new set of words and the targeted features, they need many opportunities to practice and to exercise their understandings through meaningful reading and writing experiences.

Teacher Word Walls: A New Perspective on a Common Technique

Word walls are a common sight in today's elementary classroom, especially in the primary grades, and they are easy to spot, with their brightly colored alphabet letters and the myriad words that typically accompany them spread across a wall or bulletin board. Their popularity is epitomized by the recent comment of a curriculum coordinator who shared with me that even a physical education instructor in her district had found means to incorporate use of a word wall. As a tool of reference, they serve students well in their writing, especially if the wall is not so cluttered that words are difficult to locate. In a similar vein, they can provide *teachers* with an excellent reference tool, not for writing but for reinforcing vocabulary words.

We must not underestimate the importance of developing children's general vocabulary knowledge. Readers are taught to decode unfamiliar words encountered in text with the expectation that the resulting word will map onto the learner's oral vocabulary and be "recognized." However, if the word is not in the learner's oral vocabulary, nothing will be gained from either the reader's decoding effort or the teacher's efforts to help the student learn word recognition strategies. The report of the National Reading Panel (2000) describes oral vocabulary as "a key to learning to make the transition from oral to written forms" and reading vocabulary as "crucial to the comprehension processes of a skilled reader" (pp. 4–15). The report also makes clear that multiple exposures to the words in various contexts are essential for learning them.

Thus, for words that are important to children's vocabulary knowledge and that arise through reading, word studies, or talk—especially those that are unfamiliar at present but are likely to be encountered frequently in the future (referred to as Tier 2 words by Beck, McKeown, and Kucan [2002])—we must find and create opportunities for students to visit and revisit these words in meaningful contexts so that they begin to "make them their own." The word *dash* discussed in the previous guided word walk, for example, might be such a word, as perhaps might *exhausted* or *fatigued* as synonyms for *tired*. A Teacher's Word Wall might consist of 10 to 15 such words printed on large cards or sentence strips and posted on a wall that is visible to the teacher most of the day. Posting of the words provides busy teachers with a quick and constant reminder that these words need to be used and called to children's attention on a frequent basis. Once a word starts to be assimilated into classroom use, its word card can be replaced with a different one. As with the word walls teachers create for students' use, too many words will decrease its utility. Although primarily intended as a teacher reminder, I have sometimes discovered children glancing at the wall and calling their teacher's attention to a prime opportunity for using the word! Whether for first grade or seventh grade, Teacher Word Walls have much to offer.

Using Syllabication and Morphology to Solve Word Problems

We often tell students to break words into syllables, to look for meaningful chunks, and to use context clues with the available letter–sound clues to figure out unfamiliar words. I suspect that all too often children are asked to do so without the benefit of having been taught just how to go about it. We need to *teach* strategies such as these and provide lots of opportunities for students to put them into practice under our guidance.

Syllabication

Teaching readers a few useful tips such as those that follow for dividing two-syllable words can be useful, because knowing how to separate longer words into syllables enables readers to work with more manageable chunks when decoding an unfamiliar word. If care is taken in the kinds of words chosen for practice or example, many students will learn quite early on to apply the strategy to their reading of words.

Tip 1. Common compound words such as the following provide an effective starting point, because children can be taught to look for known words: *doghouse, sidewalk, weekend, bathroom, classroom, fireman, football, mailbox, playground, hallway, afternoon.*

Tip 2. Teach students to keep a watchful eye out for double consonants. There are many such twins in the middle of words, and the syllable division is made between them. Although students are likely to read vowels in unstressed syllables as long or short vowels rather than with the schwa sound (pronounced /uh/), they will still likely recognize many of these words, provided the words are in their oral vocabulary: *puppet, traffic, passage, muffin, village,* and *sudden.*

Tip 3. Even when there are two consonants in the middle of the word that aren't twins, it is usually a good idea to try dividing the word between them: *cactus, insect, contest, pretzel, publish.*

Tip 4. Sometimes three consonants are clustered in the middle of a word. In such cases, two of the consonants will be a blend or digraph (such as *th, ch, gr, dr, pl, st,* etc.). Just as elsewhere in words, these teams usually stick together, so the division is not likely to be made between them: *athlete, merchant, pilgrim, hundred, complete, instant,* and so forth.

Tip 5. Where only one consonant appears between two vowels in the middle of a word, break the word before the consonant, give the vowel before it a long sound, and check to see whether this results in a recognizable word. An effective way to help children think about such open syllables is to use the analogy that vowels can be rather shy guys, and when left alone at the end of a syllable, they often cry out their name in fright, similar to the way a person might cry out if left alone in a room with the door open: *hotel, bacon, fever, humid, detour,* and *event.*

Tip 6. If the use of Tip 5 does not lead to a recognizable word, students should divide the word after the consonant and give the vowel a short sound. Again, the door analogy may be applied: The shy vowel feels safe and quiets its voice down when the opening is closed with a consonant: *comet, credit, talent, vanish,* and *manage.*

The preceding tips should be introduced one at a time, with lots of opportunity for practice, so students can gain control over the use of a particular strategy before being presented with a new one. Teachers can provide practice in an engaging way by challenging students, as a whole class or during small-group instruction, to decode a word-of-the-day. (See the boxed section on "Word-of-the-Day Decoding Practice with Syllabication" on the facing page.)

Morphology

Recognition of *morphemes,* or meaningful word parts, such as common prefixes, suffixes, and base words can also help students to decode unfamiliar words, words that may be composed of even more than two syllables. Consider the following example:

TEACHER: (*Writes* mistreating *on the board and thinks aloud.*) This is a pretty long word. Sometimes we can break words like this into smaller chunks that are easier to handle by looking to see if we recognize any meaningful chunks, just like we did with compound words. But

Word-of-the-Day Decoding Practice with Syllabication

The following lists of words, grouped by decoding tip and vowel pattern so teachers can control the complexity of the words they choose, may be used to model decoding strategies, as well as to engage students in solving words using the strategies. Students might also enjoy decoding names of well-known people and characters from children's books or decoding and then locating the names of cities in various parts of the United States. Morphology can be incorporated into the activity, and longer words can be created by adding a suffix and/or prefix to some of the words in the list, for example: *bordering, harvesting, incomplete, profitable, punishment, remodel,* and *sincerely.*

Tip 1: Compounds
SV: *bedbug, blacksmith, blacktop, catnip, catnap, eggshell, handspring, windmill, upset*
SLV: *bedtime, classmate, goldfish, handshake, landslide, seasick, weekend, windshield*
SLRAV: *birthstone, downpour, courtyard, earthquake, fireproof, nightmare, proofread, raindrop, throughout, warehouse, windstorm*

Tip 2: Words with Double Consonants (words may contain a schwa vowel)
SV: *attic, blossom, classic, comment, gallon, hammock, inning, muffin, stopping, tennis, traffic*
SLV: *cabbage, caddy, dizzy, follow, hollow, message, shallow, suffice, trolley, valley, willow*
SLRAV: *blizzard, blubber, cheddar, effort, guffaw, pattern, raccoon, slipper, suffer*
Note: Some students may need to have pointed out to them that final *y* and *ey* sound like long e.

Tip 3: Words with Two Consonants (words may contain a schwa vowel)
SV: *absent, album, cactus, contact, husband, napkin, picnic, plastic, pretzel, trumpet, victim*
SLV: *chimney, compose, confuse, costume, invite, reptile, rescue, texture, umpire*
SLRAV: *absorb, admire, border, cartoon, disturb, furnish, harvest, injure, lantern, mustard, observe, orbit, pardon, percent, perfume, scarlet, shelter, sincere, urgent, whimper*

Tip 4: Words with Three Consonants (words may contain a schwa vowel)
SV: *district, dolphin, express, hundred, inspect, nostril, pilgrim, pumpkin.* Also, double consonants plus *le:* If needed, point out to students the /l/ sound of *le;* the final syllable is *consonant-le: baffle, cattle, cuddle, drizzle, fiddle, huddle, pebble, scribble, sniffle, snuggle, truffle, wiggle*
SLV: *athlete, complete, conclude, control, exchange, explain, include*
SLRAV: *although, farther, marshal, merchant, monster, orchard, panther, portrait, surprise*

Tip 5: Words with VCV Open Syllables (words may contain a schwa vowel)
SLV: *agent, bacon, basic, bison, crisis, frequent, human, legal, pupil, rodent, sequel, siren, virus*
SLRAV: *acorn, crater, detour, female, flavor, major, navy, profile, radar, rotate, secure, vapor*
Note: Words with two consonants are sometimes also open: *April, migrate, program.*

Tip 6: Words with VCV Closed Syllables (words may contain a schwa vowel)
SV: *balance, cabin, camel, civil, credit, digit, finish, frigid, honest, legend, limit, mimic, model, novel, profit, rapid, satin, talon, timid, topic, punish, visit, vomit*
SLV: *figure, manage, refuge, volume*
SLRAV: *cavern, clever, forest, govern, jury, lizard, plural, rural*

Key
SV = Short vowels; **SLV** = Short and long vowels; **SLRAV** = Short, long, *r*-controlled, and abstract vowels.

this time, the chunk might not be a whole word. For example, I see *ing* on the end of this word. I know that it's found at the end of a lot of words, like *looking, reading, flying, show-ing,* and so forth, and it's pronounced /ĭng/, so I'm going to just cover that part up, because I know how to say that. (*Covers up the letters with a sticky note.*) Now, let's see, what about the rest? I see a word I know—*t-r-e-a-t,* /trēt/. (*Peels the sticky note off again.*) So the last part of the word is *treating,* and that leaves only the beginning. (*Drawing her finger under the letters as she names them*) I think *m-i-s* is also in quite a few words, like *misspell* . . . and *misuse,* . . . and *misplace* . . . and *misread*—" (*Writes each word on the board as she thinks aloud.*)

STUDENT: —And *misbehave.* My mom always says it's bad to misbehave at school.

TEACHER: Good example. . . . So *m-i-s* seems to be another meaningful chunk, and we pro-nounce it /mĭs/. Now we've got all the chunks and we can put them together, *mistreating.* Does anyone know what *mistreating* means? Our story reads: *The man was mistreating the horse.*

STUDENT: I think he wasn't treating the horse right, because when I misspell a word, I'm not spelling it right.

TEACHER: Good thinking. So if we misuse a tool, we don't use it right. And if we misplace a book, we don't put it in the right place; we put it in the wrong place. What about *misread*?

STUDENT: You read the wrong word.

TEACHER: M-*i-s* seems like a chunk we may come across again in our reading.

Using Context and Letter–Sound Clues: A Balancing Act

An effective way to teach children to take advantage of both the available letters and sounds *and* the surrounding text is with the use of sticky notes, a passage of text or a summary of a passage, and a whiteboard or chalkboard (Strickland, Ganske, & Monroe, 2002). The summary segment that follows is based on a delightful picture book by A. U'Ren titled simply *Mary Smith.* The "knocker-up" custom described has a historical basis, and the book has a surprise ending.

TEACHER: (*Records a short passage of text, covers up a few key words with sticky notes, keeping the covered lengths of similar size, and numbers the sticky notes as shown in* Figure 4; *then says*) Good readers are good word solvers. Just like a good detective uses all available clues to solve a mystery, good readers use available clues to help them solve word difficulties. They use letter–sound clues [you might also mention syllable divisions and meaningful word parts, if these have been studied] and the rest of the words in the sentence to help them figure out unfamiliar words. I've written a paragraph on the board that is about a story I'm going to read aloud later today. It's called *Mary Smith.* So that you will really concentrate on *context clues,* which are the clues we get from the other words in the sentence, I've cov-ered up a few of the words to see what you can discover just by using the context. You don't have the letters and sounds to give you any hints, but don't worry; I'll let you use those clues, too, just not yet. Let's read to the end of the sentence that has the first cov-ered-up word in it and decide what word makes sense where the sticky note is. [Reading may be choral, by individual volunteers, or silent, depending on the group of students.] Who has a guess for word #1?

The students offer *day, morning,* and *night.* The last idea spurs comments of disagreement, as students note that you "don't get up early at night." The student withdraws the suggestion, and the

Mary Smith lived long ago. She had a very unusual job. Every ▮1▮ Mary got up early and walked into town. She walked and walked, because it was a long way. As she went by the houses of sleeping people, she stopped to ▮2▮ them up. Did Mary shout? Did she ▮3▮ on the door? No. Mary took out a pea and put it in her peashooter. She hit the window with her pea. She hit it again and again until someone got up. Then she went on to the ▮4▮ house. All went well until Mary ▮5▮ home.

FIGURE 4. Balancing word recognition clues.

teacher asks students to continue reading to the end of the sentence with the second covered-up word. The process of speculating and discussion continues with the remaining masked words.

> TEACHER: Now that you've been careful to think of words that make good sense in the story for the places I've covered up, I'm going to remove some of the sticky notes, so that you can see the beginning letters for each word. If some of the guesses don't match the letters that are shown, I'm going to cross them off, because those words can't be correct.

One by one, the teacher reveals the onset of each word (see Figure 5), and the students compare the results with their guesses. If no guesses remain for a particular word after this process, new possibilities must be generated by the group. Similarly, students will need to review any words that have more than one guess remaining in order to choose the best candidate. When all of the covered words have been dealt with in this manner, the teacher reveals the correct words by removing the remaining sticky notes, as shown in Figure 6, and the group discusses any remaining errors. The teacher closes the lesson by reiterating the importance of using both context clues and letter–sound clues when solving words and by letting the children know that they will have more opportunities to try to discover the identities of hidden words.

Mary Smith lived long ago. She had a very unusual job. Every **m**▮1▮ Mary got up early and walked into town. She walked and walked, because it was a long way. As she went by the houses of sleeping people, she stopped to **w**▮2▮ them up. Did Mary shout? Did she **kn**▮3▮ on the door? No. Mary took out a pea and put it in her peashooter. She hit the window with her pea. She hit it again and again until someone got up. Then she went on to the **n**▮4▮ house. All went well until Mary **r**▮5▮ home.

FIGURE 5. Balancing word recognition clues.

Mary Smith lived long ago. She had a very unusual job. Every **morning** Mary got up early and walked into town. She walked and walked, because it was a long way. As she went by the houses of sleeping people, she stopped to **wake** them up. Did Mary shout? Did she **knock** on the door? No. Mary took out a pea and put it in her peashooter. She hit the window with her pea. She hit it again and again until someone got up. Then she went on to the **next** house. All went well until Mary **returned** home.

FIGURE 6. Balancing word recognition clues (version with words revealed).

The following section presents eight teachers who offer suggestions for other teachers based on their own successful practices in the classroom.

Teacher to Teacher: Tips from Teachers for Teachers

Lynn Dobbs, Pre-kindergarten Teacher, Dade County Schools, Georgia

With the help of an assistant, Lynn teaches 20 four-year-olds at Davis Elementary School in Trenton, Georgia; her all-day pre-K class is one of many in the state. The children's literacy levels vary greatly, so in addition to whole-class activities, Lynn incorporates small-group instruction.

The whole-class gathering time typically focuses on oral-language development and on increasing children's comprehension and concept-of-print knowledge. Books like *Five Little Monkeys Jumping on a Bed* by Eileen Christelow provide opportunities for the children to learn math concepts; to demonstrate comprehension through predicting, visualizing, sequencing, and acting out the story; to show concept-of-print understandings; to write a new version of the tale; and to engage in talk. Nursery rhymes offer many similar opportunities: each month Lynn's students learn a new rhyme and eagerly anticipate their turn to recite the rhyme to the rest of the class with a microphone.

Many of her students are three-year-olds when they start pre-K, so one of Lynn's initial aims for the large-group meeting time is just to get them to talk. She then also helps them learn new words to clarify or expand their understandings of known words. Lynn suggests that teachers "be excited about vocabulary, and teach big words; the children love it." The importance of such words to children is evident in the following vignette:

During a review of the letter *m* and its sound, a kindergarten teacher asked the children to name some words that start with /m/ and the letter *m*. After several children shared words like *man, mop,* and *monkey,* a little girl offered *metamorphosis.* Needless to say, the teacher was taken by surprise, and asked the girl where she had learned such a big word. "Ms. Dobbs taught me that," was the prompt reply, and indeed Lynn had made the word memorable by introducing it as part of a study of the life cycle and raising of butterflies.

Center time affords more opportunities for Lynn to build language. For example, one of her centers is a restaurant, complete with a variety of props. In preparation for children's use of the center, Lynn and the children create a list of restaurant-related words: *waitress, cashier, customer,* and so forth. The words are discussed and posted, then used by the children in the context of play as they work at or visit the restaurant.

Phonemic awareness and learning to listen for sounds are other areas that receive much attention in Lynn's class. Lynn knows that the children won't be able to distinguish differences in letter sounds unless they can discern differences in other types of sounds, so she incorporates many kinds of listening activities into the whole-class and small-group sessions. For example, she asks children to close their eyes and listen carefully as she drops pennies into a can and the children count them. She also asks them to listen for differences in tape-recorded sounds of everyday life: a cat meowing, a toilet flushing, or a pencil sharpener grinding. First the children listen to identify just one sound; then Lynn presents them with the much more difficult task of identifying two sounds played one after another. The students also practice listening, and they learn and review the alphabet, by engaging in Sing Your Way to [name of an alphabetic letter], an activity in which children sing the alphabet song up to a designated letter, then stop. Although the task may sound easy, it offers considerable challenge to emergent learners.

Some of the other activities used with certain children during small-group sessions include (1) sorting pictures according to sound; (2) playing sound games like Same or Different, in which children are presented orally with two names (or shown two pictures) and asked to decide whether the words begin the same or are different; (3) a blending-game variation of Simon Says (Lynn: "Simon says *j—ump*; what did Simon say?" Response: *jump*); and (4) activities in which the children create variations to the nursery rhymes they are learning, for example, when studying "Humpty Dumpty," the children change lines to such silly results as "Humpty Dumpty sat on a pear; Humpty Dumpty had curly hair."

To help prepare the children for categorizing pictures by sound, Lynn engages them in concept sorting with pictures, as described in Part 2 of this book. One activity that the children particularly like revolves around a reading of *Gregory the Terrible Eater* by Mitchell Sharmat, a story about Gregory the goat who likes to eat the food of humans rather than the expected cans, shoestrings, old tires, and the like. After reading the book, Lynn presents the children with pictures of "good food" and "bad food," and the children must choose the appropriate category for each picture. Children are active learners and thinkers in Lynn's class, with much enjoyment had by all in the process.

Helen Upperman, Reading Specialist, Washington Township School District, New Jersey

Helen is one of two reading specialists at Grenloch Terrace Early Childhood Center, which has more than 500 kindergarteners. Her role is to assist classroom teachers in promoting literacy. To do so, in addition to working with children, Helen often models lessons and coaches teachers in the classroom. There are 13 classroom teachers, but because the district provides a half-day program, there are actually 26 sessions. Helen works with 7 of the teachers and 14 classes of children. With that many teachers and groups of students, Helen has to be very organized for word study. She may be working with one group that does not recognize any letters of the alphabet, with another that may be able to distinguish the beginning sound of a word but not the ending, or with another that may be able to discern differences in vowel sounds but be uncertain as to which letters make which sound. Keeping track of the various groups presents a major challenge.

To solve the problem, Helen uses 5- × 7-inch manila envelopes to keep the materials together, and because the envelopes require limited storage space, they can be left in the classroom for students to practice with when she is not there. On the outside of the envelope, Helen writes the child's name, the child's teacher and session, and the skill being emphasized (such as short *a*/short *o*). Each time she works with the group of students, she records the date, activity, and a brief comment regarding the child's performance on the outside. An envelope might look like the following:

John Doe

Ms. Jones AM

11/4 Introduced short a and o. John seemed to hear differences and was able to sort with only 2 errors. He needed assistance in correcting.

11/11 Reviewed short a and o. Patterns are being discussed in the classroom; John made a pattern using a short a picture, then a short o picture. Made no errors in pattern.

11/18 Did quick sort. Using uncut sheet, John spelled name of each picture underneath. Did well with modeling but had difficulty independently.

11/20 Did quick sort. Students found all the pictures that rhymed and made matched sets. John was able to locate 4 of the 5 rhyming sets independently.

11/25 Did quick sort. To check sort, John finger-spelled* each item to make sure it was in the correct column. All items were correct.

Cinda Korn, First-Grade Teacher, West Windsor–Plainsboro School District, New Jersey

Organization and management are also areas of keen interest to Cinda. Throughout her 20 years of teaching first grade, Cinda has sought ways to make her job easier by turning as much responsibility as possible over to her students. When she first started using word sorts, Cinda realized that she needed (1) a system for keeping the word cards of each group separate and (2) a means for students to keep their current set of cards organized. Cinda solved the first problem by using a different color of paper for each word study group's cards: yellow, blue, green, and pink. To make it easier for students to keep track of their cards, Cinda asks them to put their *math number*, a number assigned to each student at the beginning of the year and used for a variety of purposes, on the back of each card when they cut the cards apart. To solve the second problem, Cinda collected butter and margarine tubs. Students store their cut-apart cards in the small plastic containers, which are fairly durable and easily accessed and which can readily be replaced if damaged. To aid the return of a wayward container to its proper owner, Cinda records the math number on the lid and the bottom of the container with a marker.

Students bring their containers to the gathering area when they meet with Cinda for word study. They place the containers behind them as they sit in a circle with her. After the guided word or picture walk, Cinda asks the students to complete the sort again, with their own cards. This allows her to assess their understanding of the lesson and to reteach any students who might need more support the first day.

Cinda also believes it is very important to help students make connections between word study and their reading and writing. The population of Town Center Elementary School, where she teaches, is highly diverse, with a large portion of the children coming from homes in which English is a second language. Cinda is very much aware of the special language needs of these learners. Even for children who do not participate in the school's second-language program, Cinda finds that vo-

---

*At the center, as children learn the alphabet, they also learn the hand sign for each letter.

cabulary and phrase (idiom) building are extremely important. She makes it a practice to stop to discuss the meanings of what she thinks may be unfamiliar or confusing words when she reads fiction, nonfiction, biographies, and poems aloud. The importance of this practice was brought home one day as she read *Lilly's Purple Plastic Purse* by Kevin Henkes.

> "I read the sentence 'Mr. Slinger was as sharp as a tack' and then stopped to ask if anyone knew the meaning of the phrase *as sharp as a tack*. My audience looked at me blankly for a few seconds, and then one little boy raised his hand and said, 'I know, Mrs. Korn. It means *shark attack*.' With a wide grin on my face, I proceeded to explain to the children exactly what this phrase means. In doing so, I discovered that most of the class didn't know what a *tack* was. I produced a tack and discussed with the class what it is used for and what the phrase *sharp as a tack* means. During the week, I began using the phrase in context, so the children would further understand the meaning and begin to use it themselves."

Jennifer Guht, First-Grade Teacher, Clayton School District, New Jersey

Although a veteran teacher, Jennifer is a relative newcomer to word study. When she first began to incorporate word study techniques with her first-grade class at Simmons Elementary School, she knew that time management would be a key issue. Like Cinda Korn, Jennifer color codes all of her materials to make it easy for everyone to keep track of items. She also finds it helpful to organize all of her word study materials into binders, one for the letter name stage and one for within word pattern. The binders are organized by feature and include word- and picture-card templates and a larger set of cards that Jennifer uses when she introduce a new sort to a group. She stores each "unit" in a plastic protector sheet. This sleeve is followed by another that contains homework activities that she has created, so items are easily accessible when she needs them. Jennifer's homework routine is as follows:

> *Monday*: Sort your spelling words into the pattern groups. As a bonus, see if you can add 1–2 new pattern words to each group. [A paper with the categories is included for children to record their words.]
> *Tuesday*: Choose 3 spelling words and write 3 *good* sentences. Make sure you add some details to make your sentences more interesting. Example: The *brown* dog ate the bone *in the backyard*. Please circle your spelling words. [The directions are printed at the top of lined handwriting paper.]
> *Wednesday*: Cut out the word/picture cards and play the card game Hold It [see Ganske (2000), *Word Journeys*, Chapter 3]. When you are done, glue or tape the cards into their pattern groups on the paper provided. [A sorting mat is included for this purpose.]

To assist her instructional decision making and to assess her students' understanding of the features they have studied, at the end of the week Jennifer usually dictates to the children some of the week's words, as well as three transfer words. To keep it low key, Jennifer uses a Bingo-like format for the assessment. Students record each dictated word in the box of their choosing on a template like the Spello card in Figure 7. Jennifer has several master Spello templates, each with different boxes marked for the transfer words and the *free* space. Varying the location of these adds interest when she and the children play Spello after the dictation is complete (see *Word Journeys* [Ganske, 2000]). To help children know where to write their words, Jennifer sometimes numbers each of the boxes.

Now in her second year of word study, Jennifer notes two important understandings she has gained through her experiences: (1) "All children can be successful when you take the time to in-

FIGURE 7. A completed Spello card.

struct them at their level," and (2) "Organizing your word study program so that it works for you will keep you doing it throughout your teaching."

Megan Czopek Power, Second-Grade Teacher, Poway Unified School District, San Diego, California

Megan began using word study during her first year of teaching. She, too, finds organization and management to be very important. As a second-year teacher, she notes, "Staying organized and finding a management plan that works for you is extremely important." For Megan, the best fit is a rotating schedule, in which groups get their words, complete activities, and are assessed on different days. Other management and teaching tips she suggests include:

1. Color-code word study cards, to-be-completed activities, "everything." Display a color-coded list of each group's words in a pocket chart for easy reference.

2. If students are assessed on some of their words at the end of the cycle, ask them to complete the assessment at a listening center, at which a prerecorded list of words with example sentences is provided. Each color group has its own cassette tape. Students put up their "offices" (study carrels) and plug in their earphones. Listening-center assessment is particularly valuable with a staggered schedule, as it allows Megan to work with other groups instead of reading off a list. It also eliminates the need for assessment makeups.

3. Take time to teach students word study procedures and several activities at the beginning of the year. For the first couple of weeks, Megan engages the whole class in activities with the same list of words, words the students are already proficient in using. This allows students to focus on learning the activities and routine rather than on how to spell the words. She models exactly what she wants the students to do and allows them time to practice each activity.

4. Look for ways to connect the spelling patterns children are learning to literature. One technique Megan finds effective is Phonics Pocket Poems. Each week she writes a poem for the pocket chart that emphasizes a particular phonics feature. Students read and reread the poems and use

them for word hunts. Later in the year, the students collaborate in writing their own poems. Books with poems selected for their phonic element, such as Rasinski and Zimmerman's *Phonics Poetry: Teaching Word Families*, can also be used. Megan makes a point of prompting students to notice and use the patterns they have been studying when she teaches decoding to the whole class or to guided reading groups.

5. Encourage word learning with activities such as What's That Word?, in which students share a word they know or learned outside of school that other students probably don't know. The student writes the word on the board and challenges classmates to ask questions to determine the meaning of the word. While having fun with words, students develop their vocabulary knowledge, practice asking questions, review parts of speech, and develop dictionary skills. Megan also excites her students to word learning by sharing the origins of words such as *sandwich, llama, America,* and *Tootsie Roll.* She recommends *Abracadabra to Zombie: More Than 300 Wacky Word Origins* by Don and Pam Wulffson, as "a wonderful collection of kid-friendly word origins that will have your students laughing and extremely excited about words."

Vickie Kendra, Second-Grade Teacher, Solon Public Schools, Ohio

Collecting and maintaining performance data for purposes of documenting and reporting on student learning and for instructional decision making are matters of critical importance to Vickie. As a means of keeping track of her students' progress with word study activities, including their ability to make generalizations about the features they are studying and to transfer their understandings to writing, Vickie uses a Word Study Cycle Data Collection Sheet (see Figure 8) that she devised. She keeps a data sheet for each group on a clipboard and uses them during group meetings. Like the following sample, each data sheet reflects one group's performance for the 7 days they work with a set of words. A typical 7-day cycle is as follows:

- *Day 1*: Closed sort and group discussion, with recording of students' generalizations. Students sort their words under key words or pictures. Their performance is recorded as a plus if all the words are sorted correctly; a minus sign and the number of items missed is used to document errors. During the discussion that follows, students are asked what they notice about the words. Vickie documents their thinking on chart paper and later transfers the information to the Word Study Generalization column on the data sheet, so she can compare students' final reflection to their initial one.
- *Day 2*: Independent word hunt. The children search for 10–15 minutes to find words with the week's features, while Vickie works with another group. They share and discuss their results during Day 3. At that time Vickie records their findings as a fraction: number of correct words over the total number of words found.
- *Day 3*: Speed sort with the same words used on Day 1. Speed-sort data are recorded in the same manner as the closed sort. Because there may be other trials, results from the first speed sorting are noted in the upper portion of the box; subsequent results are noted underneath. If a child is struggling, Vickie marks "SOS," as a reminder of the help she had to provide. Word hunt results are discussed after the speed sorting, and charted thoughts from Day 1 are reviewed and revised as needed.
- *Day 4*: Word study games/activities with a partner. Vickie works with another group; no data are recorded.
- *Day 5*: Speed sorting followed by one-to-one conferences with each child, using a piece of first-draft writing (3–5 minutes in duration). Students not involved in the conference are engaged in writing. If needed, Vickie completes any remaining conferences in Writer's Workshop at some

Stage: ___WWP___   Feature: ___ou-ow___

Student	Closed sort	Speed sort and glue sort	Word study generalization	Word hunt	Writing sort reflection	Writing observations
Robbie	-1	-1 -1	all words have ow /ou/	6/8	16/20 ou goes with /ou/; ow with /ow/ or /ō/	cownted first after inside played game gave room sleep there
Eric	+	+ -0	all say /ou/	3/3	20/20 sounds of ou & ow	coletion after train yard freaght lunch town road right lunch church
Gabey	-2 +	+ + -0	DK, confusing b/c too many words with ou, ow	1/1	20/20 "Nothing!"	barel prince called there barle cracker grilled came house cheese place
Sadana	+	+ + -0	lots of /ou/ vowels; spelled ou and ow	9/10	20/20 all words had o's	watch snow tarts some bear sweet part stick team close
Elana	+	-2 SOS -3 -2	ou & ow have the same sound	10/10	16/20 always √ your work	thoe starts about plan herd queen new very dress know told very tonight
Matthew	-1	+ + -0	takes a u or w after the o	7/9	20/20 ow makes 2 diff. sounds	bussie weekend cloud name called Saturday back night time again
Kyle	+	+ + -0	2 diff. ways to spell /ou/—ow & ou	7/9	20/20 ou can sound like ow	brother cards over baseball dodge played time great home both

FIGURE 8. Word study cycle data collection sheet.

point in session 7, or before the morning bell rings. During the conference, Vickie documents words with features from past and present word studies on the right-hand side of the Writing Observation column and misspelled words on the left. She chooses one or two of the latter words to discuss strategies for revising the spelling.

• *Day 6:* Word study games/activities with a partner. Vickie works with another group; no data are recorded.

• *Day 7:* Evaluation—blind writing sort, with one point for correct spelling and one for correct category placement. Four of the words are from the closed sort; the other six are different words that have the features being studied. Vickie records the total correct over the total possible in the Writing Sort Reflection column. Students also complete a Glue Sort. Using their closed sort words or pictures, the children sort the cards, glue them to a sheet of newsprint, and write a reflection about what they learned from studying the spelling feature. Vickie notes the results at the bottom of the Speed Sort/Glue Sort column and copies their reflections under Writing Sort Reflection.

Linda Zeck, Third-Grade Teacher, Washington Township Schools, New Jersey

At Birches Elementary School, Linda is part of a five-teacher team. Although each teacher engages in word study, they manage and organize their instruction in different ways. For Linda, the best fit for small-group word study is a rotating 10-day cycle. At the start of the year, as soon as she knows her students and their needs, Linda begins word study with one of the groups. The next day she begins it with another; she continues to add on a new group each day until she has met with each of the four word study groups in her class. This type of rotating schedule limits the amount of time Linda must be actively involved on any given day. For instance, on Day 1, she introduces the new sort to one group rather than to several. The rotating schedule also means that holidays or assemblies don't disrupt word study; when there is a conflict Linda simply moves that day's plans to the following day. Although Linda's activities are based on a 10-day cycle, the rotation system she uses can easily be applied to cycles with other numbers of days, such as 5 or 7.

With a rotating system, organization and management are critical to ensuring that students know what they are expected to do, and when. Before Linda forms her word study groups she teaches each of the ten activities she will be using to the whole class. She knows how important modeling is, so she demonstrates each activity. Then the class completes a unit of word study together. During this 10-day cycle students record their activity responses in their word study notebook, so they can be referred to later. Once Linda begins her groups, she uses a word study board to keep everyone informed of the day's word study task. The chart, as shown in Figure 9, is brightly colored and includes ten attached library-pockets. Each pocket is numbered and labeled with an activity.

1. Word Sort with the Teacher [guided walk or closed sort]
2. Word Sort with a Buddy [writing sort in cursive]
3. Write and Draw [for ten of the words]
4. Write Rhyming Words [for ten of the words]
5. Word Hunt [searching around the room for other words with the patterns]
6. Writing Activity [connected to mini-lessons in Writer's Workshop, or sentence writing]
7. Games Center [partner activity]
8. Spelling Bee [within the group]
9. Computer Sort [children practice sorting their words using a specially designed program (see Ganske [2000], *Word Journeys*); this year Linda substituted a Puzzle Sort, an activity in which the students create a crossword with the words]
10. Evaluation [quiz; a blind written sort]

FIGURE 9. Third grade word study board.

Four of the pockets contain a laminated index card, one for each group, currently called Butterfly, Teddy Bear, Sunshine, and Star. Appropriate symbols are stapled to the top of the corresponding index cards so that they are easily identifiable, and group members are listed below. The chart is placed in a very visible location, and each day the cards are moved to the next library pocket, so students know just which activity they are to perform. To allow children to choose a buddy for the partner activities and to ensure that each student has an opportunity to be first to select a partner, Linda places a dot next to the person's name who will be the first to select a partner; partner selection then proceeds down the remaining list of students. The following week, the dot will be placed in front of the next person's name, and that person will be first.

Linda's students truly enjoy the word study activities, which are predictable but engaging and varied, allow for choice and collaboration, and take into consideration their differences in understanding. Although everyone engages in the same activities, they do so with words and features that are developmentally appropriate.

Pam Chase, Third-Grade Teacher, Haddon Heights School District, New Jersey

Pam uses a 5-day cycle to teach her third graders at Glenview School sound, pattern, and meaning relationships. She addresses other aspects of word-learning, such as the use of context clues, during guided reading instruction. During this small-group meeting time, Pam uses the bookmark strategy (~~~d, Ganske, & Monroe, 2002) to help her students learn to monitor for meaning. The ~~~consists of a sheet of paper folded in half. On the outside flap students design an appro~~~for the book they are reading, as shown in Figure 10, of *The Littles* by John Peterson. ~~~cludes prompts for monitoring comprehension and writing space. Children learn to identify areas where their comprehension breaks down by considering prompts such as "I was confused when . . . , " and they learn to apply strategies to get past these roadblocks. Word identification provides a relatively easy starting point in this process. Although students are sometimes hesitant to reveal that they don't understand a portion of text (or they may not realize they've lost the thread of meaning), they are usually quite willing to look for "tricky," or unfamiliar, words. Focusing on one or two strategies at a time, Pam teaches her students eight ways to unlock the meaning of an unfamiliar word, including the following:

PC: Picture Clues

LC: Letter/sound Clues, chunks, or base words

RR: Reread [Back up a sentence or paragraph, and reread to try to make a link to the unfamiliar word, its meaning, or identification.]

RA: Read Ahead [Keep reading, because the author may provide more information.]

CC: Context Clues [How is the word being used? What information am I being given about the word? How can I grasp its meaning?]

AY: Ask Yourself [What personal connections can I make? Where have you heard the word used before?] [For example, during a recent reading of *Keep the Lights Burning, Abby* by Peter and Connie Roop, the phrase "trimmed the wick" was encountered. After thinking, a girl in the group recalled "My mom trims my hair" and realized that *trimmed the wick* means the character cut the wick shorter.]

D: Dictionary

AE: Ask an Expert (teacher, peer, or other adult)

FIGURE 10. Cover of bookmark for monitoring comprehension.

As she models and demonstrates use of the various strategies, Pam encourages students to reserve the Ask an Expert and Dictionary strategies for last, because they cause readers to have to stop reading the story.

The strategies are posted around the room to remind students of their many options for tackling unfamiliar words. On the portion of the bookmark devoted to tricky words, Pam has listed difficult words and the students record each word's meaning and the strategy they used (as shown in Figure 11), but as students gain confidence and competence in using the strategies, they identify tricky words themselves, note the page numbers where they were found, and then record the meanings of the words and the strategies that were used to understand them.

*   *   *

Helping students to become competent in a full repertoire of strategies that can assist them in their reading and writing is what good teaching is all about. Word learning is an area in which students sometimes encounter difficulties, particularly as novice readers and writers, whatever their age. Word studies to develop the strategies and understandings of emergent, letter name, and within word pattern spellers follow in the next parts.

To guide and maximize your use of the activities in this book, bear the following in mind:

- Answer keys, such as the one below, are included in the text for each of the sorts. Answer keys include the title and sort number, category identifiers, key words or pictures from the sort, and an alphabetical listing of the words to be sorted in each category. It should be noted that words are listed in alphabetical order merely for ease of reference. At times teachers may wish for students to alphabetize words in each category, but this should only be done *after* they have sorted them.

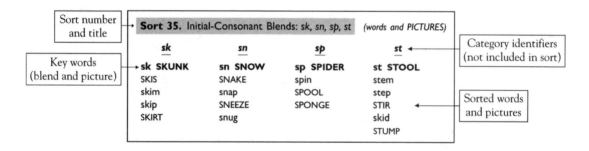

- Capital letters (SKUNK) are used in the sort answer keys to indicate that the word is represented by a picture in the actual sort.
- Slashes around letters (/m/) in category identifiers indicate that the sound rather than the letter is being referred to.
- Key words serve as exemplars of the category features and appear in boldfaced type. These may also be letters or a combination of letters, words, and pictures. Key words are included in the set of word cards and appear as the top cards of each template. If desired, they may be underlined before photocopying so that students will use the same key words each time they sort. They have not been set off in any way on the template, so as to allow flexible use of the sort. For example, teachers may wish students to complete an open sort in which they determine their own categories.
- Numerous sorts, especially in Part 4, include a sort card marked with a question mark. This card is used as a key word for the "Oddball" category. It is here that exceptions to the other categories are placed.

Page	Word	Meaning	Strategy
24	cork	a plug	CC
24	comfortably	cozy soft	PC CC
26	crumbs	bits of food	AY
27	weapons	tools	PC
29	protection	being safe	RA
29	quiver	a case for arrows	RR

FIGURE 11. Completed tricky words section of a bookmark
from *The Littles* by John Peterson.

- The templates of word cards appear with the sort number and title at the top. It is recommended that this information be removed before providing templates to students. To eliminate the sort number and title, as well as the extraneous white space surrounding the template (which frequently ends up on the floor after the cards are cut out), first photocopy the page out of the book, then trim that page down to the edge of the template, and then recopy it for students at the enlargement specified at the bottom of the sort page, usually 135%.

- Before beginning work with a feature, skim through the sorts in the text (or the list of reproducible pages) to understand the progression and to determine which of the sorts are best suited to a given group of students.

- Students need lots of opportunities to discuss how words are used and what they mean as well as how their features work. This does not mean writing out dictionary definitions and coming up with their own sentences, which all too commonly results in the following:

> regurgitate: to flow back. The tide regurgitates to the ocean.
> procrastinate: to put off. Mom said to procrastinate the lights.

It means engaging students in talk to kindle interest and appreciation for words while developing vocabulary knowledge.

- Teachers should further keep in mind that each sort may be used with more or less structure as the needs of the students require. Student engagement, the accuracy of their responses, and the insights they share as they talk about a sort provide information to guide teachers in their scaffolding of understandings and release of responsibility.

Directly following Part 4 you will find five appendices of reproducible materials: Appendices A through E. Appendix A includes several informal emergent literacy assessments. Appendix B has three sets of cards for the Oh No! card game: alphabet letter recognition cards, high-frequency word cards, and additional "For Good Measure" high-frequency word cards. Appendix C includes a variety of letter cards for Make-It, Break-It activities. Appendix D provides information and several sorts for working with Spanish-speaking English-language learners and includes Spanish-English and English-Spanish translations of the pictures used in *Word Sorts and More*. Appendix E contains blank templates, category labels, and additional pictures for some of the letter name sorts.

*   *   *

This said, and with the stage set, let's move on to the sound, pattern, and meaning explorations.

Part 2

Word Study for Emergent Learners

Learners at the emergent stage are not yet reading and writing in the conventional sense. Early on, they are likely to think of pictures as the message bearers. Those who are read to or encouraged to write come to engage in "pretend" reading and writing, characterized by the paraphrasing or retelling of a familiar text and the recording of rows and rows of squiggly lines or letter-like symbols that imitate writing. As emergent readers and writers begin to learn letters of the alphabet through the letters of their names and other adult modeling and as they gain insights about the sounds in spoken language, they come to associate spoken language with its printed form. This acquisition of the *alphabetic principle* brings changes to their reading and writing behaviors. With memory support for what a familiar text says, children begin to track print, vaguely at first but gradually becoming more accurate. They maintain their place in the text by finger-pointing to the words as they recite them, often giving careful attention to the match between their speech and the initial (or initial and final) letters of the word to which they are pointing. In writing, random-letter strings are supplanted by decipherable "words," represented by initial (and sometimes final) consonants, as for example, a former rendering of "I see Bobby" as NMBECA might now be ICBB. Concept knowledge, too, develops in contexts in which there is rich and meaningful talk, lots of storybook reading, and reinforcement activities such as those included at the end of this part of the book.

Data from informal assessments (see, for example, the letter recognition, beginning sound, and spelling assessments included in Appendix A) and from demonstrations of speech-to-print matching carried out by asking children to finger-point to previously read and reread big books, poems, and rhymes help teachers to know what children are ready to learn and to gauge their progress. Following are activities to supplement instruction in developing children's phonological awareness, alphabet knowledge, acquisition of the alphabetic principle, and concept/vocabulary development. Where included, *Try More* sections provide suggestions for extension activities, and *Read-Aloud Literature Links* reference various fiction, informational texts, and poetry to develop students' understanding of concepts through read-alouds.

Phonological Awareness (PICTURES, Numbers, and Letters)

Phonological awareness is the ability to perceive units of sound in spoken language, including the increasingly difficult-to-discern units of syllables, onsets and rimes, and phonemes. The activities that follow focus on syllable counting and identifying words with rhyming and alliteration. Activities that focus on beginning sounds are presented later. Big-book read-alouds; singing and clapping the beat to favorite rhymes, jingles, and raps; riddle guessing; and other word play are further ways to sensitize children to the sounds of our language. Begin the activities that follow with modeling and demonstration. Once children understand how to complete the task, you may want to place it in a center for additional reinforcement.

Syllables

Sorts 1 and 2 require children to categorize pictures according to the number of beats (syllables) in each word. Be sure they know the name of each picture before you begin modeling the activity. Say the word naturally so that you don't inadvertently add an extra syllable, for example: "sheep" not "she-eep."

Sort 1. Syllable Counting: 1 and 2 Syllables

1	2
SHEEP	**APPLE**
BALL	BALLOON
BELT	BUTTON
COMB	CANDLE
FISH	FEATHER
HAND	FOOTBALL
RING	MITTEN
STAMP	PUMPKIN
STAR	SANDWICH
TEETH	WAGON

Try More

Ask the children to think of or find objects in the room with names of one or two syllables.

Sort 2. Syllable Counting: 1, 2, 3, and 4 Syllables

1	2	3	4
BREAD	**SCISSORS**	**ELEPHANT**	**ALLIGATOR**
(CAR)	CRAYON	ALPHABET	ELEVATOR
PEN	FLASHLIGHT	GRASSHOPPER	THERMOMETER
SHIP	KITCHEN	INSTRUMENTS	(AUTOMOBILE)
	MOUNTAINS	KANGAROO	
	PENGUIN	OCTOPUS	
		SKELETON	
		VALENTINE	

Try More

Ask the children to think of or find objects in the room with names of one, two, three, and four syllables. Challenge them to provide a word or object with more than four syllables.

Ask students to bring in one or more magazine pictures or other cutouts, being sure that they can name the picture and the number of syllables in its name. Have a box of cutouts prepared for children who have no access at home, or give students the option to draw a picture. Play the game Can You Guess How Many Syllables? One at a time the children hold up a picture, identify it by name, and ask their peers, "Can you guess how many syllables?"

Learners might also try to recognize the number of syllables in each others' names by clapping.

Onsets and Rimes

An *onset* is the beginning element of a syllable, and a *rime* is the vowel and what follows. For example, in *bed*, *clap*, and *string*, the onsets and rimes are *b* + *ed*, *cl* + *ap*, and *str* + *ing*. Rhyming words often share a rime, as in *best* and *test*, but not always, as in *beet* and *beat*. The activities in this section center on two picture-card games, one called Odd Man Out and the other a follow-up game called Odd Man Out's Odd No More. Ten sorting sets are included, each with four games, making a total of 40 games. Sorting sets 3–7 focus on rhyming words, most of which share a common rime; sets 8–12 focus on alliteration of single-consonant onsets. Directions for the activities follow.

Directions: As shown in Figure 12, randomly place the three rhyming or alliterative words and the Odd Man card (the picture that does not rhyme or begin with the same sound as the other three) in a row or a 2 × 2 array. Be sure children know what each picture is before starting the game and be sensitive to differences: for instance, some may recognize the bag as a sack or the pail as a bucket and so forth. When necessary, discuss the word's meaning. Invite children to identify the three rhyming cards and to name the leftover Odd Man card. Provide as much support as needed through modeling. After an entire set, or after each try, children who are ready for further challenge may play Odd Man Out's Odd No More. Simply spread out the four Odd Man partner words, and ask the students to find the appropriate match to make Odd Man no longer odd, as shown in Figure 13.

FIGURE 12. Examples of layouts for Odd Man Out cards.

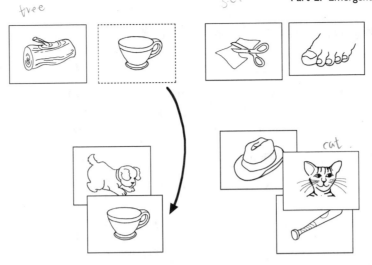

tree   *scissor*   *cat*

FIGURE 13. A correct match for Odd Man Out's Odd No More.

Sort 3. Rhyming: Odd Man Out (/ăt/, /ăg/, /ŏx/, /ŭg/)

	Try 1	Try 2	Try 3	Try 4
Rhyming Three	BAT	BAG	BOX	BUG
	CAT	FLAG	FOX	MUG
	HAT	TAG	OX	RUG
Odd Man	PUP	NUT	ROSE	DOG
Odd Man's Partner	CUP	CUT	TOES	LOG

Sort 4. Rhyming: Odd Man Out (/ĭg/, /ĕn/, /ĕt/, /ŏp/)

	Try 1	Try 2	Try 3	Try 4
Rhyming Three	DIG	HEN	JET	MOP
	PIG	PEN	PET	POP
	WIG	MEN	WET	TOP
Odd Man	MAD	SLED	YELL	PIN
Odd Man's Partner	SAD	BED	BELL	WIN

Sort 5. Rhyming: Odd Man Out (/ăn/, /ăp/, /är/, /ĭng/)

	Try 1	Try 2	Try 3	Try 4
Rhyming Three	CAN	CAP	CAR	KING
	FAN	MAP	JAR	RING
	MAN	NAP	STAR	WING
Odd Man	EGG	RIP	CORN	LAMP
Odd Man's Partner	LEG	SIP	HORN	STAMP

Sort 6. Rhyming: Odd Man Out (/âr/, /ŏk/, /ōt/, /āk/)

	Try 1	Try 2	Try 3	Try 4
Rhyming Three	BEAR	BLOCK	BOAT	CAKE
	CHAIR	LOCK	COAT	RAKE
	PEAR	SOCK	GOAT	SNAKE
Odd Man	SHIRT	TWO	DICE	SHAVE
Odd Man's Partner	SKIRT	SHOE	MICE	WAVE

Sort 7. Rhyming: Odd Man Out (/ĭk/, /ān/, /āl/, /ēp/)

	Try 1	Try 2	Try 3	Try 4
Rhyming Three	CHICK	CANE	PAIL	SHEEP
	KICK	RAIN	NAIL	SLEEP
	SICK	TRAIN	WHALE	SWEEP
Odd Man	BOOK	BEE	PIE	WELL
Odd Man's Partner	HOOK	TREE	TIE	SHELL

Sort 8. Alliteration: Odd Man Out (/b/, /m/, /r/, /s/)

	Try 1	Try 2	Try 3	Try 4
Alliterative Three	BEAR	MATCH	RING	SINK
	BIKE	MITTEN	ROCK	SIT
	BOOK	MOON	ROOF	SUN
Odd Man	MASK	ROAD	SAW	BAKE
Odd Man's Partner	MOUNTAINS	ROPE	SANDWICH	BIRD

Sort 9. Alliteration: Odd Man Out (/t/, /n/, /p/, /g/)

	Try 1	Try 2	Try 3	Try 4
Alliterative Three	TEETH	NAIL	PAIL	GAME
	TUB	NEST	PEACH	GIRL
	TURTLE	NUT	PIE	GUM
Odd Man	NAP	PEAS	GATE	TABLE
Odd Man's Partner	NEEDLE	PURSE	GHOST	TUBE

Sort 10. Alliteration: Odd Man Out (/d/, /h/, /l/, /c/)

	Try 1	Try 2	Try 3	Try 4
Alliterative Three	DEER	HAND	LAMP	CANDLE
	DISHES	HEART	LEAF	CAR
	DOLL	HORSE	LION	COMB
Odd Man	HOSE	LEMON	COT	DIVE
Odd Man's Partner	HOUSE	LOCK	COW	DOOR

Sort 11. Alliteration: Odd Man Out (/f/, /w/, /j/, /k/)

	Try 1	Try 2	Try 3	Try 4
Alliterative Three	FEET	WAGON	JACKET	KEY
	FISH	WATCH	JAM	KING
	FORK	WING	JUGGLE	KITTEN
Odd Man	WEB	JAR	KITCHEN	FEATHER
Odd Man's Partner	WINDOW	JET	KITE	FENCE

Sort 12. Alliteration: Odd Man Out (/y/, /v/, /z/, /q/)

	Try 1	Try 2	Try 3	Try 4
Alliterative Three	YARN	VAN	ZEBRA	QUEEN
	YAWN	VASE	ZIGZAG	QUESTION
	YO-YO	VEST	ZOO	QUIET
Odd Man	VACUUM	ZIPPER	QUACK	YARD
Odd Man's Partner	VINE	ZERO	QUARTER	YELL

Read-Aloud Literature Links (with Rhyme and Alliteration)

Degan, B. (1983). *Jamberry.* New York: Harper.

Dodds, D. A. (1989). *Wheel away.* New York: Harper.

Gordon, J. R. (1991). *Six Sleepy Sheep.* New York: Puffin.

Guarino, D. (1989). *Is your mamma a llama?* New York: Scholastic.

Jorgensen, G. (1988). *Crocodile beat.* New York: Scholastic.

Kuskin, K. (1990). *Road and more.* New York: Harper.

Martin, B., Jr. (1971). *"Fire! Fire!" said Mrs. McGuire.* San Diego, CA: Harcourt.

McCord, D. (1969). I want you to meet. In B. S. de Regniers (Ed.), *Poems children will sit still for: A selection for the primary grades.* New York: Macmillan.

Merriam, E. (1969). Weather. In B. S. de Regniers (Ed.), *Poems children will sit still for: A selection for the primary grades.* New York: Macmillan.

Morgan, M. (2000). *I looked through my window.* Barrington, IL: Rigby.

Prelutsky, J. (1982). *The baby uggs are hatching.* New York: Mulberry.

Weston, T. (2003). *Hey, pancakes!* San Diego, CA: Harcourt.

SORT 1 Syllable Counting: 1 and 2 Syllables

1	2	

Syllable Counting: 1, 2, 3, and 4 Syllables

1	2	3
4		
		BE MINE
98.6		
	ABCDEFGHI JKLMNOPQR STUVWXYZ	

From *Word Sorts and More* by Kathy Ganske. Copyright 2006 by The Guilford Press. Permission to photocopy this form is granted to purchasers of this book for personal use only (see copyright page for details). Enlarge 135% to fill page.

Rhyming: Odd Man Out (/ăt/, /ăg/, /ŏx/, /ŭg/)

Try 1	Try 2	Try 3	Try 4

SORT 6 Rhyming: Odd Man Out (/âr/, /ŏk/, /ōt/, /āk/)

Try 1	Try 2	Try 3	Try 4

SORT 7 Rhyming: Odd Man Out (/ĭk/, /ān/, /āl/, /ēp/)

Try 1	Try 2	Try 3	Try 4

SORT 8   Alliteration: Odd Man Out (/b/, /m/, /r/, /s/)

Try 1	Try 2	Try 3	Try 4

SORT 9 Alliteration: Odd Man Out (/t/, /n/, /p/, /g/)

Try 1	Try 2	Try 3	Try 4

SORT 10 Alliteration: Odd Man Out (/d/, /h/, /l/, /c/)

Try 1	Try 2	Try 3	Try 4

SORT 11 Alliteration: Odd Man Out (/f/, /w/, /j/, /k/)

Try 1	Try 2	Try 3	Try 4

SORT 12 Alliteration: Odd Man Out (/y/, /v/, /z/, /q/)

Try 1	Try 2	Try 3	Try 4

Alphabet Knowledge: Letter Recognition (Letters Only)

Alphabet knowledge includes recognition of letters, their production, and understanding of the sounds that go with them. With 52 letters in all, 26 upper- and 26 lowercase letters, and many similar shapes, just the process of learning to recognize their distinctive features can take considerable time. Monitoring children's progress is important because the number of letters that a kindergartener can name when presented with them in random order is nearly as accurate in predicting future reading success as an entire battery of assessments (Snow, Burns, & Griffin, 1998). The sorts that follow focus on letter identification. They may be used once students have some understanding of the basic shapes of the letters involved. The intent of the sorts is to reinforce the concept that although letters sometimes appear in slightly different shapes, there are still common traits, just as with people: Some people's faces are rounder; others longer or squarer; but nonetheless, we all have eyes, noses, and mouths as part of our faces.

Start by enlarging the letter cards, as needed. Then introduce students to the font studies with a guided walk. After the sorting, draw students' attention to the similarities and differences of each letter. Depending on the students and their level of knowledge, you may want to introduce the letters one at a time and then begin to include multiple categories, gradually working up to the four categories highlighted in the sort. As their understandings develop, you might ask them to match upper- and lowercase letters.

Sort 13–22. Letter Recognition: Upper- and Lowercase Consonants

Sort 13   B, M, R, S
Sort 14   b, m, r, s
Sort 15   T, N, P, G
Sort 16   t, n, p, g
Sort 17   D, H, L, C
Sort 18   d, h, l, c
Sort 19   F, W, J, K
Sort 20   f, w, j, k
Sort 21   Y, V, Z, X, Q

Sort 23–24. Letter Recognition: Upper- and Lowercase Vowels

Sort 23   A, E, I, O, U
Sort 24   a, e, i, o, u

Try More

Ask children to find more examples of the consonants or vowels being explored by looking in magazines or big books from shared reading experiences.

Read aloud alphabet books, such as those listed in the Literature Links at the end of the Phonemic Awareness/Alphabetic Principle section.

Letter Recognition: Uppercase Consonants (*B, M, R, S*)

B	**M**	**R**
S	*R*	**M**
M	**S**	**B**
S	R	S
B	*M*	**R**
M	*B*	S
R	B	

From *Word Sorts and More* by Kathy Ganske. Copyright 2006 by The Guilford Press. Permission to photocopy this form is granted to purchasers of this book for personal use only (see copyright page for details). Enlarge 135% to fill page.

b	m	r
s	*r*	**m**
m	*s*	b
s	r	s
b	*m*	r
m	*b*	s
r	b	

Letter Recognition: Uppercase Consonants (*T, N, P, G*)

T	N	P
G	*P*	N
N	P	T
G	G	P
T	*N*	G
N	*T*	P
G	T	

t	n	p
g	*p*	**n**
n	p	t
g	g	p
†	*n*	**g**
n	*t*	**p**
g	t	

SORT 17 Letter Recognition: Uppercase Consonants (*D, H, L, C*)

D	H	L
C	*L*	**H**
H	*C*	**D**
C	L	C
D	*H*	**L**
H	*D*	C
L	D	

SORT 18 Letter Recognition: Lowercase Consonants (*d, h, l, c*)

d	h	l
c	*l*	**h**
h	c	**d**
c	l	c
d	*h*	**l**
h	*d*	**c**
l	d	

SORT 19 Letter Recognition: Uppercase Consonants (F, W, J, K)

F	**W**	**J**
K	*J*	W
W	**K**	**F**
K	J	K
F	*W*	**J**
W	*F*	**K**
J	F	

Letter Recognition: Lowercase Consonants (*f, w, j, k*)

f	w	j
k	*j*	w
w	k	f
k	j	k
f	*w*	j
w	*f*	k
j	f	

Letter Recognition: Uppercase Consonants (*Y, V, Z, X, Q*)

Y	V	Z
X	Q	V
V	Q	Y
X	Z	Q
Y	*𝒱*	Z
V	*𝒴*	Q
Z	Y	Z

Letter Recognition: Lowercase Consonants (*y, v, z, x, q*)

y	v	z
x	q	v
v	q	y
x	z	q
y	*v*	z
v	*y*	q
z	y	z

A	E	I
O	U	*E*
U	I	*O*
O	*A*	I
A	**E**	*O*
E	*I*	U
A	*U*	

Letter Recognition: Lowercase Vowels (*a, e, i, o, u*)

a	e	i
o	u	*e*
u	i	o
o	*a*	i
a	e	*o*
e	*i*	u
a	*u*	

Phonemic Awareness/Alphabetic Principle: Beginning Sounds

(PICTURES and Letters*)

Sorts 25–34 provide emergent learners with reinforcement of initial consonant sounds. They may be used with or without the accompanying letter cards. Except for Sort 33, with the letters *y*, *v*, and *z*, each template of pictures is limited to a focus on two letters. Introduce pictures for each letter separately, then contrast them as categories in a guided walk. Be sure students can identify the pictures by name before they work with them.

As a follow-up reinforcement, students might play Picture Pool. Place all of the pictures face down in a "pool." Students take turns "fishing" for a pair; they select two cards, turn them over, and see if they make a beginning sound match. If the cards match, players keep the cards; if they do not, students must place the cards back in the pool. Teachers sometimes add an authentic element to the activity by placing magnetic tape on the back of each picture and hanging a large magnet by a string from a wooden-dowel "fishing pole."

At the letter name stage, beginning sounds are revisited as Initial Consonants, with three and four consonants contrasted at a time. Emergent learners who are ready for further challenge may progress to those. Sorts that focus on final consonant sounds are included in the sequence. For read-aloud Literature Links, see the section on initial and final consonants in Part 3.

Sort 25. Beginning Sounds (*m, s*)

m	*s*
Mm MAN	**Ss SOCK**
MAP	SANDWICH
MASK	SAW
MICE	SCISSORS
MILK	SEAL
MITTEN	SINK
MOON	SOAP
MUD	SUN

Sort 26. Beginning Sounds (*b, r*)

b	*r*
Bb BED	**Rr RING**
BALL	RAIN
BAT	RAKE
BELL	ROAD
BELT	ROOF
BIKE	ROPE
BIRD	RUG
BOOK	RUN

Sort 27. Beginning Sounds (*t, n*)

t	*n*
Tt TAPE	**Nn NOSE**
TABLE	NAIL
TEETH	NEEDLE
TENT	NEST
TOES	NET
TUBE	NINE
TURTLE	NICKEL
TWO	NUT

Sort 28. Beginning Sounds (*p, g*)

p	*g*
Pp PIG	**Gg GATE**
PAIL	GAME
PEANUTS	GAS
PEAR	GHOST
PEN	GIRL
PIE	GOAT
PUP(PY)	GUITAR
PURSE (or POCKETBOOK)	GUM

*If the letter cards are omitted, the focus is just on phonemic awareness, with beginning sounds.

Sort 29. Beginning Sounds (*d, h*)

<u>d</u>	<u>h</u>
Dd DOG	**Hh HEART**
DEER	HAM
DICE	HAND
DISHES	HAT
DIVE	HOOK
DOLL	HORN
DOOR	HORSE
DUCK	HOUSE

Sort 30. Beginning Sounds (*l, c*)

<u>l</u>	<u>c</u>
Ll LEAF	**Cc COMB**
LAMP	CAKE
LEG	CANDLE
LEMON	CAN
LETTER	CAR
LIP	COAT
LOCK	COW
LOG	CUP

Sort 31. Beginning Sounds (*f, w*)

<u>f</u>	<u>w</u>
Ff FISH	**Ww WATCH**
FAN	WAGON
FEATHER	WEB
FEET	WELL
FENCE	WIG
FIRE	WING
FIVE	WITCH
FORK	WORM

Sort 32. Beginning Sounds (*j, k*)

<u>j</u>	<u>k</u>
Jj JAR	**Kk KEY**
JACKET	KANGAROO
JEEP	KICK
JET	KING
JOG	KITCHEN
JUG	KITE
JUGGLE	KITTEN
JUMP	KIT

Sort 33. Beginning Sounds (*y, v, z*)

<u>y</u>	<u>v</u>	<u>z</u>
Yy YAWN	**Vv VAN**	**Zz ZIPPER**
YARD	VACUUM	ZEBRA
YARN	VALENTINE	ZERO
YELL	VASE	ZIGZAG
YO-YO	VEST	ZOO

Read-Aloud Literature Links

Ada, A. F. (1997). *Gathering the sun: An alphabet in Spanish and English*. New York: Lothrop, Lee & Shepard Books.—Details the life of a farm worker and his family in English and Spanish.

Aylesworth, J. (1991). *Old black fly*. New York: Holt.—Rhyming text follows a pesky fly through the alphabet as he has a busy day.

Bayer, J. (1984). *A: My name is Alice*. New York: Trumpet Club.—A rendering of the familiar alphabet name game.

Fleming, D. (2002). *Alphabet under construction*. New York: Henry Holt.—Mouse constructs an alphabet.

Howland, N. (2000). *ABC drive!* Boston: Clarion.—ABC items are encountered as a boy goes with his mother for a drive.

Inkpen, M. (2000). *Kipper's A to Z: An Alphabet Adventure*. San Diego, CA: Harcourt.—Kipper and his friend Arnold the pig go on an adventure to find items that represent each letter of the alphabet.

Johnson, S. (1995). *Alphabet City*. New York: Viking.—Photos of naturally occurring letters in the cityscape encourage listeners to look at their surroundings in a new way.

Kirk, D. (1998). *Miss Spider's ABC*. New York: Scholastic Press.—An alphabet journey with insects ends in a birthday party.

Larson, B. (2001). *Itchy's alphabet book*. Kelowna, British Columbia, Canada: ABB Creations, Ltd. (www.itchysalphabet.com).—This creative stand-up flip book devotes a page to each letter of the alphabet. The upper- and lowercase letters are shown with a picture, representing an alliterative phrase. For example: *"b" is a bat and ball* shows a picture of a bat turned on end with a ball at the bottom, creating the effect of a *b*. A second transparent page with the letter b on it fits over the top of the picture when flipped over, providing a useful mnemonic for remembering letter shape.

Metropolitan Museum of Art. (2002). *Museum ABC*. New York: Little, Brown.—Two-page spreads for each letter of the alphabet feature a simple phrase such as "F is for FEET" on the one page and details from four works of art that illustrate the word on the other.

Slate, J. (1996). *Miss Bindergarten gets ready for kindergarten*. New York: Dutton Children's Books.—An alphabet story about Miss Bindergarten's case of the flu.

Children need many opportunities to exercise their developing knowledge of letter–sound associations. Response and journal writing are an integral part of this, as are teacher modeling and demonstration. Books such as *Interactive Writing* by Andrea McCarrier, Gay Su Pinnell, and Irene Fountas (2000) provide teachers with guidance to make writing happen in the early grades. Progress in being able to approximate the spellings of words can be monitored with tools such as the *Kindergarten Inventory of Developmental Spelling* (KIDS; Ganske, 1995), included in Appendix A.

SORT 25 Beginning Sounds (*m, s*)

SORT 26 Beginning Sounds (*b, r*)

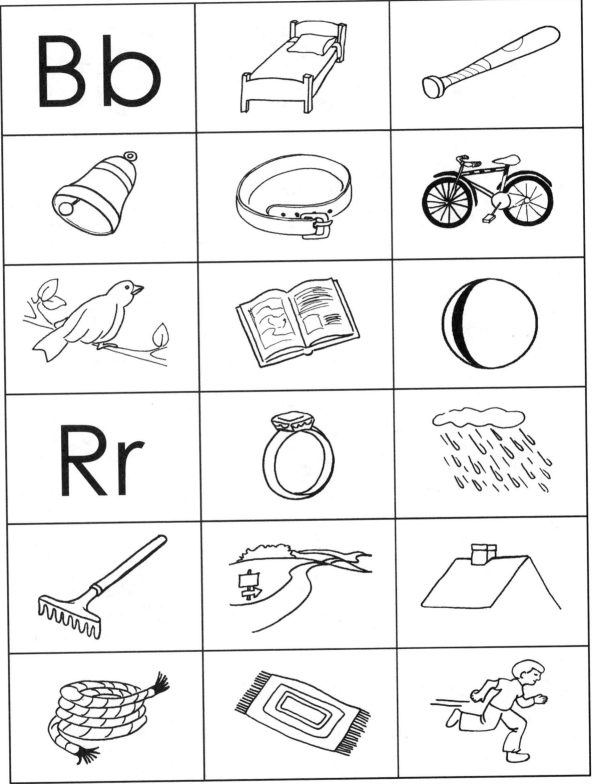

From *Word Sorts and More* by Kathy Ganske. Copyright 2006 by The Guilford Press. Permission to photocopy this form is granted to purchasers of this book for personal use only (see copyright page for details). Enlarge 135% to fill page.

Beginning Sounds (*t*, *n*)

From *Word Sorts and More* by Kathy Ganske. Copyright 2006 by The Guilford Press. Permission to photocopy this form is granted to purchasers of this book for personal use only (see copyright page for details). Enlarge 135% to fill page.

SORT 28 Beginning Sounds (p, g)

Beginning Sounds (*d, h*)

SORT 30 Beginning Sounds (l, c)

SORT 31 Beginning Sounds (*f, w*)

SORT 33   Beginning Sounds (y, v, z)

Concept of Word

Many classroom experiences with big books can be extended to provide tracking or finger-point-matching practice, as can those with nursery rhymes, poetry, jingles, raps, and dictated experience stories. It is key that the text be memorable so that familiarity with what it is supposed to say can support emergent learners in their reading efforts. Relatively short text, with rhyming or repetition lends itself well to tracking activities like those that follow. Pointing tools can be as simple as the child's finger or a pencil with an eraser tip or more elaborate, such as a dowel with a squiggly eye glued to the tip or a conductor's baton from a nearby orchestra's gift shop.

I am particularly fond of nursery rhymes for promoting concept of word. A surprisingly large number of students seem to have missed out on the experiences of "Old Mother Hubbard," "The Old Woman Who Lived in the Shoe," "Humpty Dumpty," and other favorites. Four good resources that run the gamut from the very traditional to the very contemporary and from limited in scope to comprehensive are the following:

> Ahlberg, J., & Ahlberg, A. (1978). *Each peach pear plum*. New York: Viking.—This well-loved "I spy" book is ideal in a big-book format. Children who have some background understanding of nursery rhymes will enjoy predicting the ending lines to the rhyming couplets in this book and searching out the nursery rhyme figures camouflaged in the pictures.
>
> dePaola, T. (1985). *Tomie dePaola's Mother Goose*. New York: Putnam.—Strong illustrations carry this collection of nursery rhymes.
>
> Lansky, B. (1993). *The new adventures of Mother Goose: Gentle rhymes for happy times*. New York: New Meadowbrook Press.—This book has been a favorite of mine since it was first published. It builds on children's understanding of the traditional rhymes with a modern-day spark: "Old Mother Hubbard" concludes with the "poor dog" ordering a pizza by phone, Old King Cole dances until his pants split down the middle, and the poor Old Woman just can't live in her shoe in the summer, so she packs and moves to a sandal.
>
> Grover, E. O. (Ed.). (1997). *Mother Goose* (The Original Volland Edition). New York: Derrydale Books.—This republication of the original 1915 edition offers full-page pictures with insets of 4 to 12 of the most well-known lines of the verses.

To engage students in practice with speech-to-print matching, choose a segment of text that contains at least one two-syllable word. Read, reread, and talk about the rhyme or sentence. Copy it onto chart paper and ask students to finger-point while they recite the words. Notice their pointing behaviors: Students who have much to learn may make just a vague sweep across the page. Those who are developing concept of word may point accurately overall but become confused by the strong extra beat of two-syllable words. These children will learn to self-correct errors they make with such words as their concept of word becomes stable. Follow up the pointing practice with matching activities that encourage the development of sight words, for although emergent learners initially need—and indeed rely on—pictures and pattern clues to help them recall words in the text, it is important over time to wean them away from such supports until words are recognized automatically in and out of context. The activity sequence that follows for "Old Mother Hubbard" shows attention to this need.

Concept of Word Activities with "Old Mother Hubbard"

Included on the following five pages is a sequence of activities related to the "Old Mother Hubbard" nursery rhyme. The same type of sequence may be applied to other short texts. It includes scaffolding and a gradual release of responsibility to the children through five related but different activities that promote concept of word development, sequencing, and word recognition in context and by sight. The activities are as follows:

1. Read aloud a short memorable text for enjoyment and/or information.
2. Reread and chorally read the text (with finger-pointing) so that children begin to commit it to memory.
3. Provide opportunities for emergent learners to track the text with a finger or pointing stick while they recite the words.
4. Match (and perhaps sequence) cut-apart sentence/phrase strips to the story by referring back to the original text.
5. Reconstruct sentences/phrases with individual words by referring back to the intact sentences/phrases.
6. Ask children who are ready for additional challenge to identify individual words that have been encountered in many contexts. To carry this out, simply hold up individual word cards and see which ones students can identify. Place those that are known on a metal ring or use them in a game like Oh No!, which is described in Appendix B.

Old Mother Hubbard

Old Mother Hubbard

Went to the cupboard

To get her poor dog a bone.

But when she got there

The cupboard was bare,

And so the poor dog had none.

Old Mother Hubbard

Went to the cupboard

To get her poor dog a bone.

But when she got there

The cupboard was bare,

And so the poor dog had none.

Word-to-Sentence Matching and Word Identification: Old Mother Hubbard (p. 1 of 4)

Old Mother Hubbard went to the cupboard

Old	Mother	Hubbard	went
to	the	cupboard	

To get her poor dog a bone,

To	get	her	poor
dog	a	bone	

But when she got there, the cupboard was bare,

when	she	got
the	cupboard	was
But		
there		
bare		

Word-to-Sentence Matching and Word Identification: Old Mother Hubbard (p. 4 of 4)

And so the poor dog had none.

And	so	dog
the	had	
poor	none.	

Concept Knowledge (PICTURES Only)

The importance of concept and vocabulary knowledge for reading has already been discussed in Part 1. The categorizing activities in this section encourage children to consider the traits of concepts—that is, how they are alike and different. For the sorts that follow, be sure to ask children to explain their placement of some of the cards, especially any that seem to be incorrect. Understanding the children's reasoning is just as important as noting which words they placed correctly. Furthermore, placements are not absolute, and sometimes a case may be made for a word being placed in a different category than as listed, especially words in the *Other* column. Consider, for example, Sort 34: Some zoos may have deer, leading children to place this animal under *elephant*. Choose concept sorts that are appropriate for your students. Before working with a sort, check children's identification of the pictures. If there are persistent problems with identification, omit the card(s).

Sort 34. Concept Knowledge: Zoo Animals and Farm Animals

Zoo	Farm	Other
ELEPHANT	**COW**	**?**
ALLIGATOR	CAT	DEER
BEAR	CHICK	SKUNK
GIRAFFE	DOG	
KANGAROO	DUCK	
LION	GOAT	
SEAL	HORSE	
ZEBRA	PIG	
	SHEEP	

Read-Aloud Literature Links

Bell, R. (2000). *Farm animals*. Portsmouth, NH: Heinemann.—This series provides information, supported by colorful photos, on the habits of some of the most common farm animals: chickens, cows, horses, pigs, sheep, and turkeys.

Whitehouse, P. (2003). *Zoo animals*. Portsmouth, NH: Heinemann.—This series of 12 books looks at the appearance and behaviors of the alligator, brown bear, elephant, flamingo, giraffe, hippopotamus, kangaroo, mountain goat, ostrich, sea lion, tiger, and zebra. Engaging photos and interesting facts, such as that zebras can whistle and shout, draw listeners in. Available in Spanish.

Sort 35. Concept Knowledge: You Could . . . Do It, Wear It, Smell It

Do It	Wear It	Smell It
BLOW	**BELT**	**ROSE**
CLIMB	BRACELET	FRIES
DIVE	JACKET	GAS
KICK	SCARF	LEMON
WAVE	SWEATER	SKUNK
WINK	WATCH	SMOKE
YAWN		
YELL		

Read-Aloud Literature Links

Day, E. (2003). *I'm good at....* Portsmouth, NH: Heinemann.—This series looks at what children can do with their different talents: building, dancing, helping, making art, making music, and math. As a follow-up to the reading, children might draw and label pictures of the activities they are good at doing. Available in Spanish.

Sort 36. Concept Knowledge: Tails, Tools, and Toys

Tails	Tools	Toys
BIRD	**PLIERS**	**BALL**
ELEPHANT	AXE	BLOCK
FISH	DRILL	DOLL
OX	KNIFE	GAME
PIG	RAKE	TOP
RAT	SAW	YO-YO
SHEEP		
SKUNK		

Read-Aloud Literature Links

Miles, E. (2003). *Tails.* Portsmouth, NH: Heinemann.—This book explores the size, shape, and position of common and unusual tails. It also answers the question: Do humans have something that serves the same purpose? This book is part of the *Animal Parts* series.

Sort 37. Concept Knowledge: Feelings, Food, and Furniture

Feelings	Food	Furniture
SAD	**BREAD**	**CHAIR**
HAPPY	CAKE	BED
MAD	CHEESE	CHEST
SICK	CHERRIES	CRIB
	FRIES	STOOL
	GRAPES	TABLE
	HAM	
	MILK	
	PEAR	
	PIE	

Read-Aloud Literature Links

Ehlert, L. (1989). *Eating the alphabet: Fruits and vegetables from A to Z.* San Diego, CA: Harcourt.—Alliteration abounds.

Thomas, I., & Whitehouse, P. (2005). *The colors we eat.* Portsmouth, NH: Heinemann.—This 11-book series reinforces color concepts and provides information on where we get the food we eat and how some foods are made. Available in Spanish.

Sort 38. Concept Knowledge: How Many Legs?

0 Legs	2 Legs	4 Legs	More Legs
FISH	**CHICK**	**BEAR**	**ANT**
SHARK	HEN	COW	CRAB
SNAKE	PENGUIN	FOX	FLY
WHALE	PERSON	RAT	OCTOPUS
WORM		SHEEP	SPIDER
		TURTLE	

Note: All legs may not be visible for some pictures.

Read-Aloud Literature Link

Miles, E. (2003). *Legs and feet.* Portsmouth, NH: Heinemann.—Explores differences in legs.

Sort 39. Concept Knowledge: Wings, Whiskers, and Wheels

Wings	Whiskers	Wheels	Other
BIRD	**CAT**	**CAR**	**?**
BAT	FOX	BIKE	JET
BEE	LION	BUS	
FLY	SEAL	SCOOTER	
HEN	MAN	TRACTOR	
	(SHAVE)		
SWAN		TRUCK	
		WAGON	

Note: A jet has wings and wheels, so it has been placed in the *Other* category. Because the wheels are not visible in the picture, you may want to discuss their placement and use with young children.

Sort 40. Concept Knowledge: Parts

People	Animals	Plants
HAND	**BEAK**	**LEAF**
CHIN	CLAW	STEM
ELBOW	FIN	THORN
HEEL	MANE	TWIG
LEGS	TRUNK	
LIPS	WING	
NECK		
NOSE		
THUMB		
TOES		

Note: Arrows are used to point out the targeted part in several of the pictures for this sort. These may make the sort confusing for some young children.

Read-Aloud Literature Links

Arnold, T. (1997). *Parts*. New York: Puffin Books.—A humorous rhyming tale of a boy who imagines his body is falling apart.

Miles, E. (2003). *Animal Parts*. Portsmouth, NH: Heinemann.—This series considers everything from ears, eyes, and noses to fur and feathers, paws and claws.

Schaefer, L. M. (2003). *It's my body*. Portsmouth, NH: Heinemann.—This series provides first explorations of various body parts. It's also available in Spanish.

Whitehouse, P. (2002). *Plants*. Portsmouth, NH: Heinemann.—This series looks at roots, leaves, flowers, and seeds and is told from a child's perspective. The *Plant ABC* book presents a different plant for each letter. Big-book and Spanish formats are available.

As children develop their knowledge of concepts and acquire the alphabetic principle and a concept of word, they start to read, and they begin to spell more conventionally. Part 3 addresses how to further their understandings.

SORT 34 Concept Knowledge: Zoo Animals and Farm Animals

Concept Knowledge: You Could . . . Do It, Wear It, Smell It

SORT 36 Concept Knowledge: Tails, Tools, and Toys

SORT 37 Concept Knowledge: Feelings, Food, and Furniture

Concept Knowledge: How Many Legs?

SORT 39   Concept Knowledge: Wings, Whiskers, and Wheels

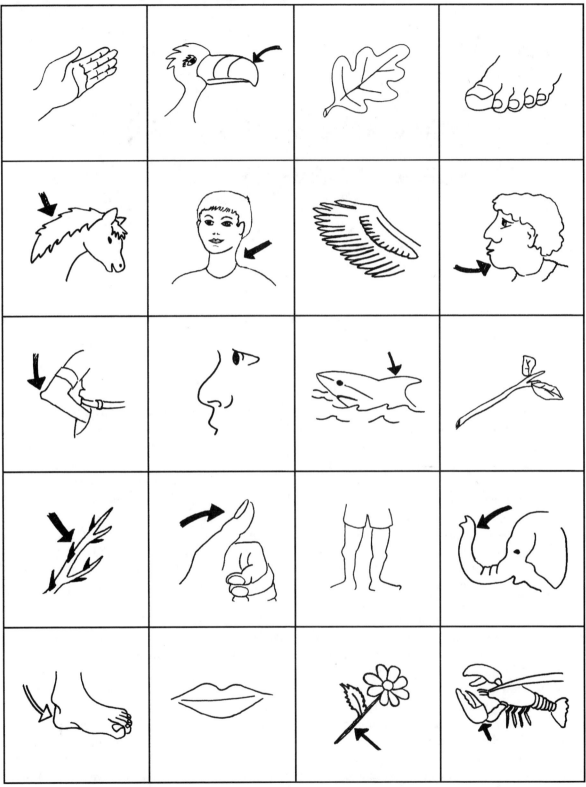

From *Word Sorts and More* by Kathy Ganske. Copyright 2006 by The Guilford Press. Permission to photocopy this form is granted to purchasers of this book for personal use only (see copyright page for details). Enlarge 135% to fill page.

Part 3

Word Study for Letter Name Spellers

Learners at the letter name stage have a stable concept of word and are beginning to associate the sounds of initial and final consonants with some degree of accuracy. Both reading and writing are slow processes due to limited sight-word knowledge and a limited writing vocabulary. Initial and final blends and digraphs and short vowels are at the heart of word study at this stage. Pictures and word families are used extensively to provide support for these novice readers and writers. Card games such as Oh No! (Strickland, Ganske, & Monroe, 2002), included in Appendix B, can be used to help beginning readers develop recognition of high-frequency words.

Wise teachers use informal assessments to guide their planning of instruction. They know which features students are ready to tackle and which they already know how to use. Teachers who are using the *Developmental Spelling Analysis* (DSA) for this purpose will find a notation of the corresponding DSA feature at the beginning of each section, as for example: "Initial and Final Consonants (DSA Feature A)." Thus, students whose assessment results indicate a need for work on Feature A would benefit from the activities described in that section.

Information for each featured group of sorts includes an identification of *What Is Known* and *What Is New*, so teachers can tell what kind of foundational knowledge students should have and how it is being extended. Most sorts should be introduced with teacher guidance. Occasionally, one of the alternative approaches described in Part 1 may be used to add interest or challenge or to focus children's attention more on sound and less on pattern. Whether pictures, words, or a combination of pictures and words are used, it is important to verify that the children can identify them. The few minutes it takes to do this can save much time and confusion later on. Some of the sorts presented at the end of this stage include Oddball words, words that not only encourage students' thinking but that also often provide reinforcement of high-frequency words. After students have been introduced to a set of word or picture cards, they typically work with them in different kinds of practice and application activities for the rest of the week (such as partner sorting, making and breaking words with the letter cards included in Appendix C, drawing and labeling, writing and drawing, and word and picture hunts) and then move on to a new set of cards the following week. Occasionally, as noted in the Tips for Teachers section of Part 1, teachers opt to use an alternative sequence for the study. For a lengthy discussion of planning and managing for a cycle of word study, see Chapter 3 of *Word Journeys* (Ganske, 2000).

Also included for sorts at this stage is a *Try 5* listing of five transfer words, which can be used to check understanding of the features being studied. The words are presented in alphabetical order but should be dictated randomly. Try 5 words are sometimes the alien words previously mentioned, namely, words that may be nonsense but more often than not are real words unfamiliar to students or real syllables of familiar but longer words. Depending on which features have already been studied and which one is currently under study, students may be held accountable for only a portion of the word, such as an initial consonant or blend. By not limiting students to common three- or four-letter words, it is hoped that they will begin to apply the features they have studied when reading and writing other longer words. Try 5 checks may be carried out orally or by asking students to record their responses. Additional checks for understanding may be carried out with the week's cards by asking students to write as much of the word as they can while you randomly call out a few of the words. As an alternative, when pictures are used, several may be placed in a jar at a center with directions for the children to pull out five, glue them on a sheet of paper, and record after each picture as much of the word as they can.

Links to literature (fiction, informational texts, and poetry) are made as well, especially in the early part of this stage, with attention to vocabulary building and extending. Each text cited includes a listing of *related* and/or *extension words* (see the sorts that follow for examples of each.) The former includes words or patterns from the word study lesson that are highlighted in the text and that may be used to clarify or enhance children's vocabulary knowledge. When the connection to the lesson is obvious because the word appears in the title, no separate indication for related words is included in the text citation. Words identified as *extension words* are also from the work cited; they are presented to extend children's vocabulary. Actions, drawings, the creation of word webs with connections to other words, and the Teacher's Word Wall are means for teachers to develop children's understanding of the words and to encourage their use in everyday speech and writing. As children gain beginning competence in reading, fewer texts are cited. However, the practice of extending and clarifying vocabulary should continue. Words from guided- or shared-reading texts may be targeted and highlighter tape used to call attention to the words in context.

Initial and Final Consonants (DSA Feature A) (PICTURES and Letters)

Initial Consonants

This section builds on understandings about initial consonants from the Beginning Sounds sorts of Part 2. There consonants were explored singly and in pairs. The sorts that follow include three to four contrasts, so children have more to consider as they refine their understanding of consonants. Although pictures are used exclusively, known words may be added to any of the sorts. Initially introduce sorts with a guided walk that provides considerable support (see Part 1, p. 5). As students gain greater competence, the level of support may be decreased. Be sure students can identify the words and that they understand their meanings.

Sort 1. Initial Consonants: *m, s, b*

m	*s*	*b*
Mm MAN	**Ss SOCK**	**Bb BAT**
MASK	SANDWICH	BEE
MITTEN	SAW	BELL
MICE	SINK	BOOK
MILK	SIX	BOY
MOON	SOAP	BUS
MOP	SUN	

Note: Here and elsewhere in this section, some students may misclassify words such as *mice* (S), *soap* (B), *mop* (B), and *bus* (S) on the basis of a salient or dominant ending sound.

Try 5: Expect feature only—*best, make, more, send, soon*

Sort 2. Initial Consonants: *m, s, b, r*

m	*s*	*b*	*r*
Mm MUD	**Ss SAD**	**Bb BUG**	**Rr RUN**
MAP	SCISSORS	BEAR	RAKE
MATCH	SEAL	BIKE	RAT
MEN	SIT	BIRD	RING
MOUNTAINS		BOX	RIP
MUG			

Try 5: Expect feature only—*burp, by, made, rain, see*

Literature Links

Boiko, C. (1998). The seal. In R. Alexander (Ed.), *Poetry place anthology.* New York: Scholastic.—Extension words: *squeal, sleek, swift,* and *jet* (a black coal used for jewelry).

Brett, J. (1989). *The mitten.* New York: Putnam.—Extension word: *cozy.*

Fyleman, R. (1988). Mice. In B. S. de Regniers (Ed.), *Sing a song of popcorn: Every child's book of poems.* New York: Scholastic.—Extension word: *nibble.*

Glaser, S. (2005). *The big race.* New York: Hyperion.—Listeners can have a never-ending race by turning the book around to start the next stretch.

Lane, L. (2003). *Snuggle mountain.* New York: Clarion Books.—Extension words: *snuggle, crevice, peak,* and *valley.*

Shulman, L. (2002). *Old MacDonald had a woodshop.* New York: Putnam's Sons.—Related word: *saw.* The many sound words will make this book enjoyable for students to join in.

Tarpley, N. A. (2002). *Bippity bop barbershop.* Boston: Little, Brown.—Related words: Title words with alliterative /b/ sounds. Extension words: The book provides a good description of the concepts of *nervousness* and *anticipation.*

Van Dusen, C. (2003). *A camping spree with Mr. Magee.* San Francisco: Chronicle Books.—Related words: *bear* and *mountains* and the alliterative *Mr. Magee.* Extension word: *spree.*

Wilson, K. (2002). *Bear snores on.* New York: Margaret K. McElderry Books.—Extension words: *cave, den, lair, blustery,* and several synonyms for *growl.*

Sort 3. Initial Consonants: t, n, p

t	*n*	*p*
Tt TOP	**Nn NUT**	**Pp PIG**
TAPE	NAIL	PAIL
TENT	NEEDLE	PEAS
TIRE	NEST	PENGUIN
TOAST	NET	PIE
TOES	NOSE	PUP
TWO		PURSE (or POCKETBOOK)

Try 5: Expect feature only—*new, name, page, pay, tell*

Sort 4. Initial Consonants: t, n, p, g

t	*n*	*p*	*g*
Tt TAG	**Nn NET**	**Pp PAN**	**Gg GUM**
TABLE	NAP	PEANUTS	GAME
TEN	NECK	PEAR	GHOST
TUB	NICKEL	PIN	GIRL
TURTLE		PUMPKIN	GOAT
			GUITAR

Try 5: Expect feature only—*get, pick, near, nice, take*

Considerations: Just as some children may refer to the purse picture as a *pocketbook*, so, too, some children may call the pail a *bucket*. In the latter case, the picture may be placed in an Oddball category. It is important for teachers to be sensitive about such differences in dialect.

Literature Links

Bennett, R. (1988). Necks. In B. S. de Regniers (Ed.), *Sing a song of popcorn: Every child's book of poems*. New York: Scholastic.—Extension word: *shaggy*.

Black, S. (1999). *Plenty of penguins*. New York: Scholastic.—Extension words: *rookeries* and *colonies*.

Hobby, H. (1997). *Toot and Puddle*. Boston: Little, Brown.—Another tale of adventure and friendship with two pigs whose names begin with letters being explored.

Lawson, J. (2002). *Audrey and Barbara*. New York: Atheneum Books for Young Readers. A girl seeks adventure but has trouble convincing her cat friend that it's a good idea. Related words: *tub* and *nap*; the tub depicted looks very much like the picture card. Extension words: *adventure* and *friendship*.

Smith, W. J. (1998). The toaster. In R. Alexander (Ed.), *Poetry place anthology*. New York: Scholastic.—The toaster is used as a metaphor for a dragon. Extension word: *scale*.

West, C. (1991). Norman Norton's nostrils. In B. Lansky (Ed.), *Kids pick the funniest poems: Poems that make kids laugh*. New York: Meadowbrook Press.—Related word: *nose*. Extension words: *nostril, inhale,* and *vanish*.

Wood, A. (1984). *The napping house*. Orlando, FL: Harcourt Brace.

Wood, A. (2001). *The little penguin*. New York: Dutton Children's Books.—Extension word: *nuzzling*.

Sort 5. Initial Consonants: *d, h, l*

d	*h*	*l*
Dd DOG	**Hh HAT**	**Ll LEGS**
DEER	HAND	LAMP
DICE	HEART	LETTER
DIG	HELMET	LION
DISHES	HIVE	LIPS
DUCK	HOP	LOG
	HORN	
	HOUSE	

Try 5: Expect feature only—*dark, day, have, home, like*

Sort 6. Initial Consonants: *d, h, l, c*

d	*h*	*l*	*c*
Dd DOLL	**Hh HORSE**	**Ll LEAF**	**Cc CAR**
DESK	HAM	LEMON	CAKE
DIVE	HIT	LETTERS	CAT
DOOR	HOSE	LOCK	COAT
	HUG		COMB
			CORN
			COW

Try 5: Expect feature only—*down, him, hurt, look, come*

Literature Links

Belloc, H. (2003). The lion. In G. Hale (Ed.), *An illustrated treasury of read-aloud poems for young people.* New York: Black Dog & Leventhal.—Extension words: *dwells,* the *waste, stark,* and *grim.*

Buzzeo, T. (2003). *Dawdle duckling.* New York: Dial Books for Young Readers.—Related word: *duck* and numerous alliterative words. Extension words: *dawdles, preen, downy,* and *dunk.*

Chute, M. (1988). Dogs. In B. S. de Regniers (Ed.), *Sing a song of popcorn: Every child's book of poems.* New York: Scholastic.—Extension word: *fluff.*

Driscoll, L. (1997). *The bravest cat! The true story of Scarlett.* New York: Scholastic.—Extension words: *hero* and *brave.*

Durston, G. R. (1998). The hippopotamus. In R. Alexander (Ed.), *Poetry place anthology.* New York: Scholastic.—Related words: Much repetition of the /h/ sound. Extension words: *rank* and the nonsense words *squdgy* and *oozely.*

Hall, K. (1995). *A bad, bad day.* New York: Scholastic.—Related words: Many words beginning with H.

Hartung, S. K. (2002). *One leaf rides the wind.* New York: Viking.—Extension words: *grasp, startled, miniature, prowl.* Haiku can also be considered an extension word, because the text is composed of 10 haiku poems.

Meisel, P. (2003). *Zara's hats.* New York: Dutton's Children's Books.—Extension words: *extraordinary, astonishment, melancholy, fabulous, amazing,* and *stupendous.*

Rockwell, A. (2005). *Honey in a hive.* New York: HarperTrophy.

Shannon, D. (2002). *Duck on a bike.* New York: Blue Sky Press.

Sort 7. Initial Consonants: *f, w, j*

f	*w*	*j*
Ff FORK	**Ww WELL**	**Jj JOG**
FEATHER	WATCH	JACKS
FENCE	WAVE	JAR
FISH	WET	JEEP
FIVE	WIG	JET
FOOTBALL	WING	
FOX	WITCH	
	WORM	

Try 5: Expect feature only—*first, for, with, joke, junk*

Sort 8. Initial Consonants: *f, w, j, k*

f	*w*	*j*	*k*
Ff FAN	**Ww WEB**	**Jj JUG**	**Kk KING**
FEET	WAGON	JACKET	KANGAROO
FIN	WIN	JUGGLE	KEY
FOUR	WINDOW	JUMP	KICK
	WINK		KITCHEN
			KITE
			KITTEN

Try 5: Expect feature only—*fun, will, would, jeans, keep*

Considerations: Because several of the words in Sort 8 are verbs, you might ask students to demonstrate their understanding of these words.

Literature Links

Bennett, R. (1988). From *The witch of Willowby Wood*. In B. S. de Regniers (Ed.), *Sing a song of popcorn: Every child's book of poems*. New York: Scholastic.—Extension words: *weird, snarled, gnarled,* and *rickety*.

Carle, E. (2000). *Does a kangaroo have a mother, too?* New York: HarperCollins.

Cowley, J. (2003). *Mrs. Wishy-Washy's farm*. New York: Philomel Books.—Related words: *farm* and *feathers* and the repetitive /w/ sound. Extension words: *anxious* and *stampede*.

Pfeffer, W. (1997). *Wiggling worms at work*. New York: HarperTrophy.

Reeves, J. (1969). W. In B. S. de Regniers (Ed.), *Poems children will sit still for: A selection for the primary grades*. New York: Macmillan.

Taback, S. (2000). *Joseph had a little overcoat*. New York: Viking.—Related word: *jacket*. Extension word: *overcoat*.

Uegaki, C. (2003). *Suki's kimono*. Toronto, Ontario, Canada: Kids Can Press.—Extension words: *kimono* and *festival*.

Sort 9. Initial Consonants: *y, v, z, q*

y	*v*	*z*	*q*
Yy YELL	**Vv VAN**	**Zz ZIPPER**	**Qq QUEEN**
YARD	VACUUM	ZEBRA	QUACK
YARN	VEST	ZERO	QUARTER
YAWN	VINE	ZIGZAG	QUESTION
YO-YO		ZIP CODE	QUIET
		ZOO	

Try 5: Expect feature only—*voice, very, your, yuck, zap*

Literature Links

Brown, M. W. (2003). *The fierce yellow pumpkin*. New York: HarperCollins.—The seasonal nature of this book may make it inappropriate at times. Related words: *yellow* and *zigzag*. Extension word: *fierce*.

Ellingwood, L. B. (1998). At the zoo. In R. Alexander (Ed.), *Poetry place anthology*. New York: Scholastic.—Extension words: *gamboled, pattered, clambered, frolic, hullabaloo,* and *vast.*

Mauchan, W. L. (1998). Quiet. In R. Alexander (Ed.), *Poetry place anthology*. New York: Scholastic.—Extension word: *fleecy.*

Taback, S. (2000). *Joseph had a little overcoat*. New York: Viking.—Related word: *vest.*

Thompson, L. (2003). *Little Quack*. New York: Simon & Schuster Books for Young Readers.

Final Consonants

This is the first study of consonants in the final position of words. Students may demonstrate some confusion over focusing on the ending sound. During interactive modeling of writing, give added attention to the final consonant sound. The consonants dealt with here are *b, d, f, g, l, m, n, p, r, s, t,* and *v.* Expectations for spelling sort words should be limited to what children know. For example HS and HUS are acceptable spellings for *house* at this time, as are SM and SEM for *swim.*

Sort 10. Final Consonants: *b, m, s, r*

b	*m*	*s*	*r*
b TUB	**m HAM**	**s HOUSE**	**r CAR**
COB	GAME	BUS	DOOR
CRAB	GUM	GAS	FOUR
ROBE	JAM	VASE	JAR
WEB	SWIM		PEAR
			STAR

Try 5: Expect feature only—*him, more, rub, some, this*

Sort 11. Final Consonants: *t, n, p, f*

t	*n*	*p*	*f*
t BOAT	**n MAN**	**p CUP**	**f LEAF**
BAT	BONE	CAP	KNIFE
CUT	BUN	MOP	ROOF
COAT	CANE	SHEEP	
KITE	MOON	SOAP	
NUT	SWAN		

Try 5: Expect feature only—*green, night, off, on, snap*

Sort 12. Final Consonants: *g, d, l, v*

g	*d*	*l*	*v*
g BAG	**d MUD**	**l BELL**	**v FIVE**
DIG	BREAD	BALL	DIVE
DOG	MAD	DOLL	HIVE
JOG	SAD	SEAL	STOVE
MUG	ROAD		WAVE
RUG			

Try 5: Expect feature only—*big, call, give, good, school*

SORT 1 Initial Consonants: *m, s, b*

Mm	Ss	Bb

SORT 2 Initial Consonants: *m, s, b, r*

Mm	**Ss**	**Bb**
Rr		

Tt	Nn	Pp

SORT 4 Initial Consonants: *t, n, p, g*

Tt	Nn	Pp
Gg		
10		

From *Word Sorts and More* by Kathy Ganske. Copyright 2006 by The Guilford Press. Permission to photocopy this form is granted to purchasers of this book for personal use only (see copyright page for details). Enlarge 135% to fill page.

Initial Consonants: *d, h, l*

Dd	Hh	Ll

SORT 6 Initial Consonants: *d, h, l, c*

Dd	Hh	Ll
Cc		

From *Word Sorts and More* by Kathy Ganske. Copyright 2006 by The Guilford Press. Permission to photocopy this form is granted to purchasers of this book for personal use only (see copyright page for details). Enlarge 135% to fill page.

Ff	Ww	Jj

From *Word Sorts and More* by Kathy Ganske. Copyright 2006 by The Guilford Press. Permission to photocopy this form is granted to purchasers of this book for personal use only (see copyright page for details). Enlarge 135% to fill page.

SORT 8 Initial Consonants: *f, w, j, k*

Ff	Ww	Jj
Kk		
4		

Yy	Vv	Zz
Qq		
0		

From *Word Sorts and More* by Kathy Ganske. Copyright 2006 by The Guilford Press. Permission to photocopy this form is granted to purchasers of this book for personal use only (see copyright page for details). Enlarge 135% to fill page.

SORT 10 Final Consonants: *b, m, s, r*

b 🛁	**m** 🍖	**s** 🏠
r 🚗	(vase)	(web)
(swimmer)	(gum)	(jar)
(crab)	(door)	(corn)
(gas pump)	(pear)	(game)
(robe)	(bus)	(star)
4	(jam)	

Final Consonants: *t, n, p, f*

t		n		p	
f					

SORT 12 Final Consonants: *g, d, l, v*

g		d		l	
v	5				

Same-Vowel Word Families: Introducing Short Vowels (DSA Feature C)

(Words and PICTURES)

Word families, or phonograms, are introduced in this part. Their study also initiates the study of short vowels, a theme that will be revisited and built on throughout the letter name stage. By this time, students should be somewhat confident in their use of initial and final consonants, although they may still exhibit some confusions over consonants such as *w* and *y*. Also, some of their spellings are likely to include vowels (such as JOP for *jump*, PEK for *peek*, and YAT for *wait*).

Eleven sorts are included in this section. Each focuses on a particular vowel's word families. The first one, Sort 13, isn't really a sort at all, as it does not involve a contrast. You may choose to use Sort 13 just to introduce the concept of a word family to the children, and then move on to Sort 14, which does have a contrast. Vowel *a* is covered thoroughly in Sorts 13–16 in order to build students' background knowledge for word families—*what is known*. Families for the other vowels are not covered as exhaustively. Because the even-numbered sorts that follow build on the odd-numbered ones through the inclusion of an additional family (such as adding *am* in Sort 16 to *ad*, *ag*, and *ap* in Sort 15), you may wish to omit the odd-numbered sorts for more capable students. Due to the limited pool of three-letter words available, numerous words are repeated in Sorts 13–24.

As children begin to work with word families in this and later sections, Make-It, Break-It activities with letter tiles (see Appendix C) can provide practice and reinforcement at centers or for independent work.

Sort 13. Same-Vowel Word Families: *at*   (Words with Their PICTURES)

at

fat
bat (ball)
bat (animal)
cat
hat
mat
pat
rat

Introduce students to the concept of word family by engaging them in a matching activity. Place the pictures in a row or column in front of the students and ask them to identify the name of each with you. Then say, "What do you notice about all of these words? How are they alike?" Once it has been pointed out that they all rhyme or sound alike, spread out the word cards in front of the children. Ask the students to try to find the word card that matches the first picture. Allow a volunteer to place it beside the picture; then direct students to try to find the word that matches the next picture. Continue the matching until all of the cards have been used. Then ask the students to look carefully at the words and to tell what they notice. With prompting, they should observe that all of the words rhyme *and* that they all end with *at*. Celebrate their discovery by reading aloud a book that includes numerous *at* family words, such as Dr. Seuss's *The Cat in the Hat*. The next day, present students with the following set of words and pictures:

Sort 14. Same-Vowel Word Families: *at, an*   *(Words with Their PICTURES)*

at	*an*
fat	**fan**
bat (ball)	can
hat	man
mat	pan
	ran
	van

After placing the key pictures, *fat* and *fan*, in front of the students, remind them of the family of words they explored the previous day, pointing out that *fat* was a member of the family and so was *bat*. Draw their attention to *fan* and ask if they think this word is also a member of the family. (If they focus on the *f* in both words, refocus their attention to the way *fat* and *bat*, which are in the same family rhyme.) Follow up with "What makes you think that?" Students should conclude that *fan* belongs to a different family because it doesn't rhyme. Next, place one of the remaining *an* pictures in front of the students and ask if this word rhymes with *fat* or with *fan*. Once it is identified, move the card to the *fan* column, correcting any misunderstandings, and point out that it is a member of the *an* family because it rhymes with *fan*. Continue in like manner with the remaining pictures.

Then spread the word cards out in a line in front of the children. As on the previous day, ask students to match up the words with their pictures, one at a time. When all of the matches are made, ask the children to join you in reading each of the lists. After each list is read, discuss how the words are alike: "They all rhyme" should be part of the response. Then ask how the words under *fat* are different from those under *fan*. They should note that all the words in the *fat* category end in *at*, and that all the words in the *fan* category end in *an*.

Close the session by asking students to spell an alien *at* or *an* word or by redoing the sort. For the latter, collect and randomly distribute the word cards to the children; leave the picture cards in a line. Beginning with the first picture (leftmost or top), ask the group to check their card(s) to see if they have the match. When a match is found, tell the student to read the word and place it next to the picture, just as before. Continue in like manner until all of the words have been sorted.

Sort 15. Same-Vowel Word Families: *ad, ag, ap*   *(Words with Their PICTURES)*

ad	*ag*	*ap*
sad	**tag**	**cap**
dad	bag	lap
mad	sag	map
pad	wag	nap

Try 5: bad, had, gap, rag, rap

Sort 16. Same-Vowel Word Families: *ad, ag, ap, am*   *(Words and PICTURES)*

ad	*ag*	*ap*	*am*
dad	**bag**	**lap**	**ham**
bad	FLAG	CLAP	dam
had	rag	gap	jam
MAD	tag	map	
pad	wag	nap	
sad		tap	
		zap	

Try 5: *fad,* **hap**py, *nag, ram, yam.* When dictating Try 5 words with more than one syllable, say something like "The next one is *hap … hap …* as in *happy.*" Expect only the bolded portion of *happy.*

Considerations: Because words are included for each picture in Sort 15 (as well as Sorts 17, 19, 21, and 23), the sort may be introduced in the same manner as Sorts 13–14. Also, as previously indicated, students who are able to move along more quickly may skip Sort 15; all three of its categories are included in Sort 16. Except where otherwise noted, the remaining sorts in Part 3 may be introduced to students through closed sorting with teacher direction, such as a guided word walk. Many additional experiences should be provided to enable children to practice and apply their understandings.

Literature Links

Bang, M. (1999). *When Sophie gets angry—Really, really angry.* New York: Blue Sky Press.—Related word: *mad.*

Dyer, J. (2002). *Little Brown Bear won't take a nap!* Boston: Little, Brown.—Extension word: *hibernation,* although it does not appear in the text.

Krosoczka, J. J. (2002). *Baghead.* New York: Knopf.

Prelutsky, J. (1984). I wonder why Dad is so thoroughly mad. In *The new kid on the block.* New York: Scholastic.—Extension word: *thoroughly.*

Sort 17. Same-Vowel Word Families: *ig, in, ip*   *(Words with Their PICTURES)*

ig	*in*	*ip*
dig	**chin**	**lip**
big	fin	rip
pig	pin	sip
wig	win	zip

Try 5: *bin, dip, fig, jig, tin*

Sort 18. Same-Vowel Word Families: *ig, in, ip, it* (Words and PICTURES)

ig	*in*	*ip*	*it*
wig	**pin**	**zip**	**hit**
big	CHIN	dip	bit
dig	FIN	lip	fit
fig	tin	SHIP	pit
	win	tip	kit
			sit

Try 5: dinner, hip, nip, lit, rig. Expect first syllable only in multisyllabic words, as with Sort 16.

Considerations: Be sure students know what the words mean; if possible, it may be helpful to bring in a *fig* to illustrate this word. *Tin* is also likely to be unfamiliar to many students. Students who are able to move along more quickly may skip Sort 17; all three of its categories are included in Sort 18.

Literature Links

Davis, A. (1997). *The enormous potato.** Ontario, Canada: Kids Can Press.
Peck, J. (1998). *The giant carrot.** New York: Dial.
Prelutsky, J. (1990). Something big has been here. In *Something big has been here*. New York: Scholastic.
Tolstoy, A. (2003). *The enormous turnip** (S. Goto, Illus.). San Diego, CA: Harcourt.

*These three books provide a wonderful opportunity for reading and writing follow-up stories related to other humungous vegetables. *Big* is a related word for all three books. Ask students to brainstorm other words that mean big, besides *giant* and *enormous*. Depict the results in a word web.

Sort 19. Same-Vowel Word Families: *og, op, ot* (Words with Their PICTURES)

og	*op*	*ot*
frog	**hop**	**dot**
dog	mop	cot
log	pop	hot
jog	top	pot

Try 5: fog, got, hog, lop, not

Sort 20. Same-Vowel Word Families: *og, ot, ob* (Words and PICTURES)

og	*ot*	*ob*
dog	**cot**	**sob**
bog	dot	bob
fog	got	cob
FROG	hot	gob
hog	jot	job
LOG	lot	mob
	not	ROB
	rot	

Try 5: cog, **lob**ster, **gog**gles, **slot**, tot. Expect first syllable only in multisyllabic words; see Sort 16 for guidance in dictating words with multiple syllables. Also, incomplete renderings of blends and digraphs (*slot* as SOT) are to be expected at this time.

Considerations: Students who are moving along quickly may skip Sort 19. Due to the limited pool of words, Sort 20 maintains three categories rather than increasing to four.

Literature Links

Egan, B. (1996). *"Pop" pops the popcorn.* Parsippany, NJ: Modern Curriculum Press. (Ready Readers series).
Geisel, T. S. [Dr. Seuss]. (1963). *Hop on pop.* New York: Random House.
Gregorich, B. (1996). *Jog, frog, jog* (Start to Read series). Grand Haven, MI: School Zone.

Sort 21. Same-Vowel Word Families: eg, en, et   *(Words with Their PICTURES)*

eg	*en*	*et*
leg	**ten**	**pet**
beg	den	jet
peg	hen	net
	men	wet
	pen	

Try 5: Ben, get, let, Meg, Ted

Sort 22. Same-Vowel Word Families: eg, en, et, ed   *(Words and PICTURES)*

eg	*en*	*et*	*ed*
peg	**pen**	**net**	**bed**
beg	den	get	fed
leg	hen	met	led
	men	PET	red
	ten	set	SHED
		wet	SLED
		yet	

Try 5: Greg, **ken**nel, **let**ter, fed, wed. Expect first syllable only in multisyllabic words. Initial blend may be incomplete in *Greg.* See Sort 16 for guidance in dictating multisyllabic words.

Considerations: (For Sorts 21–22) *Bear Snores On* by Karma Wilson includes pictures of a den and synonymous words: *lair* and *cave.* Also, students who are moving along quickly may skip Sort 21.

Literature Links

Douglas, L. A. (2003). The hen. In G. Hale (Ed.), *An illustrated treasury of read-aloud poems for young people.* New York: Black Dog & Leventhal.
Galdone, P. (1985). *The little red hen.* Boston: Clarion.

Plath, S. (1995). From *The bed book*. In E. H. Sword (Ed.), *A child's anthology of poetry*. Hopewell, NJ: Ecco Press.—Extension words such as "tucked-in-tight little, nighty-night little, turn-out-the-light little bed."

Viorst, J. (1971). *The tenth good thing about Barney*. New York: Aladdin.

Sort 23. Same-Vowel Word Families: *ug, un, ut* (Words with Their PICTURES)

ug	un	ut
jug	sun	cut
bug	bun	hut
hug	run	nut
mug		
rug		
tug		

Try 5: *but, dug, lug, fun, rut*

Sort 24. Same-Vowel Word Families: *ug, un, ut, ub* (Words and PICTURES)

ug	un	ut	ub
bug	run	hut	tub
dug	bun	but	cub
hug	fun	CUT	hub
JUG	sun	nut	rub
mug			sub
PLUG			
rug			
tug			

Try 5: *bubble, hub, mutter, slug, spun*. Expect first syllable only in multisyllabic words, and do not hold students accountable for the blend, just the initial consonant, as blends have not yet been studied. See Sort 16 for guidance in dictating multisyllabic words.

Considerations: Students who are moving along quickly may skip Sort 23.

Literature Links

Asch, F. (1988). Sunflakes. In B. S. de Regniers (Ed.), *Sing a song of popcorn: Every child's book of poems*. New York: Scholastic.—Related word: *sun* appears in many imaginative words, such as *sunman, sunball, sunbanks*, and *sunmobile*.

Ehlert, L. (1993). *Nuts to you*. San Diego, CA: Harcourt Children's Books.

Fredericks, A. D. (2000). *Slugs*. Minneapolis, MN: Learner.

Richstone, M. (1998). Tug-of-war. In R. Alexander (Ed.), *Poetry place anthology*. New York: Scholastic.—Extension words: *marvel, brace,* and *extend*.

Simmie, L. (1991). Bug. In B. Lansky (Ed.), *Kids pick the funniest poems: Poems that make kids laugh*. New York: Meadowbrook Press.

Same-Vowel Word Families: *at*

fat	bat	mat
bat	cat	pat
rat	hat	

SORT 14 Same-Vowel Word Families: *at, an*

fat	fan	can
hat	pan	van
man	ran	mat
bat		

Same-Vowel Word Families: *ad, ag, ap*

sad	tag	cap
sag	nap	dad
lap	bag	mad
pad	map	wag

Same-Vowel Word Families: *ad, ag, ap, am*

dad	bag	lap
ham	wag	had
tap	zap	dam
sad	rag	gap
nap	jam	bad
tag	pad	map

dig	chin	lip
fin	zip	big
sip	wig	pin
win	pig	rip

SORT 18 Same-Vowel Word Families: *ig, in, ip, it*

wig	pin	zip
hit	dip	fit
rip	pit	tip
win	sit	big
bit	fig	kit
dig	lip	tin

frog	hop	dot
mop	dog	top
pot	jog	cot
hot	pop	log

Same-Vowel Word Families: *og, ot, ob*

dog	cot	sob
hog	got	fog
job	mob	lot
not	dot	bog
cob	jot	rot
hot	bob	gob

Same-Vowel Word Families: *eg, en, et*

leg	ten 10	pet
men	peg	den
jet	hen	beg
pen	wet	net

peg	pen	net
bed	get	men
wet	fed	leg
hen	set	led
yet	beg	red
ten	met	den

jug	sun	cut
bun	mug	hug
rug	run	nut
hut	tug	bug

bug	run	hut
tub	hub	rug
tug	nut	sub
but	dug	bun
cub	fun	hug
sun	mug	rub

Initial Consonant Digraphs and Blends (DSA Feature B)

(PICTURES Only, Except as Noted)

Digraphs and blends are frequently incomplete at the letter name stage, so contrasts that focus on this feature build on children's more secure knowledge of single consonants. Thus, for Sort 25, the *s* and the *h* are the *what is known*, and *what is new* is the digraph *sh*. Sort 28 provides an example of how the *new* can become the *known* after students have worked with the feature. In Sort 28, *t* and *th* have been studied (are known) and *wh* is new. Seven sorts follow with a focus on digraphs; these are followed by numerous blend-related sorts. Be sure to check picture identification and to discuss the meanings of any unfamiliar words before modeling and demonstrating the sort. As with the previous study of word families, be sensitive to your students' needs; all of the sorts may not be necessary.

Sort 25. Initial-Consonant Digraphs: *s, h, sh*

<u>s</u>	<u>h</u>	<u>sh</u>
s SIT	**h HOP**	**sh SHOP**
SANDWICH	HAND	SHADOW
SEVEN	HEART	SHAVE
SINK	HIT	SHED
SIP	HOUSE	SHEEP
SOAP		SHELL
SOCK		SHIP
		SHOE

Try 5: Expect feature only—*how, seat, send, shake, short*

Literature Link

Stevenson, R. L. (2003). My shadow. In G. Hale (Ed.), *An illustrated treasury of read-aloud poems for young people.* New York: Black Dog & Leventhal.

Sort 26. Initial-Consonant Digraphs: *c, h, ch*

<u>c</u>	<u>h</u>	<u>ch</u>
c CUP	**h HIT**	**ch CHIN**
cake	ham	chain
candle	hat	chair
comb	haystack	check
cow	hook	cheese
cut	horn	chick
		chimney
		chop

Try 5: Expect feature only—*check, child, color, came, here.* See Sort 16 for guidance in dictating multisyllabic words.

Literature Links

Prelutsky, J. (1990). Last night I dreamed of chickens. In *Something big has been here*. New York: Scholastic.

Rossetti, C. (2003). Caterpillar. In G. Hale (Ed.), *An illustrated treasury of read-aloud poems for young people*. New York: Black Dog & Leventhal.

Sort 27. Initial-Consonant Digraphs: *t, h, th*

t	*h*	*th*
t TENT	**h HOT**	**th THINK**
TABLE	HARP	THERMOS
TIE	HILL	THERMOMETER
TOES	HOLE	THIMBLE
TURTLE	HOSE	THIRTY
TWO	HUG	THORN
	HUMP	THUMB

Try 5: Expect feature only—*hello, tale, thing, thunder, title*. See Sort 16 for guidance in dictating multisyllabic words.

Literature Links

Killon, B. (1998). Think of it. In R. Alexander (Ed.), *Poetry place anthology*. New York: Instructor.—Related word: *think*. Extension words: *darting, soaring, strolling*, and *oozing*.

Merriam, E. (1998). A cliché. In R. Alexander (Ed.), *Poetry place anthology*. New York: Instructor.—Related word: *think*. Extension words: *cliché, fleecy*, and *scuttling*.

Nash, O. (1988). The camel. In B. S. de Regniers (Ed.), *Sing a song of popcorn: Every child's book of poems*. New York: Scholastic.—Related word: *hump*. Extension word: *dromedary*.

Sort 28. Initial-Consonant Digraphs: *h, th, wh*

h	*th*	*wh*
h HILL	**th THINK**	**wh WHIP**
HEEL	THERMOMETER	WHALE
HELMET	THERMOS	WHEEL
HEN	THIRTEEN	WHEELBARROW
HIVE	THORN	WHISKERS
HOOK	THUMB	WHISPER
HORSE		WHISTLE

Try 5: Expect feature only—*hiccough, hurt, thank, where, why*

Literature Link

Hubbell, P. (1998). Our washing machine. In R. Alexander (Ed.), *Poetry place anthology*. New York: Scholastic.—Related words: Numerous sound words, several with /wh/, are included.

Prelutsky, J. (1984). We heard Wally wail. In *The new kid on the block*. New York: Scholastic.

Rossetti, C. (2003). What is pink? In G. Hale (Ed.), *An illustrated treasury of read-aloud poems for young people.* New York: Black Dog & Leventhal.—*What* appears repeatedly in the poem. Extension words: *brink, mellow,* and *twilight.*

Sort 29. Initial-Consonant Digraphs: *ch, sh, th, wh*

ch	*sh*	*th*	*wh*
ch CHEESE	**sh SHEEP**	**th THUMB**	**wh WHISTLE**
CHECK	SHARK	THIMBLE	WHALE
CHERRIES	SHAVE	THINK	WHEEL
CHEST	SHIRT	THIRTY	WHIP
CHICK		THORN	WHISKERS
CHOP			

Try 5: Expect feature only—*chose, sharp, there, those, what*

Considerations: Some children may be able to skip Sort 29; the same categories are covered in Sort 30. The difference lies in the fact that Sort 29 consists of pictures only, whereas Sort 30 has pictures and words.

Sort 30. Initial-Consonant Digraphs: *ch, sh, th, wh*   (Words and PICTURES)

ch	*sh*	*th*	*wh*
ch CHICK	**sh SHELL**	**th THIMBLE**	**wh WHEEL**
CHERRIES	SHADE	them	WHALE
CHIEF	shot	then	WHEELBARROW
chip	SHIRT	THERMOS	when
	shut	THIRTEEN	whip
		this	

Try 5: Expect feature only—*chocolate, shout, they, thought, which.* See Sort 16 for guidance in dictating multisyllabic words.

For Sorts 31–45, the focus shifts from consonant digraphs to blends. As with the digraphs, the contrasts build on the known, which is, again, knowledge of initial consonants. Pictures are used for all but three of the sorts (Sorts 35, 38, and 45), and those sorts are composed of pictures and words. Additional known words may be included in the sort, if desired. The pictures draw students' attention to sound distinctions, and they increase the number of words these novice readers can explore. Some children may require assistance in blending together individual consonants.

Sort 31. Initial-Consonant Blends: *s, t, st*

s	*t*	*st*
s SIX	**t TUB**	**st STOP**
SAIL	TIE	STAMP
SIP	TEETH	STAR
SIT	TOES	STEM
SOAP	TOP	STICK
SOB	TUG	STIR
		STOOL
		STUMP

Try 5: Expect feature only—*silly, sort, still, stand, tongue.* See Sort 16 for guidance in dictating multisyllabic words.

Literature Link

Cannon, J. (1993). *Stellaluna.* San Diego, CA: Harcourt, Brace.—Repetition of *st* in Stellaluna, the bat's name. Extension words: *swooped, clambered, perched, sultry,* and *clutched.*

Taylor, J. (2003). The star. In G. Hale (Ed.), *An illustrated treasury of read-aloud poems for young people.* New York: Black Dog & Leventhal.—The most well known of star poems in its entirety.

Welte, L. A. (1998). Start of a storm. In R. Alexander (Ed.), *Poetry place anthology.* New York: Scholastic.—Extension phrase: "yellow stabs the sky."

Sort 32. Initial-Consonant Blends: *s, p, sp*

s	*p*	*sp*
s SINK	**p PEN**	**sp SPOON**
SAD	PAIL	SPEAR
SANDWICH	PEACH	SPIDER
SAW	PENGUIN	SPIN
SCISSORS	PIPE	SPONGE
SEAL	PUP	SPOOL
	PURSE	SPOT

Try 5: Expect feature only—*pencil, people, sale, spend, sports*

Considerations: Some children may confuse *pinwheel* with *spin.* Point out the action lines to them. If the problem persists, allow them to sort it under *p.*

Literature Link

Jacobson, E. (1998). The spider. In R. Alexander (Ed.), *Poetry place anthology.* New York: Scholastic.—Extension words: *entertain, relations, woe, wary, accomplished,* and *murmurs.*

Monks, L. (2004). *Aaaarrgghh! Spider!* Boston: Houghton Mifflin.

Sort 33. Initial-Consonant Blends: *st, sp, sk, sn*

st	*sp*	*sk*	*sn*
st STAMP	**sp SPIN**	**sk SKIRT**	**sn SNAIL**
STAIRS	SPILL	SKATE	SNAKE
STING	SPONGE	SKELETON	SNEEZE
STIR	SPOON	SKULL	SNOW
		SKIS	SNOWMAN
		SKIP	
		SKUNK	

Try 5: Expect feature only—*sky, snarl, sneakers, spoil, stapler.* See Sort 16 for guidance in dictating multisyllabic words.

Literature Links

Cannon, J. (1997). *Verdi.* San Diego, CA: Harcourt, Brace.—Related word: *snake.* Extension words: *dawdled* and *ventured.*

Milne, A. A. (1988). The more it snows. In B. S. de Regniers (Ed.), *Sing a song of popcorn: Every child's book of poems.* New York: Scholastic.—Repetition of "tiddely-pom" creates a feeling of snow hitting against a window.

Sort 34. Initial-Consonant Blends: *sc, sm, sl, sw*

sc	*sm*	*sl*	*sw*
sc SCARF	**sm SMELL**	**sl SLED**	**sw SWIM**
SCALE	SMASH	SLEEP	SWAN
SCOOTER	SMILE	SLEEVE	SWEATER
SCORE	SMOKE	SLIDE	SWING
SCOUT		SLIP	SWITCH
		SLIPPER	

Try 5: Expect feature only—*scare, smart, smooth, slow, sweat*

Literature Links

Andersen, H. C. (1999). In *The ugly duckling* (J. Pinkney, Illus.).—Related word: *swan.*

Coatsworth, E. (1995). Swift things are beautiful. In E. H. Sword (Ed.), *A child's anthology of poetry.* Hopewell, NJ: Ecco Press.—Extension words: *swallows, bright-veined, meteors, strong-withered,* and *ember.*

Sierra, J. (1998). Penguins' first swim. In *Antarctic antics: A book of penguin poems.* San Diego, CA: Harcourt Brace and Company. Extension words: *hesitate, huddle,* and *fidget.*

Stevenson, R. L. (1995). The swing. In E. H. Sword (Ed.), *A child's anthology of poetry.* Hopewell, NJ: Ecco Press.

U'Ren, A. (2003). *Mary Smith.* New York: Farrar, Straus & Giroux.—Related words: Mary *Smith,* which is repeated numerous times in the text.

Sort 35. Initial-Consonant Blends: *sk, sn, sp, st* *(Words and PICTURES)*

sk	*sn*	*sp*	*st*
sk SKUNK	**sn SNOW**	**sp SPIDER**	**st STOOL**
SKIS	SNAKE	spin	stem
skim	snap	SPOOL	step
skip	SNEEZE	SPONGE	STIR
SKIRT	snug		STUMP
skid			

Try 5: Expect feature only—*skill, snack, snore, special, stomach*. See Sort 16 for guidance in dictating multisyllabic words.

Considerations: The use of words and pictures for this sort allows children to apply their knowledge of blends to spell entire words, while still working with a relatively large pool of words.

Sort 36. Initial-Consonant Blends: *sl, gl, pl*

sl	*gl*	*pl*
sl SLIP	**gl GLOBE**	**pl PLANT**
SLED	GLASS	PLAID
SLEEP	GLASSES	PLANE
SLEEVE	GLOVE	PLATE
SLIDE	GLUE	PLIERS
SLING		PLUG
SLIPPER		PLUM
		PLUS

Try 5: Expect feature only—*glow, play, please, sloppy, slush*. See Sort 16 for guidance in dictating multisyllabic words.

Sort 37. Initial-Consonant Blends: *bl, cl, fl*

bl	*cl*	*fl*
bl BLOUSE	**cl CLOWN**	**fl FLOWER**
BLANKET	CLAP	FLAG
BLINDFOLD	CLAW	FLAME
BLOCK	CLIMB	FLASHLIGHT
BLOW	CLIP	FLIP
	CLOCK	FLOAT
	CLOUDS	FLUTE
		FLY

Try 5: Expect feature only—*blue, blink, clay, clothes, flea*

Literature Links

McCord, D. (1996). Every time I climb a tree. In *A jar of tiny stars: Poems by NCTE award-winning poets*. Honesdale, PA: Boyds Mills Press.—Extension word: *dodge*.

Rossetti, C. (1988). Clouds. In B. S. de Regniers (Ed.), *Sing a song of popcorn: Every child's book of poems*. New York: Scholastic.—Sheep are used as a metaphor for clouds.

Sort 38. Initial-Consonant Blends: *cl, fl, pl, sl* (Words and PICTURES)

cl	*fl*	*pl*	*sl*
cl CLOCK	fl FLY	pl PLATE	sl SLEEP
clap	flag	PLANT	slip
CLAW	flap	PLIERS	SLEEVE
CLOWN	flip	plug	SLIDE
	FLOWER	plus	slop
	FLOAT		

Try 5: Expect feature only—*close, closet, flock, planet, sliver*. See Sort 16 for guidance in dictating multisyllabic words.

Considerations: The use of words and pictures for this sort allows children to apply their knowledge of blends to spell entire words, while still working with a relatively large pool of words.

Literature Links

Adams, P. (1988). *There was an old lady who swallowed a fly*. China: Child's Play International.—Extension word: *wriggled*.

Spence, R., & Spence, A. (1999). *Clickety clack*. New York: Puffin Books.—Extension words: *yak, caboose*, and *acrobat*.

Sort 39. Initial-Consonant Blends: *b, bl, br*

b	*bl*	*br*
b BEE	bl BLOCK	br BRUSH
BAKE	BLANKET	BRACELET
BEAK	BLINDFOLD	BRAID
BELL	BLOUSE	BREAD
BELT	BLOW	BRICK
BIKE		BRIDE
BIRD		BRIDGE
		BROOM

Try 5: Expect feature only—*back, been, breathe, brother, blame*. See Sort 16 for guidance in dictating multisyllabic words.

Sort 40. Initial-Consonant Blends: *cl, fl, cr, fr*

cl	*fl*	*cr*	*fr*
cl CLIP	**fl FLAG**	**cr CRAYON**	**fr FRUIT**
CLIMB	FLASHLIGHT	CRAB	FRAME
CLOUDS	FLIP	CRACK	FRECKLES
CLOWN	FLOWER	CRIB	FRIES
	FLUTE	CROWN	FROG
	FLY		

Try 5: Expect feature only—*class, crash, cry, floor, friend*

Literature Links

Angelou, M. (2003). Life doesn't frighten me. In G. Hale (Ed.), *An illustrated treasury of read-aloud poems for young people.* New York: Black Dog & Leventhal.

Watts, M. (1998). Freckles. In R. Alexander (Ed.), *Poetry place anthology.* New York: Scholastic.—Extension word: *speckles.*

Sort 41. Initial-Consonant Blends: *gl, pl, gr, pr*

gl	*pl*	*gr*	*pr*
gl GLASSES	**pl PLANE**	**gr GRAPES**	**pr PRETZEL**
GLOBE	PLANT	GRASS	PRAY
GLOVE	PLATE	GRASSHOPPER	PRESENT
GLUE	PLIERS	GRILL	PRICE
	PLUG	GROCERIES	PRIZE
	PLUS		

Try 5: Expect feature only—*glance, great, plenty, promise, pretty*

Sort 42. Initial-Consonant Blends: *d, r, dr*

d	*r*	*dr*
d DOLL	**r RUG**	**dr DRUM**
DAD	RAKE	DRAGON
DEER	RING	DRAWER
DESK	ROBE	DREAM
DICE	ROCK	DRESS
DIME	ROOF	DRIP
DUCK		DRIVE

Try 5: Expect feature only—*day, dollar, drink, rest, room.* See Sort 16 for guidance in dictating multisyllabic words.

Literature Links

Funk, A. L. (1998). My dream. In R. Alexander (Ed.), *Poetry place anthology*. New York: Scholastic.
Hughes, L. (1994). Dreams. In *The dream keeper and other poems*. New York: Scholastic.—Extension
      words: *hold fast* and *barren*.

Sort 43. Initial-Consonant Blends: *t, r, tr*

t	r	tr
t TEN	**r ROPE**	**tr TREE**
TAG	RAIN	TRACTOR
TAPE	RAN	TRAIN
TIE	RIP	TRAMPOLINE
TOAST	ROAD	TRIANGLE
TOES		TRUCK
TUBE		TRUNK
TWO		

Try 5: Expect feature only—*right, talk, teacher, trash, try*. See Sort 16 for guidance in dictating multisyllabic words.

Literature Links

Palmer, T. H. (1995). Try, try again. In E. H. Sword (Ed.), *A child's anthology of poetry*. Hopewell, NJ: Ecco
      Press.
Silverstein, S. (1964). *The giving tree*. New York: HarperCollins.

Sort 44. Initial-Consonant Blends: *dr, gr, tr*

dr	gr	tr
dr DRESS	**gr GRASS**	**tr TRUCK**
DRAGON	GRAPES	TRACK
DRAWER	GRASSHOPPER	TRACTOR
DREAM	GRILL	TRAMPOLINE
DRILL	GROCERIES	TRAY
DRIP		TREE
DRIVE		TRIANGLE
		TRUNK

Try 5: Expect feature only—*drew, dread, ground, grow, trail*

Literature Links

Prelutsky, J. (1984). Drumpp the grump. In *The new kid on the block*. New York: Scholastic.—Related
      word: *gruff*; as well as the title words; also includes several *d, g,* and *r* words.

Sort 45. Initial-Consonant Blends: *cr, dr, gr, tr* *(Words and PICTURES)*

cr	*dr*	*gr*	*tr*
cr CROWN	**dr DREAM**	**gr GRILL**	**tr TRAIN**
CRAB	drag	GRAPES	TRAP
crib	DRIP	GRASS	TREE
crop	drop	grid	TRUCK
	DRUM	grip	trim
			trip

Try 5: Expect feature only—*crowd, drizzle, green, trick, troll*. See Sort 16 for guidance in dictating multisyllabic words.

Considerations: The use of words and pictures for this sort allows children to apply their knowledge of blends to spell entire words, while still working with a relatively large pool of words.

Sort 46. Initial-Consonant Blends and Digraphs: *sw, wh, qu, tw*

sw	*wh*	*qu*	*tw*
sw SWING	**wh WHISPER**	**qu QUACK**	**tw TWELVE**
SWAN	WHALE	QUARTER	TWEEZERS
SWIM	WHEEL	QUEEN	TWENTY
SWITCH	WHIP	QUESTION	TWINS
	WHISTLE	QUIET	TWIRL
			TWIST

Try 5: Expect feature only—*quit, sweet, twinkle, wheat, while*. See Sort 16 for guidance in dictating multisyllabic words.

Literature Link

McKinney, J. B. (1998). Twins. In R. Alexander (Ed.), *Poetry place anthology*. New York: Scholastic.

Initial-Consonant Digraphs: *s, h, sh*

s	h	sh

Initial-Consonant Digraphs: *c, h, ch*

c	h	ch

Initial-Consonant Digraphs: *t, h, th*

t	h	th
30		
	98.6	
	2	

SORT 28 Initial-Consonant Digraphs: *h, th, wh*

h	th	wh
		13

ch	sh	th
wh		30

ch	sh	th
wh		when
		shot
this	whip	
	13	them
shut		chip
	then	

Initial-Consonant Blends: *s, t, st*

s	t	st

Initial-Consonant Blends: *s, p, sp*

s	p	sp

SORT 33 Initial-Consonant Blends: *st, sp, sk, sn*

st	sp	sk
sn		

SORT 34 Initial-Consonant Blends: *sc, sm, sl, sw*

sc	sm	sl
sw		

Initial-Consonant Blends: *sk, sn, sp, st*

sk	sn	sp
st		
skim		stem
	snap	skip
snug		skid
	step	
spin		

From *Word Sorts and More* by Kathy Ganske. Copyright 2006 by The Guilford Press. Permission to photocopy this form is granted to purchasers of this book for personal use only (see copyright page for details). Enlarge 135% to fill page.

sl	gl	pl

SORT 37 Initial-Consonant Blends: *bl, cl, fl*

bl	cl	fl

cl	fl	pl
sl	clap	
flag		plug
	slip	flip
flap		
	plus	
slop		

SORT 39   Initial-Consonant Blends: *b, bl, br*

b	bl	br

SORT 40 Initial-Consonant Blends: *cl, fl, cr, fr*

cl	fl	cr
fr		

Initial-Consonant Blends: *gl, pl, gr, pr*

gl	pl	gr
pr		

Initial-Consonant Blends: *d, r, dr*

d	r	dr

SORT 43 Initial-Consonant Blends: *t, r, tr*

t 10	r	tr
		2

SORT 44 Initial-Consonant Blends: *dr, gr, tr*

dr	gr	tr

Initial-Consonant Blends: *cr, dr, gr, tr*

cr	dr	gr
tr		
trip		drag
	grid	
crop		trim
	drop	crib
grip		

SORT 46 Initial-Consonant Blends and Digraphs: *sw, wh, qu, tw*

sw	wh	qu
tw		

Different-Vowel Word Families (DSA Feature C)
(Words and PICTURES, Except as Noted)

In this section, several word families from the same-vowel word families study are combined and ex-amined across different vowels. Although nearly all of the word families included are *known*, com-paring them in mixed groups is *new*. These types of contrasts will move learners closer to examining short vowels by helping them begin to notice differences in the sounds of the vowels themselves. Because the spellings provide strong visual cues, a few pictures have been included in each sort to encourage attention to sound as well as pattern. In addition, blind sorting should be incorporated into the activity routine.

All of the Try 5 words in this section are real words. However, students may not be familiar with them. If preferred, words from previous sorts may be used, with the aim of checking long-term retention of the spellings rather than providing learners with opportunities to apply their new un-derstanding. Where applicable, the relevant sorts are noted after the Try 5 words.

After students identify the words, discuss any unfamiliar word meanings; then introduce Sorts 48–50 in a manner similar to the following: Ask students to help you sort the word cards by group-ing together those that have the same rhyming pattern, such as *cap/clap*. Present one word at a time and provide modeling support as needed. Next, ask them to read with you through each column of words, discussing how the words in each category are alike. Then bring out the picture cards and ask if anyone can tell where the first picture should go. Continue in like fashion with the remaining pictures. Once placed, ask students to provide spellings for the picture words. Finally, help them to make generalizations about the sounds and patterns under study; for example, "The words under *cap* all end in *a-p*, and they have the /ăp/ sound." Refine students' thinking so that it encompasses the fact that in all of the *ap* words the vowel has a short sound /ă/, and so on. Sorts 48–50 may be taught in a similar manner.

Sort 47. Different-Vowel Word Families: *ap, ip, op*

ap	*ip*	*op*
cap	**sip**	**top**
clap	clip	flop
LAP	dip	plop
NAP	FLIP	POP
snap	hip	SHOP
slap	LIP	
	ship	
	skip	
	tip	

Try 5: blip, lop, pip, prop, yap. See also Sorts 15–20.

Sort 48. Different-Vowel Word Families: *at, et, ot*

at	*et*	*ot*
hat	**pet**	**pot**
BAT (animal)	get	COT
FAT	JET	got
flat	let	rot
sat	met	shot
that	vet	SPOT
	WET	trot

Try 5: brat, bet, chat, slot, yet. See also Sorts 13–14 and 19–22.

Sort 49. Different-Vowel Word Families: *ag, ig, og, ug*

ag	*ig*	*og*	*ug*
sag	**big**	**jog**	**rug**
BAG	fig	bog	dug
brag	twig	DOG	MUG
nag		fog	PLUG
snag		clog	TUG
		hog	
		LOG	

Try 5: shag, brig, blog, chug, rig. See also Sorts 15–20 and 23–24.

Sort 50. Different-Vowel Word Families: *ab, ub, ad, id*   (Words Only)

ab	*ub*	*ad*	*id*
crab	**tub**	**mad**	**lid**
blab	cub	bad	did
cab	rub	fad	hid
jab	sub	had	kid
tab	stub	glad	slid

Try 5: brad, dub, flub, nab, rid. See also Sorts 15–16 and 24.

Considerations: Although word families with *ub* and *ad* have previously been explored, the *ab* and *id* families are new in this sort.

Different-Vowel Word Families: *ap, ip, op*

cap	sip	top
	plop	skip
tip		clap
	dip	snap
clip		flop
slap	hip	
	ship	

Different-Vowel Word Families: *at, et, ot*

hat	pet	pot
	rot	met
flat		trot
	let	that
get	shot	
	vet	sat
got		

Different-Vowel Word Families: *ag, ig, og, ug*

sag	big	jog
rug	nag	
brag		fog
hog		
twig	dug	fig
clog		bog
	snag	

crab	tub	mad
lid	fad	did
rub	kid	sub
had	jab	hid
tab	cub	bad
stub	glad	cab
blab	slid	

Short Vowels (DSA Feature C)

Note: Except for key words, PICTURES only are used for Sorts 51–57 and words only for Sorts 58–61.

Sorts 51–61 focus on short vowels, but without the support of word families. Additional known words may be added to any of the sorts, if desired. Initially, vowels that novice spellers typically confuse are not contrasted in the same sort. For example, short *a* and short *e* are contrasted only after each has been explored separately, with other vowels. The same is true for *e* and *i*. Except for Sorts 57, 60, and 61, Try 5 words for this section consist of *review words*—words that have already been studied. In addition, a few multisyllabic words are listed. These may replace some of the review words or they he used as challenge words.

Begin the session by making sure that everyone can identify the pictures; discuss meanings as necessary. Then proceed with the guided walk, modeling as much as necessary to gain students' active involvement. Discuss the sort and, if time allows, follow up with a quick check on students' understanding (see Part 1). When asking students to spell words from this exploration, take into consideration that final blends and digraphs have not yet been the focus of instruction. To prevent students from missing many of the words, hold them accountable for just the onset and vowel, unless the word ends in a single final consonant.

Sort 51. Short Vowels: *a, i*

<u>*a*</u>	<u>*i*</u>
cat	**pig**
CLAP	DISHES
CRACK	DRIP
GAS	FISH
LAMP	LID
MASK	MILK
PAD	MIX
RAT	SKIP
SAG	SWING
STAMP	WINK

Try 5: *big, sit, skim, snap, wag.* Also **silver**, **tablet**, **plas**tic—expect first syllable only. See Sort 16 for guidance in dictating multisyllabic words.

Sort 52. Short Vowels: *e, o, u*

<u>*e*</u>	<u>*o*</u>	<u>*u*</u>
bed	**mop**	**sun**
BEG	BLOCK	BUG
CHECK	CHOP	BRUSH
DRESS	DOLL	CUT
NEST	FROG	HUMP
WELL	SPOT	SKUNK
YELL	STOP	

Try 5: *jot, them, met, slop, plug.* Also, **dentist**, **pol**ish, **publish**—expect first syllable only. See Sort 16 for guidance in dictating multisyllabic words.

Sort 53. Short Vowels: *a, i, u*

a	i	u
cat	**pig**	**sun**
BAT	CRIB	BUS
CAP	FLIP	CUP
GLASS	SHIP	JUMP
PLANT	SINK	MUD
TACK	WIN	SKULL
	ZIP	STUMP

Try 5: flat, *plum, snug, spin, that*. Also *happen, signal, **muffin***—expect first syllable only. See Sort 16 for guidance in dictating multisyllabic words.

Sort 54. Short Vowels: *a, e, o*

a	e	o
cat	**bed**	**dot**
BAT	CHEST	FOX
CAB (taxi)	MEN	POD
CRAB	SHELF	ROCK
GRASS	STEM	SHOP
HAM	TENT	SOCK
QUACK	WEB	

Try 5: blab, *mob, pat, pet, slop, yet*. Also, *rapid, lemon, **problem***—expect first syllable only. See Sort 16 for guidance in dictating multisyllabic words.

Sort 55. Short Vowels: *e, i, o, u*

e	i	o	u
bed	**pig**	**dot**	**sun**
BELT	BRICK	BOX	BUN
NET	CLIP	CLOCK	DRUM
SHELL	GRILL	POP	THUMB
VEST	RING		TUG
	SLING		

Try 5: did, *pen, plus, spin, trot*. Also *level, **limit**, **solid**, **pun**ish*—expect first syllable only. See Sort 16 for guidance in dictating multisyllabic words.

Sort 56. Short Vowels: *a, e, i, o, u*

a	*e*	*i*	*o*	*u*
cat	**bed**	**pig**	**dot**	**sun**
FLAG	BELL	DRILL	COB	DUCK
HAND	DESK	FIN	LOCK	GUM
MAD	SLED	SIP		PLUG
		STICK		

Try 5: drop, flat, leg, plum, twig. Also, **na**pkin, **me**nu, **in**sect, **con**test, **sud**den—expect first syllable only. See Sort 16 for guidance in dictating multisyllabic words.

Sort 57. Initial Short Vowels: *a, e, i, o, u*

a	*e*	*i*	*o*	*u*
a APPLE	**e EGG**	**i IGLOO**	**o OCTOPUS**	**u UMBRELLA**
ALLIGATOR	ELBOW	INCH	OLIVES	UMPIRE
ALPHABET	ELEPHANT	INSECTS	OTTER	UNDER
ANIMALS	ELF			UP
AXE	ENGINE			
	ESKIMO			

Considerations: Two-letter high-frequency words could be added to this sort: *am, an, at, is, it, in, if, on, up.*

Try 5: Expect feature only—**a**stronaut, **e**cho, **i**tch, **o**strich, **u**ncle

Sort 58. Short Vowels: *a, e, o*

a	*e*	*o*	**Oddball**
cat	**bed**	**dot**	**?**
cab	bet	fox	was
has	let	lot	for
lab	set	mob	
sat	web	mom	
tax	yes	nod	

Try 5: can, met, not, sob, tap

Sort 59. Short Vowels: e, i, u

e	i	u	Oddball
bed	**pig**	**sun**	**?**
led	did	bud	her
pep	fit	hum	put
red	fix	lug	
	lid	mud	
	him	sum	
	his		
	six		

Try 5: bus, kid, rip, rub, web

Sort 60. Short Vowels: a, e, o

a	e	o	Oddball
crab	**sled**	**stop**	**?**
clam	fret	crop	from
grab	shed	flop	what
scab	step	plot	
slam		shop	
than		slot	
that			
wham			

Reinforcement of Blends and Digraphs

s-blends	l-blends	r-blends	digraphs	Oddball
scab	clam	crab	shed	slam
step	flop	crop	shop	sled
stop	plot	fret	that	slot
		from	than	
		grab	wham	
			what	

Try 5: Expect first syllable only—*channel, pretzel, problem, shadow, whopper.* See Sort 16 for guidance in dictating multisyllabic words for the Try 5 activity.

Considerations: Although most children will perceive *from* as an Oddball, due to dialect differences, some may categorize it under *stop.* Also, as a review of blends and digraphs, ask students to re-sort the short vowel words into the categories of s-blends, l-blends, r-blends, digraphs, and *Oddball. Sled, slot,* and *slam* may cause some confusion because they are both s-blends and l-blends.

Sort 61. Short Vowels: *e, i, u*

e	i	u	Oddball
stem	**clip**	**plus**	**?**
bled	crib	club	does
step	grip	glum	
them	skin	plum	
when	slim	snug	
	swim	stub	
	this		
	whip		

Reinforcement of Blends and Digraphs

s-blends	*l-blends*	*r-blends*	**digraphs**	**Oddball**
skin	bled	crib	them	does
snug	clip	grip	this	slim
sped	club		when	
stem	glum		whip	
stir	plum			
stub	plus			
swim				

Try 5: Expect first syllable only—*clutter, litter, shiver, slender, spinach*

Considerations: Call students' attention to the tricky and frequently occurring *does*, which seems to wear a disguise. Although it has no *u* in it, the vowel sound is short *u*. You might challenge students to be on the lookout for this trickster so that it doesn't fool them into a misspelling. As a review of blends and digraphs, ask students to re-sort the short vowel words into the categories of *s*-blends, *l*-blends, *r*-blends, digraphs, and Oddball. *Slim* may cause some confusion because it is both an *s*-blend and an *l*-blend.

cat	pig	

From *Word Sorts and More* by Kathy Ganske. Copyright 2006 by The Guilford Press. Permission to photocopy this form is granted to purchasers of this book for personal use only (see copyright page for details). Enlarge 135% to fill page.

bed	mop	sun

SORT 53 Short Vowels: *a, i, u*

cat	pig	sun

Short Vowels: *a, e, o*

cat	bed	dot

Short Vowels: *e, i, o, u*

bed	pig	dot
sun		

SORT 56 Short Vowels: *a, e, i, o, u*

cat	bed	pig
dot	sun	

a	e	i
o	u	

SORT 58 Short Vowels: *a, e, o*

cat	bed	dot
sat	fox	mom
web	was	nod
cab	mob	set
for	let	lab
tax	lot	yes
bet	has	?

Short Vowels: *e, i, u*

bed	pig	sun
did	sum	him
lug	red	lid
put	fit	bud
pep	six	her
his	hum	mud
fix	led	?

Short Vowels: *a, e, o*

crab	sled	stop
fret	what	scab
slam	crop	from
shop	wham	shed
that	slot	than
plot	step	clam
grab	flop	?

SORT 61 Short Vowels: *e, i, u*

stem	clip	plus $2+2=$
slim	does	them
crib	step	swim
grip	plum	skin
stub	this	when
bled	snug	glum
club	whip	?

More Initial Blends and Digraphs, with Affricate Sounds (DSA Feature D)

(Words and PICTURES)

Note: For more contrasts with affricates, see pages 130, 132, 137, and 138.

Because learners sometimes confuse the spellings of affricate sounds, three additional sorts follow to address any persistent uncertainty that some students may have. All students are not likely to need additional work in this area. If *tr, dr,* and *ch* are being used correctly, as well as the consonants *j, g,* and *h,* Sorts 62–63 should be skipped or used as an open sort for students' enjoyment and your information. For everyone else, introduce the sorts with a guided word walk that provides sufficient support and ample challenge.

Sort 62. More Initial Blends and Digraphs, with Affricates: *dr, d, j*

dr	d	j	Oddball
drum	**dim**	**jug**	**?**
DRAGON	dab	jam	gas
DRESS	DECK	JAR	
drink	DESK	jet	
drip	DIVE	JOG	
DRIVE	do	JUMP	
	DOOR		

Try 5: Expect first syllable only for multisyllabic words—*dizzy, drab, dribble, dud, jiggle.* See Sort 16 for guidance in dictating multisyllabic words.

Sort 63. More Initial Blends and Digraphs, with Affricates: *ch, h, tr, t*

ch	h	tr	t
chop	**had**	**trap**	**tub**
CHAIN	hem	TRAIN	tab
chat	hit	TRAY	tan
CHECK	HOLE	TRIANGLE	TEETH
CHIMNEY	HORN	trim	TIE

Try 5: children, habit, travel, temper, tunnel. See Sort 16 for guidance in dictating multisyllabic words.

More Initial Blends and Digraphs, with Affricates: *dr, d, j*

drum	dim	jug
		gas
	do	
drip		dab
	jet	
		jam
drink		?

More Initial Blends and Digraphs, with Affricates: *ch, h, tr, t*

chop	had	trap
tub		
	hit	tab
trim		
	tan	hem
chat		

From *Word Sorts and More* by Kathy Ganske. Copyright 2006 by The Guilford Press. Permission to photocopy this form is granted to purchasers of this book for personal use only (see copyright page for details). Enlarge 135% to fill page.

Final Digraphs and Blends (DSA Feature E) (Words Only, Except as Noted)

The sorts in this final section focus on final digraphs and blends, including word families, such as *ack*, *ick*, *ock*, and so forth. Although errors will still occur, students should be gaining competence in their use of initial consonant digraphs and blends and short vowels. Some final digraphs and blends are the same as those used at the onset of words, for example, *st*, *sh*, and *ch*. However, there are many new combinations, as *ft*, *ng*, and *ld*, which do not occur in the initial position of words. As with the study of initial consonant digraphs and blends, contrasting can be approached by building on what is *known*, namely, the single consonants that make up the digraph or blend (as *g*, *n*, *ng*, and *nk*), as well as by comparing similar blends, such as those involving a nasal consonant before a final consonant, as *mp*, *nd*, and *nt*.

The series that follows introduces students to final clusters with word families that end with *ck* and *ll*. Review of short vowels can be integrated into the study of Sorts 65 and 66 by incorporating blind sorting, even through the word walk. For example, after placing the key words in front of the students, select a card, look at it without showing it to the group, and then think aloud to determine its placement. After completing the same process for one or two more pictures, select a card, read the word, and then ask for a volunteer to name its category. When the card is placed in its category, attention may be called to its spelling. Other sorts in this section can be introduced with one of the closed-sort word walks described in Part 1. Whatever the approach, be sure students can identify the words or pictures, and be sure to discuss any unfamiliar meanings.

Sort 64. Final Digraphs with Word Families: *ack, eck, ick, ock, uck* (PICTURES)

ack	*eck*	*ick*	*ock*	*uck*
ack CRACK	**eck CHECK**	**ick KICK**	**ock BLOCK**	**uck DUCK**
JACK	DECK	BRICK	CLOCK	TRUCK
QUACK	NECK	CHICK	LOCK	
TACK		SICK	ROCK	
TRACK		STICK	SOCK	

Try 5: back, buck, dock, speck, tick

Literature Link

Silverstein, S. (1995). Sick. In E. H. Sword (Ed.), *A child's anthology of poetry*. Hopewell, NJ: Ecco Press.— Extension words: *instamatic, rash, wrenched,* and *numb*.

Sort 65. Final Digraphs with Word Families: *ack, ick, ock, uck*

ack	*ick*	*ock*	*uck*
crack	**kick**	**block**	**duck**
black	lick	dock	luck
pack	pick	flock	pluck
rack	sick	shock	stuck
snack	thick		yuck
	trick		

Note: The words *kick* and *sick* were included in the previous sort as pictures.

Try 5: cluck, flick, smock, stack, tack

Sort 66. Final Digraphs with Word Families: *all, ell, ill*

all	*ell*	*ill*	Oddball
wall	**well**	**will**	?
all	fell	drill	pull
call	sell	fill	
fall	smell	hill	
hall	spell	pill	
small	tell	spill	
		still	

Note: Optional pictures for this sort are included in Appendix E.

Try 5: chill, dill, tall, stall, swell

Considerations: Introduce students to two other double-consonant clusters: *ff* and *ss*. As with *ck* and *ll*, there are families of words: *stiff/cliff gruff/puff, grass/glass, dress/mess, cross/toss*. Help students to realize that knowing how to spell one of the words can assist with spelling others.

Sort 67. Final Digraphs: *ch, th, sh*

ch	*th*	*sh*	Oddball
much	**bath**	**dash**	?
such	cloth	blush	class
rich	math	dish	
which	path	fish	
	with	flush	
		fresh	
		rush	
		smash	
		trash	
		wish	

Try 5: beach, breath, gash, mouth, swish. With the exceptions of *gash* and *swish,* expect correct spelling of only the beginning consonant or blend and the final digraph.

Considerations: To reinforce short vowels, ask students to re-sort the words according to short vowel sounds (a, e, i, o, u) and then to examine each category for words that rhyme (for example, *dash, crash, smash, trash; blush, flush, rush; dish, fish, wish;* etc.). If there is no rhyme, students may try to brainstorm a match, such as *flesh* for *fresh*.

Sort 68. Final Blends: t, ft, lt, st

t	ft	lt	st
shut	**raft**	**malt**	**best**
brat	craft	felt	just
grit	drift	tilt	lost
	gift	wilt	must
	left		nest
	soft		twist
			trust

Note: Optional pictures for this sort are included in Appendix E.

*Try 5: blast, **built**, cost, swift, **wait**.* For *built* and *wait*, students are likely to omit the silent *u* and *i*.

Considerations: To reinforce short vowels, ask students to re-sort the words according to short vowel sounds (*a, e, i, o, u*) and then to search for rhyming words (*just, must, trust*, etc.) within each category. If there is no rhyme, students may try to brainstorm a match, such as *theft* for *left*.

Sort 69. Final Blends: mp, nd, nt

mp	nd	nt
bump	**sand**	**went**
camp	land	hunt
limp	lend	print
pump	pond	rent
ramp	send	slant
stump	spend	want
	stand	
	wind	

Note: When sorting by vowels, *want* is an oddball. Also, optional pictures are included in Appendix E.

Try 5: brand, chant, dent, slump, tend

Literature Link

Crandell, R. (2002). *The hands of the Maya: Villagers at work and play.* New York: Holt.—A beautiful look at the busy hands of the Maya.

Considerations: *Wind* may be pronounced as /wĭnd/ and /wīnd/. To reinforce short vowels, ask students to re-sort the words according to short vowel sounds (*a, e, i, o, u*) and then to search for rhyming words within each category (for example, *bump, dump, pump, lend, send, spend;* etc.). If there is no rhyme for a word, students may try to brainstorm a match (for example, *punt* for *hunt*).

Sort 70. Final Blends: *g, n, ng, nk*

_g_	**_n_**	**_ng_**	**_nk_**
wig	**win**	**wing**	**wink**
rag	grin	bring	blink
slug	scan	long	dunk
	thin	rang	pink
		song	thank
		swing	think
		thing	

Note: Optional pictures for this sort may be found in Appendix E.

Try 5: *chunk, fang, shin, prong, yank*

Considerations: For reinforcement, ask students to re-sort the words according to short vowel sounds (*a, i, o*), and then to search for rhyming words within each category. They may try to generate rhyming words for those with no match.

SORT 64 Final Digraphs with Word Families: *ack, eck, ick, ock, uck*

ack	eck ✔	ick
ock	uck	

Final Digraphs with Word Families: *ack, ick, ock, uck*

crack	kick	block
duck	shock	pack
snack	yuck	pick
trick	black	sick
flock	thick	luck
rack	stuck	dock
pluck	lick	

wall	well	will
still	sell	small
hall	tell	fill
pull	fall	spill
all	spell	call
pill	fell	hill
smell	drill	?

Final Digraphs: *ch, th, sh*

much	bath	dash
blush	dish	cloth
smash	rich	wish
math	rush	with
such	flush	class
fresh	which	path
fish	trash	?

shut	raft	malt
best	just	craft
grit	soft	nest
trust	brat	tilt
left	twist	must
wilt	lost	drift
gift	felt	

Final Blends: *mp, nd, nt*

bump	sand	went
send	limp	wind
print	land	camp
pump	hunt	spend
want	pond	ramp
lend	rent	stand
slant	stump	

SORT 70 Final Blends: *g, n, ng, nk*

wig	win	wing
wink	bring	thank
long	blink	rang
thing	grin	song
dunk	pink	rag
scan	think	swing
thin	slug	

Putting It All Together: Short Vowels, Blends, and Digraphs

Words in the two sorts that follow include key features studied at the letter name stage: initial and final blends and digraphs and short vowels. Besides sorting by vowel sound, students might be asked to group their words according to whether they begin with a single consonant or a blend or digraph. Or they might be asked to look for words with the same beginning blend or digraph (*r*-blends, *s*-blends, *l*-blends, digraphs). They might also check for common ending clusters (*st*, *pt*, *nd*, *nt*, and so forth).

Sort 71. Putting It All Together with Blends and Digraphs: Short *a, e, o*

<u>a</u>	<u>e</u>	<u>o</u>	**Oddball**
flash	**help**	**sock**	**?**
ask	blend	blond	walk
blank	chess	floss	
damp	next	fond	
draft	shelf	frost	
grand	slept		
last	test		

Note: Optional pictures for this sort are included in Appendix E.

Try 5: grasp, honk, mend, self, task

Considerations: Ask students to use the key words as guides and to sort their words according to the short vowel sound: /ă/, /ĕ/, and /ŏ/. Go over and discuss the results.

Sort 72. Putting It All Together with Blends and Digraphs: Short *e, i, u*

<u>e</u>	<u>i</u>	<u>u</u>	**Oddball**
desk	**chick**	**brush**	**?**
chest	crisp	crush	push
kept	hint	grunt	
flesh	milk	slush	
press	shift	skunk	
swept	sift		
	sling		
	stink		

Note: Optional pictures for this sort are included in Appendix E.

Try 5: chimp, crept, dust, pest, risk

Considerations: As with Sort 71, ask the students to sort the words according to vowel sound: /ĕ/, /ĭ/, and /ŭ/. Discuss the categories.

Putting It All Together with Blends and Digraphs: Short *a, e, o*

flash	help	sock
draft	fond	blank
next	walk	test
blend	last	damp
grand	frost	slept
blond	chess	floss
shelf	ask	?

Putting It All Together with Blends and Digraphs: Short *e, i, u*

desk	chick	brush
slush	flesh	hint
crisp	grunt	kept
swept	crush	stink
sift	press	shift
sling	skunk	push
chest	milk	?

Looking Ahead to Long Vowels

The final sort presented in this part requires students to separate short vowels from long vowels in a Short, Not Short activity. Short vowels are the *known* and Not Short are the *new*, namely, long vowels, which are explored in depth in Part 4. There are no Try 5 words for this activity, as this group of words is not intended to require a week-long study. The words should serve as an introduction to word explorations at the within word pattern stage.

After checking for picture recognition, ask the students to sort the words into two categories, Short and Not Short. When they have finished, ask them to describe what they notice. They should mention that the long vowels say their name. You might ask them to brainstorm additional long vowels. If time allows, you might also have them re-sort the words under ANT, NEST, FISH, SOCK, BRUSH, and ? to reinforce short vowels.

Sort 73. Looking Ahead to Long Vowels: Short, Not Short

Short	Not Short
ANT	BRAID
BRUSH	CHEESE
BOX	DIME
DUCK	FEET
FISH	TOAST
KICK	TUBE
LAMP	VASE
MAD	
NEST	
PEN	
SIX	
SKUNK	
SOCK	

With a working knowledge of short vowels and consonant blends and digraphs and an increasing sight vocabulary, learners prepare to negotiate the many long vowel patterns of English through word study for within word pattern spellers, the focus of Part 4.

		?
	UNITED STATES OF AMERICA	
6		

Part 4

Word Study for Within Word Pattern Spellers

Students at the within word pattern stage are typically in the second-grade to mid-fourth-grade range. They have developed sufficient sight vocabularies to read more fluently than their word-by-word counterparts at the letter name stage; they have also entered the world of chapter books, such as those by Cynthia Rylant and Arnold Lobel, as well as more sophisticated books such as those in the *Magic Tree House* series. Similarly, their longer and more conventional writing reflects a stronger understanding of words and how they work. Students at this stage have a working knowledge of short vowels, blends, and digraphs in single-syllable words and are ready to confront the pattern issues associated with the within word pattern stage. Pictures are still used at the beginning of this stage to focus children's attention on sound. Although they are soon supplanted by words so that pattern issues can also be explored, inclusion of Oddball words (and the use of blind sorting as an activity) prompts learners to continue considering sound.

Within word pattern learners enjoy riddles and jokes such as those included in Hall and Eisenberg's *Turkey Riddles*, Rosenbloom's *Biggest Riddle Book in the World*, and Shel Silverstein's latest book *Runny Babbit: A Billy Sook*, so this is perhaps an ideal time to introduce students to the hidden meanings of idioms. Idioms that relate to words being studied receive considerable attention in this part. Besides being sources of humor and enjoyment, idioms are also the source of much confusion for English-language learners and can be, too, for others who struggle with literacy. Attention to idioms can develop appreciation for language and increase vocabulary knowledge and often adds a bit of humor to the group session. Children might be encouraged to role play the literal and actual meaning of idiomatic phrases or be asked to illustrate the two possibilities. Books from the *Amelia Bedelia* series by Peggy Parish might also be incorporated, as they are written on levels accessible to most within word pattern spellers and provide a wonderful look at the sometimes not-so-humorous confusions to which misinterpretation of idioms can lead. Or you might share the meanings and origins of common idiomatic phrases, such as *to let the cat out of the bag*. Marvin Terban's *Scholastic Dictionary of Idioms* includes more than 600.

Recommended Literature Links continue in this part but with much less emphasis than at the two previous stages, because such connections can be provided by many books, including the current read-aloud, guided reading texts, shared reading material, and even content area material.

Throughout Part 4, much attention is given to describing aspects of the small-group instruction: vocabulary that might warrant attention, information about why particular features work the way they do, help in answering questions that may arise, suggestions for introducing certain sorts, and so forth. Most of the sorts in this part require students to contrast several different features. For example, rather than contrasting various short vowels, the student may be asked to compare a short vowel (*dash*) with a long vowel pattern (*face*) and an *r*-controlled pattern (*card*). So that teachers know the level of understanding students are assumed to have in order to engage in a particular word study, beginning with Sort 6, each of the sorts described includes the sections *What Is Known* and *What Is New*. This information will assist teachers who wish to omit certain sorts or use them in a different order; they will know where they may need to scaffold to ensure that students are not left confused. As described in Part 1, teachers should be sure that students can read the words being used and should check students' understanding of meanings. The various introductory word walks described in Part 1 are equally applicable to learners at this stage of spelling development. Before embarking with students on the explorations that follow, teachers should informally assess their understandings with the Developmental Spelling Analysis or other assessment instrument to ensure that instruction is matched to the child.

Introducing Long Vowels (PICTURES Only)

The five sorts that follow introduce students to long vowels via picture sorting. Spelling of the words is not an aim of the study, as words of various patterns are included. In all cases, short vowels are the *known*, and the long vowel sound is *what is new*. Each of the sorts can be introduced in a similar manner: After checking picture recognition and understanding, place the key words in front of the students and begin modeling with a think-aloud. Release responsibility to the students as they come to understand the features under study. Follow up the sorting with a discussion of the categories. Ask the students to re-sort their words independently, or rely on one of the approaches described in Part 1 to verify students' awareness of the targeted features. You might also engage students in The Long or Short of It. Simply, call out words with short or long vowels, then ask students to respond with "short" or "long" to indicate the type of vowel in the word.

Sort 1. Introducing Long Vowels: Short *a* and Long *a*

Short *a*	Long *a*	Oddball
CAT	**LAKE**	**?**
BAG	EIGHT	SHIRT
BAT	HAY	
FAN	MANE	
GRASS	PAIL	
LAMP	RAIN	
RAT	SCALE	
WAG	SLEIGH	
	TAPE	
	TRAY	
	WHALE	

Considerations: Children may identify *bag* as *sack* or *pail* as *bucket*; in the latter case, the picture should be placed under the Oddball category. Drawing attention to the action lines for *wag* should reduce any confusion with *tail*.

Sort 2. Introducing Long Vowels: Short *e* and Long *e*

Short *e*	Long *e*	Oddball
BED	**SHEEP**	**?**
BEAD	BEAK	STAR
BELT	BEE	
EGG	CHEESE	
NET	FEET	
SHELL	HEEL	
TENT	QUEEN	
WEB	SLEEP	
	SLEEVE	
	SWEEP	
	TEETH	

Sort 3. Introducing Long Vowels: Short *i* and Long *i*

Short *i*	Long *i*	Oddball
PIG	**LINE**	**?**
BRICK	CLIMB	WATCH
CLIP	CRY	
DRIP	DIME	
HILL	FLY	
MILK	KNIFE	
MIX	KNIGHT	
THINK	PIE	
TWIST	TIE	
WINK		

Literature Link

Prelutsky, J. (1984). Nine mice. In *The new kid on the block*. New York: Scholastic.—Long *i* words abound. Extension words: *despite* and *trice*.

Sort 4. Introducing Long Vowels: Short *o* and Long *o*

Short *o*	Long *o*	Oddball
DOT	**BONE**	?
BLOCK	BOAT	LEAF
COB	COAT	
DOLL	COMB	
OX	GLOBE	
POT	GOAT	
STOP	ROAD	
TOP	SNOW	
	SOAP	
	TOAST	
	TOES	

Sort 5. Introducing Long Vowels: Short *u* and Long *u*

Short *u*	Long *u*	Oddball
SUN	**TUBE**	?
HUMP	FLUTE	BALL
MUD	FRUIT	
PLUS	GLUE	
PUP	MOON	
RUG	ROOF	
RUN	SCHOOL	
THUMB	SHOE	
TUG	SPOON	
	STOOL	

Literature Link

Lansky, B. (1991). How I quit sucking my thumb. In B. Lansky (Ed.), *Kids pick the funniest poems: Poems that make kids laugh*. New York: Meadowbrook Press.—Other short *u* words include *such* and *dumb*.

Prelutsky, J. (1984). Jellyfish stew. In *The new kid on the block*. New York: Scholastic.—Long *u* words abound. Extension word: *revolting*.

Introducing Long Vowels: Short *a* and Long *a*

ă	ā	
		?

From Word Sorts and More by Kathy Ganske. Copyright 2006 by The Guilford Press. Permission to photocopy this form is granted to purchasers of this book for personal use only (see copyright page for details). Enlarge 135% to fill page.

SORT 2 Introducing Long Vowels: Short e and Long e

ĕ 🛏	ē 🐑	
		?

From *Word Sorts and More* by Kathy Ganske. Copyright 2006 by The Guilford Press. Permission to photocopy this form is granted to purchasers of this book for personal use only (see copyright page for details). Enlarge 135% to fill page.

SORT 3 Introducing Long Vowels: Short *i* and Long *i*

ĭ	ī	
		?

From *Word Sorts and More* by Kathy Ganske. Copyright 2006 by The Guilford Press. Permission to photocopy this form is granted to purchasers of this book for personal use only (see copyright page for details). Enlarge 135% to fill page.

Introducing Long Vowels: Short *o* and Long *o*

Ŏ	Ō	
E		
		?

SORT 5 Introducing Long Vowels: Short *u* and Long *u*

ŭ ☀	ū 🧴	🏠
👟	🍎🍐	🐕
🪑	2+2=	✋
🏃	🎶	👟
🌙☆	🤼	🍯
🐫	🌑	🥄
🏠	🧶	?

Long Vowels with VCe, Including Sorts with Magic e (DSA Feature F)

(Words Only, Except as Noted)

The following series of sorts relies mainly on words. It includes three "magic e" sorts. The words in these sorts are such that each short-vowel word can be changed into a VCe word by simply adding *e*. Although the three sorts target different vowels, they can be collapsed into one sort, with or without all of the words, if desired. If this option is chosen, the best time to present the words is at the beginning of this section.

Sort 6. Long Vowels with VCe: Short *a* and Long *a* with Magic e

a	*a*Ce
cap	**cape**
at	ate
can	cane
mad	made
man	mane
pal	pale
pan	pane
plan	plane
tap	tape
van	vane

What Is Known: Long/short *a* sounds; short *a* pattern

What Is New: Magic or silent e to make long *a*

Considerations: Introduce the words for this lesson as follows:

1. Record the list of short vowel words on the board twice, side by side.
2. Ask students to read the first word.
3. Using the adjacent list, show them what happens when you add e to the word (*cap* becomes *cape*). Say something like, "Just like magic, the e makes a new word, so some people call it *magic* e. Because the e doesn't make a sound, sometimes people also call it *silent* e. Let's try another one."
4. After the next modeling example, invite students to make the changes; discuss each.
5. When the last word has had the e added, discuss the two categories and any unfamiliar word meanings; draw students' attention to differences in sound and pattern. Let them know that they will be working more with magic or silent e.

Integrating Idioms

"My little sister was **as mad as a wet hen** when Mom told her she couldn't go to the movies." (was really angry)

Literature Link

Hays, A. J. (2004). *Here comes silent e!* New York: Random House.—Many magic e words put into a story about a personified magic e.

Sort 7. Long Vowels with VCe: Short *a* and Long *a*   *(Words and PICTURES)*

a	*a*Ce	Oddball
cat	lake	?
bad	came	have
CRAB	crate	saw
fast	FLAME	
flat	gave	
glad	late	
glass	WAVE	
	lane	
	same	
	shape	
	SHAVE	

What Is Known: Long/short *a* sounds; short *a* pattern; long *a* with magic e

What Is New: Extending VCe beyond magic e

Considerations: Discuss the meanings of *crate* and *lane*.

Integrating Idioms

"You sure **let the cat out of the bag** when you told the teacher you are going to have a new brother." (gave away a secret)

Sort 8. Long Vowels with VCe: Short *i* and Long *i* with Magic e

i	*i*Ce
pin	pine
bit	bite
dim	dime
fin	fine
hid	hide
kit	kite
slid	slide
slim	slime
rip	ripe
twin	twine

What Is Known: Long/short *i* sounds; short *i* pattern

What Is New: Magic e to make long *i*

Integrating Idioms

"You don't have to **bite my head off** just because I forgot to take the dog out." (get really angry)

"**Go fly a kite, will ya?**" ("Go away and don't bother me.")

Sort 9. Long Vowels with VCe: Short *i* and Long *i*   *(Words and PICTURES)*

i	*iCe*	Oddball
pig	**line**	**?**
drink	DIVE	give
list	FIVE	
rim	life	
miss	like	
skill	pile	
SPIN	PRIZE	
stiff	ride	
	size	
	spice	
	while	

What Is Known: Long/short *i* sounds; short *i* pattern; long *i* with magic e

What Is New: Extending *i*Ce beyond magic e

Integrating Idioms

"When I asked why were having pancakes for dinner, Dad smiled and said, '**Variety is the spice of life.**'" (It's good to have a few changes; they add interest.)

Literature Links

Jenkin, S. (2005). *Actual size*. Boston: Houghton Mifflin.—Interesting facts.
Prelutsky, J. (1984). When Tillie ate the chili. In *The new kid on the block*. New York: Scholastic.—This poem can bring to life the idiom listed for this sort. Although the word *spice* is not used, Tillie's experience shows that a little *spice* can go a long way. Extension words: *amok* and *wheezed*.

Sort 10. Long Vowels with VCe: Short *a* and *i*, Long *a* and *i*

a	*i*	*aCe*	*iCe*
last	**fish**	**gate**	**smile**
band	bring	date	nice
clash	film	make	shine
cram	mint	place	side
		safe	time
		space	wife

What Is Known: Short *a* and *i*; *a*Ce and *i*Ce

What Is New: Contrasting *a* and *i* long and short vowels

Considerations: Discuss the meanings of *clash* and *cram* and the multiple meanings of words such as *band, film, mint,* and *date.*

Integrating Idioms

"Can you **crack a smile for once**?" (smile a little even though you may not feel like it)

Literature Link

Editors of *Time* for Kids. (2005). *Planets! Discover our solar system*. New York: HarperTrophy.—Related word: *space*.

Sort 11. Long Vowels with VCe: Short *o* and *u*, Long *o* and *u* with Magic *e*

o	oCe	u	uCe
not	note	cut	cute
glob	globe	cub	cube
hop	hope	plum	plume
rob	robe	us	use
slop	slope		
tot	tote		

What Is Known: Long/short *o* and *u* sounds; short *o* and *u* pattern

What Is New: Magic e to make long *o* and *u*

Considerations: Discuss the meaning of *plume* and of the expression "a plume of smoke." The meanings of *tot* and *tote* may also need to be addressed.

Integrating Idioms

"Since the present you're making is for your grandma, don't **cut corners**." (take short cuts and do a poor job)

Sort 12. Long Vowels with VCe: Short *o* and Long *o* (Words and PICTURES)

o	oCe	Oddball
dot	bone	?
boss	broke	done
CHOP	chose	how
crop	close	
cross	drove	
doll	home	
(ROCK)	rode	
SOB	ROPE	
	(STONE)	
	those	
	vote	

What Is Known: Long/short *o* sounds; short *o* pattern; long *o* with magic e

What Is New: Extending oCe beyond magic e

Considerations: Some children may call the rock a *stone;* categorize it accordingly. If discussion high-lights both terms, you may want to place it under the Oddball category. Remind students of the impor-tance if thinking about sound as well as pattern as they sort the words. As a follow-up to sorting, ask how *d-o-n-e* would be pronounced if it was placed in the oCe category (with a long o: dōn).

Integrating Idioms

"I have to **bone up on** my math facts tonight." (review and study carefully)

Sort 13. Long Vowels with VCe: Short *u* and Long *u*

u	*uCe*
sun	**tube**
drum	CUBE
dull	FLUTE
gruff	huge
HUG	JUNE
hush	MULE
jump	rude
just	tune
rung	
rust	
such	
tusk	

What Is Known: Long/short *u* sounds; short *u* pattern; long *u* with magic e

What Is New: Extending uCe beyond magic e

Considerations: Discuss the animal-related meaning for *mule:* an offspring of a male donkey and a fe-male horse. Students may also know this word as an open-heeled shoe or a stubborn person. The meaning of *rust* may need to be clarified, as well as *gruff, rude,* and *dull.*

Integrating Idioms

"As soon as our friend comes back, he'll **be singing a different tune.**" (changing his manner)

"As the athlete stumbled at the finish line, a **hush fell over** the crowd." (Everyone became very quiet.)

"You watch the lemonade stand while I go **drum up some business.**" (try to find customers)

Sort 14. Long Vowels with VCe: Short *o* and *u*, Long *o* and *u*

<u>o</u>	<u>u</u>	<u>oCe</u>	<u>uCe</u>	Oddball
blot	**dust**	**code**	**prune**	**?**
fond	cuff	froze	flute	come
prong	husk	hole	mule	some
	lump	mope	rule	
	stung	stove		
		woke		

What Is Known: Long and short *o* and *u* sounds and the VCe pattern

What Is New: Contrasting the two vowels in their long and short forms

Considerations: Some students may be unfamiliar with the meanings of *prong, husk,* and *mope.* Discuss as needed. Also, the five categories in this sort may be overly challenging for some children; if so, delete the oddball words. Finally, this sound and pattern sort may be completed as a sound sort, with *come* and *some* placed in the short *u* category, or as a pattern sort with two categories: CVC words (all the short vowel words) and VCe words (those with *oCe, uCe,* plus the Oddballs).

Integrating Idioms

"As a **rule of thumb**, to cut apart your word cards, first cut along the two vertical lines; then stack the three strips and cut along the lines that are left." (a general or accepted practice [from the use of one's thumb to estimate measurements])

Long Vowels with VCe: Short *a* and Long *a* with Magic *e*

cap	cape	pal
vane	tap	mane
can	pane	at
ate	plan	mad
pan	cane	plane
tape	made	van
man	pale	

cat	lake	
late	fast	have
	came	glad
gave	same	
glass		shape
lane	bad	flat
saw	crate	?

pin	pine	bit
bite	rip	slim
fin	twine	hid
twin	slime	dime
kite	dim	slide
slid	ripe	fine
hide	kit	

pig	line	skill
rim	while	miss
	like	
ride	give	drink
stiff		spice
pile	size	list
5	life	?

Long Vowels with VCe: Short *a* and *i*, Long *a* and *i*

last	fish	gate
smile	nice	place
bring	time	cram
make	date	film
space	clash	wife
band	side	safe
shine	mint	

SORT 11 Long Vowels with VCe: Short *o* and *u*, Long *o* and *u* with Magic *e*

not	note	cut
cute	tot	hope
robe	cube	plum
use	glob	plume
cub	tote	rob
hop	us	slope
globe	slop	

Long Vowels with VCe: Short *o* and Long *o*

dot	bone	home
crop	close	cross
broke		chose
	how	doll
drove	boss	
vote	done	those
	rode	?

Long Vowels with VCe: Short *u* and Long *u*

sun	tube	tusk
just	such	June
huge	jump	hush
		gruff
dull		rung
	rude	tune
rust	drum	

Long Vowels with VCe: Short *o* and *u*, Long *o* and *u*

blot	dust	code
prune	mule	froze
cuff	some	husk
rule	fond	hole
stung	flute	lump
prong	come	woke
mope	stove	?

R-Controlled Vowels with Short Vowel Patterns (DSA Feature G) (Words Only)

Note: R-controlled vowels with long vowel patterns follow the section on other long vowel patterns.

It is likely to take some time for children to master *r*-controlled vowels. Although the distinctly different sounds of *ar* and *or* provide students with clues to spelling the patterns correctly, the sound-alike patterns of *er*, *ir*, and *ur* are more challenging. Because sound is of no help in distinguishing among these three, children must learn to pay careful attention to the pattern. Short vowels and the VC*e* long vowel pattern provide the *known* and, as such, are reinforced as students compare and contrast them with the newly introduced *r*-controlled vowels. Be sure to provide sufficient support during the guided word walk. It's easier to reduce your involvement than it is to increase it after you realize students are not getting the sort.

Sort 15. R-Controlled Vowels: Short *a*, Long *a*, and R-Controlled *a* (*a*, *aCe*, *ar*)

a	*aCe*	*ar*	Oddball
dash	face	card	?
camp	grade	art	are
crash	save	bark	
hand	tame	barn	
swam	vase	far	
wax		hard	
		start	
		yard	

What Is Known: Short *a* and long *a* (VC*e*)

What Is New: *ar*

Considerations: Discuss the multiple meanings of *yard* and *bark*, and check for understanding of *tame*.

Integrating Idioms

"Don't worry; my brother's **bark is worse than his bite.**" ("He may threaten but he won't cause much harm.")

Sort 16. R-Controlled Vowels: Short *i*, Long *i*, and R-Controlled *i* (*i*, *iCe*, *ir*)

i	*iCe*	*ir*	Oddball
snip	mine	bird	?
cliff	five	chirp	worm
cling	mile	first	
lift	pride	girl	
skit	wide	skirt	
will	write	stir	
		third	

What Is Known: Short *i* and long *i* (VCe)

What Is New: *ir*

Considerations: Point out to students the importance of remembering that *write*, like several other words in sorts at this stage, includes a tricky silent letter. Also, check students' understanding of the meanings of *cliff, cling, skit,* and *pride.*

Integrating Idioms

"We're going to head over to the game at 5:00; don't you know **the early bird catches the worm?**" (Arriving early gives someone an advantage.)

Literature Link

Ciardi, J. (1991). The early bird. In B. Lansky (Ed.), *Kids pick the funniest poems: Poems that make kids laugh.* New York: Meadowbrook Press.—Related words: *bird, first,* and *worm.*

Sort 17. *R-Controlled Vowels: Short o, Long o, and R-Controlled o (o, oCe, or)*

o	oCe	or	Oddball
drop	**spoke**	**horn**	**?**
flock	choke	born	lose
moth	doze	north	word
prop	mole	sort	
stomp	whole	sport	
	zone	storm	
		thorn	

What Is Known: Short *o* and long *o* (VCe)

What Is New: *or*

Considerations: Point out the importance of remembering the tricky silent letter in *whole.* Discuss the meanings of *flock, moth, prop, doze, thorn,* and *mole* as needed. Note that due to their pronunciation of *moth* some children may think the Oddball category a better place for the word. Also, check for possible confusion of *loose* with *lose.*

Integrating Idioms

"Sometimes you just have to **toot your own horn.**" (praise yourself)

Literature Links

Kulling, M. (2000). *Escape north!: The story of Harriet Tubman.* New York: Random House.
Stanford, N. *The bravest dog ever: The true story of Balto.* New York: Random House.—Related word: *storm.* Extension word: *blizzard.*

Sort 18. R-Controlled Vowels: Short *u*, Long *u*, and R-Controlled *u* (*u*, *uCe*, *ur*)

u	*uCe*	*ur*	Oddball
club	**tube**	**burp**	**?**
bulb	crude	burn	four
crush	dude	curb	your
junk	dune	curl	
plump		fur	
thumb		hurt	
		surf	
		turn	

What Is Known: Short *u* and long *u* (VCe)

What Is New: *ur*

Considerations: In a sound sort, students may sort *your* under the *ur/burp* category. This is also correct. Also, taking note of the silent letter in *thumb* will help students to include it when spelling the word. Discuss the meanings of *crude, dude, dune,* and *surf* as needed.

Integrating Idioms

"Don't **try to turn the tables**; you know it was your fault." (place blame on the other person)

"The report is due tomorrow, so I'll just have to **burn the midnight oil**." (stay up late working)

Literature Link

Prelutsky, J. (1984). My mother says I'm sickening. In *The new kid on the block*. New York: Scholastic.— Related word: *crude*. Extension word: *catapult*.

Sort 19. R-Controlled Vowels: *ar, or, ir*

ar	*or*	*ir*	*er*	Oddball
dark	**fork**	**dirt**	**fern**	**?**
cart	cord	firm	clerk	more
farm	corn	shirt	jerk	work
park	horse	twirl		
scarf	short			
snarl				

What Is Known: R-controlled *a* and *o*

What Is New: Two spellings for the /ər/ r-controlled vowel: *ir* and *er*

Considerations: Start with a sound sort for the study of these words. *More* would be placed with words such as *fork*. Discuss the results; then ask students to consider pattern by separating out words that have the same sound but a different pattern. See the sort above for the outcome. Some students may be inclined to place *horse* in the Oddball category, due to the final e. This is fine.

Integrating Idioms

"Hey, **keep your shirt on**." (Don't get impatient)

Literature Links

Parks, R. (1997). *I am Rosa Parks*. New York: Penguin Books.—Related word: *segregation*.

Prelutsky, J. (1984). Ma! Don't throw that shirt out. In *The new kid on the block*. New York: Scholastic.— Additional related word: *dirt*. Extension words: *peculiar, infested, regiment, frazzled*.

SORT 15
R-Controlled Vowels:
Short *a*, Long *a*, and *R*-Controlled *a* (*a, aCe, ar*)

dash	face	card
yard	hard	swam
grade	crash	vase
wax	bark	camp
hand	far	save
start	tame	art
barn	are	?

R-Controlled Vowels:
Short i, Long i, and R-Controlled i (i, iCe, ir)

snip	mine	bird
write	cling	wide
lift	worm	skirt
girl	five	skit
cliff	third	pride
mile	first	stir
chirp	will	?

SORT 17
R-Controlled Vowels:
Short o, Long o, and R-Controlled o (o, oCe, or)

drop	spoke	horn
zone	north	stomp
choke	flock	thorn
word	born	prop
doze	storm	sort
whole	mole	moth
lose	sport	?

club	tube	burp
fur	your	crush
dune	four	curb
plump	surf	bulb
curl	junk	turn
hurt	burn	dude
thumb	crude	?

R-Controlled Vowels: ar, or, ir

dark	fork	dirt
fern	horse	farm
snarl	corn	firm
more	work	jerk
twirl	short	scarf
park	cord	shirt
clerk	cart	?

Other Common Long Vowel Patterns (DSA Feature H) (Words Only)

There are many ways to spell long vowels. The most common pattern is VC*e*; however, numerous other patterns occur in many words. These are explored in this section. Some students may benefit from completing all of the sorts, but others will be able to move through this feature more quickly by completing just some of the sorts. Because patterns are often revisited in a subsequent sort, more capable students may be able to complete one sort with two (or occasionally three) new patterns, rather than three sorts, each with one new pattern. Keep in mind, however, that moving too quickly may result in an overload of issues for learners and confuse them. For Feature H, the essential sorts are 22, 24, 25, 26, 28, 31, and 33. Also, consider that students may demonstrate understanding of certain vowels, such as the *a* and *i* patterns, and need to work on just some of the patterns, such as the *e*, *o*, and *u* patterns. Periodic informal assessments and ongoing observation enable teachers to make appropriate instructional decisions.

Sort 20. Other Common Long Vowel Patterns: Short *a* and Long *a* (*a, aCe, ay*)

a	*aCe*	*ay*	Oddball
grass	**shade**	**play**	**?**
fact	base	day	hey
rash	cave	gray	they
slam	chase	may	
wrap	fake	say	
	gaze	way	
	stage		

What Is Known: Short *a*, and long *a* spelled VC*e*

What Is New: Long *a* spelled *ay*

Considerations: Point out to students the importance of remembering *wrap* as a tricky word with a silent letter. This word is a homophone, so be sure they also understand its meaning. Discuss the meanings of *rash*, *fake*, and *gaze* as well.

Integrating Idioms

"He'll let us go with him: he **always caves in**." (agrees to something someone is asking)

"This is just **a wild goose-chase**; we'll never find the store." (a worthless pursuit)

Sort 21. Other Common Long Vowel Patterns: Short *a* and Long *a* (*a, aCe, ay, ai*)

a	*aCe*	*ay*	*ai*	Oddball
past	**shake**	**stay**	**chain**	**?**
cash	blame	pay	brain	said
grab	male	sway	mail	swamp
than	trade		paint	
	wade		tail	
			wait	

What Is Known: Short *a*, and long *a* spelled *a*Ce and *ay*

What Is New: Long *a* spelled *ai*

Considerations: Inclusion of the homophones *male* and *mail* in this sort make this an ideal time to caution spellers that rhyming words with long vowel sounds may have different spelling patterns. If in doubt, students should be encouraged to refer to the text, an expert, a dictionary, or a spell checker to verify the correct spelling. Also, because the word *than* is sometimes confused with *then*, be sure that students understand the meaning of this word.

Integrating Idioms

"That cat has food **on the brain**." (is obsessed with, can't think about anything else)

Sort 22. Other Common Long Vowel Patterns: Short *a* and Long *a* (*a*, *a*Ce, *ai*, *ei*)

a	aCe	ai	ei	Oddball
flash	state	paid	eight	?
draft	brake	claim	freight	wand
lamp	grave	main	neigh	wash
pass	race	stain	vein	
		waist	weigh	

What Is Known: Short *a*, and long *a* spelled *a*Ce and *ai*

What Is New: Long *a* spelled *ei*

Considerations: Be sure students understand the meanings of the homophones *brake*, *main*, *waist*, *vein*, and *weigh*, as well as other words that may be confusing. You may also want to call students' attention to the fact that the sound of *a* when preceded by a *w* is often different as in *wand* and *wash*, and also in *swan*, *swamp*, *swat*, *wad*, *wasp*, and so forth.

Integrating Idioms

"We had to **race against time** to finish the project." (Time was running out and they had to hurry.)

Sort 23. Other Common Long Vowel Patterns: Short *e* and Long *e* (*e*, open *e*, *ee*)

e	Open e	ee	Oddball
desk	he	keep	?
dent	be	creep	ski
mess	she	feel	new
rest	we	free	these
swell		meet	
		greet	
		speed	
		week	

What Is Known: Short e, and the sound of long e

What Is New: Long e with an open syllable and long e spelled ee

Considerations: The absence of a final consonant in the word *free* may cause students to consider it an Oddball. Also, draw students' attention to the fact that *the* is sometimes pronounced as a member of the *he* category, especially when the word that follows it begins with a vowel, as in *the entrance*.

Integrating Idioms

There are many idioms with the word *keep*. Here are some common ones:

"You're doing well learning the math facts; **keep the ball rolling**." (continue the progress)

"I know you can't find your homework, but **keep cool**." (stay calm)

"I know you're late, but **keep a stiff upper lip** when you talk to your mom." (be calm in time of trouble)

"How can you **keep a straight face** when you tell me that the cat ate your homework?" (not show smiles or laughter)

Sort 24. Other Common Long Vowel Patterns: Short e and Long e (e, ee, ea)

e	ee	ea	Oddball
kept	need	beat	?
best	deep	clean	break
text	seed	dream	great
less	sheet	mean	
	steep	neat	
	wheel	real	
	weed	teach	

What Is Known: Short e, and long e spelled ee

What Is New: Long e spelled *ea*

Considerations: Discuss the meanings of *beat, text, break,* and any other words that may be confusing. Because some of the patterns have multiple sounds, if time allows, you might ask the students to sort first by sound, then by pattern, then by sound and pattern (as shown).

Integrating Idioms

"Quit **beating about the bush** and get to the point." (stop wasting time)

Sort 25. Other Common Long Vowel Patterns: Short e and Long e (e, ee, ea, ie)

e	ee	ea	ie	Oddball
west	**sweep**	**peach**	**chief**	**?**
bend	beef	feast	brief	friend
fresh	seem	east	field	lie
then	sleek	leave	thief	
		meal		
		team		

What Is Known: Short e, and long e spelled ee and *ea*

What Is New: Long e spelled *ie*

Considerations: Recalling the phrase "*I* am your friend to the *end*" may help students to remember the *iend* spelling in *friend*. The final e on *leave* is not part of a VCe pattern but rather it serves as a partner for the *v*, which in English does not end a word. *Sleeve* is another example of this. You may want to suggest that students keep a sharp eye out for more words of this type in future sorts, as others are included. Discuss the meaning of *sleek*.

Sort 26. Other Common Long Vowel Patterns: Short e and Long e (e, ee, ea, ea)

e	ee	ea	Short ea	Oddball
pest	**green**	**reach**	**bread**	**?**
guess	bleed	heat	breath	been
melt	preen	sneak	dead	read
yell	sweet	steal	head	
			meant	
			sweat	

What Is Known: Short e spelled with just an e, and long e spelled with ee and *ea*

What Is New: Short e spelled *ea*

Considerations: In *guess* the u is not part of the vowel pattern but makes the g sound like /g/ rather than /j/, as it also does in *guitar, guest,* and *guide*. *Read* may be pronounced with either a long or a short e sound. Also, thinking of the smaller word *mean* can aid students in remembering the correct spelling of *meant*. Finally, point out the difference between *breath* (listed) and *breathe* (not listed). As with *leave* in the previous sort, the e at the end of the latter word is also not part of a VCe pattern; here the e serves to give the *th* its characteristic voiced /th/ sound. Be sure students understand the meaning of *preen*.

As with many sorts in this feature, this one can be sorted in multiple ways: sound, pattern, or sound and pattern (as shown). When completing the sort as a sound sort, be sensitive to dialect differences. Some children may hear the ee in *been* as a short e, others as a short *i*, and still others as long e. The ultimate goal of this sort should be for learners to be able to sort by sound and pattern.

Integrating Idioms

"Mom said she'd take us to the movies Friday night, but **don't hold your breath.**" (It might not happen, so you'd be holding your breath for a very long time.)

"Why not **reach for the sky**?" (set your goals high)

Sort 27. Other Common Long Vowel Patterns: Short *i* and Long *i* (*i, iCe, y, igh*)

i	*iCe*	*y*	*igh*	Oddball
clip	**wipe**	**why**	**light**	**?**
blink	file	by	bright	tie
crisp	prize	dry	high	
fist	tide	shy	might	
		sky	sigh	
		try		

What Is Known: Short *i*, and long *i* spelled with *iCe*

What Is New: Long *i* spelled with *y* and with *igh*

Considerations: Be sure students understand the meanings of *crisp, file,* and *tide.*

Integrating Idioms

"I said she could go to the movie, and **in the blink of an eye** she had left." (in a very short period of time)

"Let's go to bed early so that tomorrow you are **bright-eyed and bushy-tailed.**" (wide awake and energetic, like a squirrel)

Literature Link

Kennedy, X. J. (1992). Paperclips. In B. S. Goldstein (Ed.), *Inner chimes: Poems on poetry.* Honesdale, PA: Boyds Mills Press.—Related words: In addition to *clip,* there is *high, bright,* and several other words with short or long *i* in them.

Sort 28. Other Common Long Vowel Patterns: Short *i* and Long *i* (*i, iCe, igh, iCC*)

i	*iCe*	*igh*	*iCC*	Oddball
grin	**white**	**right**	**find**	**?**
risk	glide	fight	blind	live
skid	guide	night	child	wind
	rice	slight	climb	
		tight	mind	
			wild	

What Is Known: Short *i*, and long *i* spelled with *iCe* and with *igh*

What Is New: Long *i* spelled *iCC*

Considerations: *Wind* and *live* have been placed in the Oddball category because they can be pronounced with either a long or a short vowel sound: *wind blows* and *wind the clock*; *live in a house* and *live animals in the box*. Students need to think carefully when reading words such as *wind* with an *iCC* pattern. They need to consider context clues and whether a long or a short vowel sound will lead to a known word. You might also ask them to think about which final consonants seem to signal a long vowel sound, such as *–nd* and *–ld*. Note that the *u* in *guide* is not part of the vowel pattern but makes the *g*, have a hard sound, as it also does in *guitar* and *guest*.

Integrating Idioms

"After four days of rain, the children were starting to **climb the walls**." (become totally bored)

Literature Links

Hurwitz, J. (1997). *Helen Keller: Courage in the dark*. New York: Random House.—Related word: *blind*.

Sort 29. Other Common Long Vowel Patterns: Short *o* and Long *o* (*o*, *oCe*, *oa*)

o	oCe	oa	Oddball
fog	**rope**	**float**	**?**
cloth	dome	road	move
golf	owe	loan	none
long	phone	oak	
moss	tone	roast	
plot		toad	
prompt			

What Is Known: Short *o*, and long *o* spelled *oCe*

What Is New: Long *o* spelled *oa*

Considerations: Discuss the meanings of words that may be somewhat unfamiliar to students, such as *dome*, *moss*, *plot*, *prompt*, and *tone*.

Integrating Idioms

"Come on; let's **hit the road**." (be on our way)

Literature Links

Sandburg, C. (1995). Fog. In E. H. Sword (Ed.), *A child's anthology of poetry*. Hopewell, NJ: Ecco Press.

Sort 30. Other Common Long Vowel Patterns: Short *o* and Long *o* (*o, oCe, oa, oCC*)

o	oCe	oa	oCC	Oddball
lost	**nose**	**loaf**	**hold**	**?**
smog	pose	boast	cold	gone
wrong	stole	coax	both	month
		foam	post	
		groan	roll	
		moan	told	

What Is Known: Short *o*, and long *o* spelled with *oCe* and *oa*

What Is New: Long *o* spelled *oCC*

Considerations: Point out to students the importance of remembering that *wrong* is one those tricky words with a silent letter. Also, just as with the *iCC* long vowel pattern, long *o* spelled *oCC* can be confusing, especially when it is encountered during reading, because it can have either a long or a short sound. Again, context clues must be used to determine which sound is appropriate. Discuss the meanings of *smog, pose, coax, boast,* and *post.*

Integrating Idioms

"Dad says it's **a lost cause**, but I'm going to keep on trying anyway." (hopeless situation)

Sort 31. Other Common Long Vowel Patterns: Short *o* and Long *o* (*o, oa, oCC, ow*)

o	oa	oCC	ow	Oddball
clog	**soak**	**most**	**blow**	**?**
cost	coast	bold	know	now
sock	goal	fold	show	
toss	load	ghost	slow	
	toast	mold		
		scold		

What Is Known: Short *o*, and long *o* spelled with *oa* and with *oCC*

What Is New: Long *o* spelled with *ow*

Considerations: Be aware that students may notice the slight variations in the vowel sound of the short *o* words. Also, point out to students the importance of remembering that *know* is another one of those tricky words with a silent letter. Discuss the meanings of *toss* and *mold.*

Integrating Idioms

"She was ready to **blow her top** when she saw the grade on my test." (get really angry)

"They don't have **a ghost of a chance** of winning." (not even the slightest possibility)

Sort 32. Other Common Long Vowel Patterns: Short *u* and Long *u* (*u*, *uCe*, *ue*, *ew*)

u	*uCe*	*ue*	*ew*	Oddball
dump	**June**	**glue**	**drew**	**?**
crumb	fume	blue	blew	bush
gulp	refuse	clue	chew	push
stuff		due	few	
		hue	stew	
		true		

What Is Known: Short *u*, and long *u* spelled *uCe*.

What Is New: Long *u* spelled with *ue* and with *ew*

Considerations: Discuss the meanings of *fume* and *hue*, as well as the homophones *due* and *dew*, and *blue* and *blew*, if necessary. Help students to realize that spelling final long *u* is difficult due to the numerous ways that the sound can be spelled: *ue* and *ew* as in the sort and occasionally other ways, as in *do* and *too*. Also point out the importance of remembering that *crumb* has a silent letter. [*Refuse* is a homograph that can be pronounced as (rĭ•fyooz′) and (rĕf′•yoos), the latter meaning *trash*. It is unlikely that students will be aware of the second meaning and pronunciation.]

Integrating Idioms

"Remember you're already taking piano lessons; don't **bite off more than you can chew**." (take on more than you can deal with)

Sort 33. Other Common Long Vowel Patterns: Short *u* and Long *u* (*u*, *ew*, *ui*, *oo*)

u	*ew*	*ui*	*oo*	Oddball
crust	**crew**	**fruit**	**room**	**?**
fuss	flew	bruise	bloom	build
gulf	grew	cruise	noon	does
slump		juice	proof	
		suit	soon	
			pool	

What Is Known: Short *u*, and long *u* spelled with *ew*.

What Is New: Long *u* spelled with *ui* and with *oo*. [Note that the *oo* pattern will be revisited later, when abstract vowels and words such as *foot* and *book* are explored.]

Considerations: Discuss the meaning of *gulf*. You may want to point out the *Gulf* of Mexico or some other *gulf* on a map. Students may have heard of another use of the word: "wide gap," such as people can have in understanding one another. *Cruise*, too, may need discussing. Also, note that the final *e* on *bruise*, *cruise*, and *juice* is not part of the vowel pattern. The vowel pattern in all three words is *ui*. In the first two words, the *e* signals the /z/ sound for the preceding *s*; in *juice* it ensures a soft /s/ sound for the *c*.

Integrating Idioms

"I told her my project is going to be the best of all, but she just said, '**The proof is in the pudding**.'" (Whether or not it is the best will be seen by the finished product.)

SORT 20 Other Common Long Vowel Patterns:
Short *a* and Long *a* (*a*, *a*Ce, *ay*)

grass	shade	play
cave	way	fake
gray	slam	say
wrap	they	chase
base	may	rash
hey	gaze	day
stage	fact	?

past	shake	stay
chain	said	wade
sway	paint	than
brain	male	wait
trade	swamp	mail
cash	pay	grab
tail	blame	?

flash	state	paid
eight	lamp	vein
stain	neigh	grave
pass	wash	freight
weigh	claim	brake
waist	wand	main
race	draft	?

SORT 23 Other Common Long Vowel Patterns:
Short e and Long e (e, open e, ee)

desk	he	keep
we	meet	dent
new	ski	greet
these	feel	she
swell	creep	speed
free	week	mess
rest	be	?

kept	need	beat
best	real	sheet
mean	wheel	clean
deep	text	break
weed	neat	seed
less	dream	teach
great	steep	?

SORT 25 Other Common Long Vowel Patterns:
Short e and Long e (e, ee, ea, ie)

west	sweep	peach
chief	meal	friend
team	fresh	beef
sleek	east	lie
leave	field	bend
thief	seem	feast
then	brief	?

pest	green	reach
bread	head	yell
steal	sweet	read
preen	meant	guess
been	sneak	dead
bleed	breath	heat
sweat	melt	?

clip	wipe	why
light	sky	tide
prize	high	tie
shy	blink	dry
might	try	fist
crisp	sigh	bright
by	file	?

grin	white	right
find	slight	glide
rice	climb	wind
child	risk	night
fight	blind	live
skid	guide	wild
mind	tight	?

fog	rope	float
long	roast	none
toad	moss	phone
owe	loan	golf
cloth	move	road
dome	oak	plot
prompt	tone	?

lost	nose	loaf
hold	boast	smog
pose	told	groan
foam	month	both
roll	moan	wrong
gone	coax	post
cold	stole	?

SORT 31 Other Common Long Vowel Patterns:
Short o and Long o (o, oa, oCC, ow)

clog	soak	most
blow	ghost	fold
now	toast	sock
coast	show	goal
mold	cost	bold
know	load	slow
toss	scold	?

Other Common Long Vowel Patterns:
Short *u* and Long *u* (*u*, *u*Ce, *ue*, *ew*)

dump	June	glue
drew	true	crumb
stuff	blew	clue
few	refuse	push
due	chew	hue
bush	stew	gulp
blue	fume	?

crust	crew	fruit
room	bruise	soon
flew	does	slump
pool	juice	bloom
suit	gulf	proof
build	noon	cruise
fuss	grew	?

Advanced R-Controlled Vowels with Long Vowel Patterns (DSA Feature G)
(Words Only)

Note: Students should have some prior knowledge of long vowel patterns before working with these sorts.

The sorts that follow extend students' understandings of *r*-controlled vowels to include the influence of *r* on long vowel patterns. The sorts also reinforce previously studied *r*-controlled vowels, because those patterns are among the contrasts included in the sorts. Students will learn that there are often multiple patterns for the same sound, so care must be taken when writing words with *r*-controlled vowels and when learning to spell them.

Sort 34. Advanced *R*-Controlled Vowels: *R*-Controlled *a* and Long *a*
(*ar, aCe, ai, are*)

ar	aCe	ai	are	Oddball
arm	**case**	**rain**	**care**	**?**
chart	age	aim	dare	warm
part	crane	faint	glare	where
sharp	sale	laid	rare	
	rate		spare	

What Is Known: *R*-controlled pattern *ar* and long vowel patterns *aCe* and *ai*.

What Is New: *R*-controlled vowel with a long vowel pattern, *are*

Considerations: Discuss the multiple meanings of *crane*: to stretch your neck to see better, a machine for raising heavy objects, and a wading bird with long legs. Also, talk about the meanings of the homophone *sale* and its absent partner *sail* and the effect of *w* on the sound of *a* in *warm*; compare the pronunciations of *warm* and *arm*. Finally, a usage discussion for the word *laid* may be beneficial for some students: *He laid his paper on the table* and *Earlier today, she lay on the couch and napped.*

Integrating Idioms

"Can I **twist your arm** into going?" (convince or persuade you)

"The new baseball glove cost **an arm and a leg**." (cost too much)

Sort 35. Advanced *R*-Controlled Vowels: *R*-Controlled *a* and Long *a*
(*ar, ai, are, air*)

ar	ai	are	air	Oddball
smart	**trail**	**share**	**air**	**?**
harm	braid	bare	chair	heart
scar	drain	fare	hair	
spark	gain	scare	pair	
	snail	stare	stair	

What Is Known: R-controlled patterns *ar* and *are* and long vowel pattern *ai*

What Is New: R-controlled pattern *air*

Considerations: Discuss the meanings of the homophones *bare, fare, stare, stair, hair,* and *pair* and the absent *bear, fair, hare,* and *pear.* Also, draw students' attention to spelling similarities and differences between *scar* and *scare* and to their differences in pronunciation. Students may be able to think of other such pairs, such as *star* and *stare, far* and *fare, bar* and *bare,* and *car* and *care.* Include a sound sort as part of the study of these words, as that will place *heart* with such words as *smart.* Discuss spelling differences in the categories. Then move to a sound and pattern sort, as shown.

Integrating Idioms

"He's **full of hot air** when he says it will take an hour to get there." (talking nonsense)

Sort 36. Advanced *R*-Controlled Vowels: *R*-Controlled *e* and Long *e* (*er, ea, ee, eer*)

er	ea	ee	eer	**Oddball**
perch	**seat**	**sleep**	**cheer**	**?**
nerve	beach	cheek	deer	dear
stern	cream	cheese	peer	near
serve	treat	heel	steer	
term		sleeve		

What Is Known: R-controlled pattern *er* and long vowel patterns *ea* and *ee*

What Is New: R-controlled pattern *eer*

Considerations: Discuss the meanings of the homophones *heel, deer, dear,* and *peer* and the absent *heal* and *pier.* Students will likely benefit from a discussion of *nerve* and *steer* as well. In the latter case, although students may be familiar with the driving connection, many will be surprised to learn that the word also refers to animals from which we get beef. Also, if students don't call attention to the final *e* in *serve, nerve,* and *sleeve,* do so, reminding them that it is there for the *v* and not as part of the vowel pattern. Similarly, the final *e* in *cheese* provides the *s* with a /z/ sound. If time allows, this set of words may be introduced as a sound sort with the category headers *perch, seat,* and *cheer.* This will lead to words in the *sleep* column being placed under *seat* and the two Oddballs under *cheer.* Following a discussion of the categories, engage students in re-sorting the words according to sound and pattern, as shown.

Integrating Idioms

"I wonder what **she has up her sleeve**." (what surprise idea she is thinking of)

Literature Link

Prelutsky, J. (1984). What nerve you've got, Minerva Mott! In *The new kid on the block.* New York: Scholastic.

Sort 37. Advanced *R*-Controlled Vowels: *R*-Controlled *e* and Long *e* (*er, ear, ea, ear*)

er	*ear* (short)	*ea*	*ear* (long)	Oddball
herd	**learn**	**meat**	**clear**	**?**
verb	earn	breathe	beard	here
swerve	earth	leash	fear	tear
	heard	wheat	hear	
	pearl		smear	
			year	

What Is Known: R-controlled pattern *er* and long e pattern *ea*

What Is New: R-controlled counterpart to the *ea* in *bread* (*ear* as in *learn*) and r-controlled counterpart to the *ea* in *meat* (*ear* as in *clear*)

Considerations: Discuss meanings of the homophones *hear, here, herd, heard,* and *meat* and its absent partner, *meet.* Also talk about the two different pronunciations and meanings of the homograph *t-e-a-r*: *a rip in a piece of paper* and *a droplet of water in the eye.* Students may be able to recall other such words (*read, bow,* etc.). Also, because several examples of words with a final e after a *v* have previously been encountered, students may point out *swerve* as one more instance. If they do not, call their attention to it. Similarly, as previously noted in Sort 26, the final e in *breathe* is there to give the *th* the sound heard in *this*, rather than as in *thing.* Have students compare this word with *breath.*

Students must learn to approach words flexibly in their reading. Imagine for a moment that a student comes across an unfamiliar word such as *yearn* and applies the vowel sound in *year* in an effort to read it. Assuming that the reader has heard of the word, when the attempt fails to produce a recognizable word, the flexible reader with a good knowledge of strategies will then apply the vowel sound heard in *earn.*

When it comes to writing words, students need to be aware that there are multiple ways to represent a particular sound. Although there are sometimes clues that can assist in determining the correct spelling (for example, *I hear with my* **ear**, and *heard* is merely *hear* with a *d* added), the bottom line is simply awareness. A wise speller realizes that, according to the sound /yûrn/, the spelling could be either *yern* or *yearn*, and, if uncertain, he or she knows the word will need to be checked with the aid of the teacher, a class expert, or a dictionary or other resource. The same need applies when a speller must choose between other sound-alike patterns, such as between *ear* and *eer.*

Integrating Idioms

"Don't **breathe** a word about the surprise party." (keep quiet)

Literature Links

Kenah, K. (2004). *Destruction earth.* Columbus, OH: Children's Publishing.—Extension words: *volcanoes, continental drift, earthquake, tsunami, glaciers,* and *meteor.*

Sort 38. Advanced *R*-Controlled Vowels: *R*-Controlled *i* and Long *i* (*ir*, *iCe*, *igh*, *ire*)

ir	*iCe*	*igh*	*ire*	**Oddball**
sir	**crime**	**sight**	**tire**	**?**
birth	price	flight	fire	world
swirl	tribe	fright	hire	worm
whirl	twice	thigh	wire	
	whine			
	wise			

What Is Known: *R*-controlled pattern *ir* and long vowel patterns *iCe* and *igh*

What Is New: *R*-controlled pattern *ire*

Considerations: Students may notice that *swirl* and *whirl* are very close in meaning. Discuss other word meanings as needed. Although Sort 38 involves categorizing by sound and pattern, you may also want to include a sound sort in the study of these words. It would include three categories, with *worm* and *world* sorted with words such as *sir* and with the *crime* and *sight* columns collapsed into one. Point out to students that *w* affects the sound of the *or* in many words, making it sound like /ər/. See if they can brainstorm other such words (for example, *word*, *work*, *worst*, and so forth. They may recall that *w* also affects the vowel *a* when it precedes it, as in *dwarf*, *war*, *warm*, and *warn*.

Integrating Idioms

"Have you noticed how they seem to **worm their way out of everything**?" (avoid a problem or responsibility)

Literature Link

Smith, D. J. (2002). *If the world were a village: A book about the world's people*. Tonawanda, NY: Kids Can Press.—This book looks at our global village as though it had only 100 people.

Sort 39. Advanced *R*-Controlled Vowels: *R*-Controlled *o* and Long *o* (*or*, *oa*, *ore*, *oar*)

or	*oa*	*ore*	*oar*	**Oddball**
fort	**goat**	**score**	**roar**	**?**
cork	moat	chore	board	floor
form	roam	shore	oar	
pork		snore	soar	
torch		store		
		tore		
		wore		

What Is Known: *R*-controlled pattern *or*, and long vowel pattern *oa*

What Is New: R-controlled patterns *ore* and *oar*

Considerations: Discuss the meanings of the homophones *wore, oar,* and *soar* and the absent *war, or,* and *sore.* After checking students' recognition and understanding of the words in this sort, ask them to categorize the words according to vowel sound; *fort* and *goat* can serve as the key words. Discuss the results. Next, ask students to review each of the categories and to separate out the different patterns. This will yield results similar to Sort 39. During the follow-up discussion, students should realize that when /ôr/ is involved, a wise speller is either certain of the correct spelling or knows to check it out.

Literature Link

Prelutsky, J. (1984). Louder than a clap of thunder! In *The new kid on the block.* New York: Scholastic.— Related word: though not in the text, *snore* is clearly described. Extension words: *blunder, ogre, stampeding, tidal wave.*

arm	case	rain
care	faint	sharp
age	rare	where
laid	part	sale
rate	warm	dare
chart	glare	crane
spare	aim	?

From *Word Sorts and More* by Kathy Ganske. Copyright 2006 by The Guilford Press. Permission to photocopy this form is granted to purchasers of this book for personal use only (see copyright page for details). Enlarge 135% to fill page.

smart	share	trail
air	braid	fare
drain	chair	scar
spark	pair	stare
scare	heart	gain
hair	stair	bare
harm	snail	?

perch	seat	sleep
cheer	treat	nerve
beach	dear	steer
near	term	deer
cheek	heel	serve
stern	peer	cheese
sleeve	cream	?

herd	learn	meat
clear	here	wheat
earth	breathe	earn
leash	verb	beard
hear	pearl	year
swerve	tear	heard
smear	fear	?

sir	crime	sight
tire	worst	swirl
fright	twice	wire
birth	flight	price
whine	world	fire
hire	thigh	tribe
whirl	wise	?

From *Word Sorts and More* by Kathy Ganske. Copyright 2006 by The Guilford Press. Permission to photocopy this form is granted to purchasers of this book for personal use only (see copyright page for details). Enlarge 135% to fill page.

fort	goat	score
roar	moat	store
shore	board	pork
oar	cork	tore
roam	floor	chore
form	wore	soar
snore	torch	?

Complex Consonant Patterns (DSA Feature I) (Words Only)

Words in the following sorts contain short, long, *r*-controlled, and (rarely) abstract vowels. Certain sorts such as 40 and 41, may be completed much earlier in the stage. As previously noted in the discussion of other long vowel patterns, students may not need to complete all of the sorts.

Sort 40. Complex Consonant Patterns: Final /k/ (*ck, ke*)

ck	*ke*	**Oddball**
back	**bake**	**?**
brick	bike	look
buck	flake	think
click	smoke	
dock	snake	
neck	take	
pack	wake	
pick		
sack		
tack		
wreck		

What Is Known: Final *ck* in the context of word families and VCe as a pattern for long vowels. Because the knowledge base for this sort was formed at the previous stage and with the first sorts of Part 4, this sort and the one that follows could be used early on at this stage.

What Is New: Examination of the different ways to spell final /k/

Considerations: A note about how final /k/ works: When the vowel is short, the spelling of /k/ is usually *ck*, unless a consonant sound is heard before the /k/, as in *think*. By contrast, long vowel words are usually vowel-*ke* (V*ke*). Long e words are exceptions because the VCe pattern is rare. These words, as well as words with *oo*, as in *look*, and with the /ô/ sound, as in *chalk* and *squawk*, are spelled with just *k*.

You may need to discuss the meanings of *buck, click,* and *dock*. Also, students should take special note of the silent letter in *wreck* to help them remember the spelling. They may recall *wrap* from a previous word study (see Sort 20).

Begin the lesson with a guided walk that focuses on sound: short vowels, long vowels, and other. Then ask students to look carefully at the columns of words to see if they can determine how the words in each category are alike. Their hypotheses should reflect key aspects of the information discussed at the beginning of this *Considerations* section. Blind sorting opportunities will help students pay attention to sound, as well as pattern, distinctions.

Integrating Idioms

"That really **takes the cake!**" (wins the prize for the best or worse)

"I have a **bone to pick with you.**" (a concern to talk over)

Literature Links

Cronin, D. (2000). *Click, clack, and moo: Cows that type.* New York: Scholastic.—Extension words: *neutral,*
    ultimatum, and *to go on strike.*
Editors of *Time for Kids.* (2005). *Snakes!* New York: HarperTrophy.
Holub, J. (2004). *Why do snakes hiss?* New York: Puffin Books.
Penner, F. (2005). *The cat came back.* New Milford, CT: Roaring Book Press.—Extension words: *absurd,*
    humane, amuck.

Sort 41. Complex Consonant Patterns: Final /k/ (*ck, ke, k* with C*k* blend)

ck	*ke*	*k* (C*k* blend)	**Oddball**
sick	**poke**	**silk**	**?**
black	duke	ask	creek
flick	mike	blank	took
jack	stroke	bunk	
knock		disk	
speck		honk	
stock		link	

What Is Known: Use of *ck* with short vowels and *ke* with long vowels

What Is New: When a consonant is heard before the /k/ sound and after the short vowel, the ending
is just *k*, not *ck*

Considerations: You may need to discuss the meanings of *duke, stroke, bunk, disk,* and *link.* Also, students may need to be reminded that *mike* (microphone) and *jack* (toy or tire-fixing tool), are not capi-
talized here because they are not being used as names of people. Finally, point out to students the importance of remembering the silent letter in *knock.* As with the previous sort, begin with a sound sort
that focuses on the vowel: short, long, and other. Discuss the results and generate ideas related to the
spellings in each category. With teacher guidance, students should extend their ideas from the previous
lesson to include the use of just *k* when a consonant precedes the final /k/ of a word with a short
vowel. (It is also used with long *e*; with the *oa* pattern, as in *soak*; and with abstract vowels, but this does
not need to be brought to students' attention unless they express curiosity regarding the matter.)

Integrating Idioms

"You're **asking for trouble** if you go over to his house." (doing something that will cause trouble)

Sort 42. Complex Consonant Patterns: Final /k/ Sound (ck, ke, k with Ck blend and VVk pattern)

| | | k | |
ck	ke	Ck blend	VVk
snack	**hike**	**mark**	**book**
deck	drake	bank	leak
pluck	fluke	chunk	peek
slick	stake	dusk	seek
stack			shook
tick			speak

What Is Known: Final /k/ with ck, ke, and Ck

What Is New: Use of final k with long e and with abstract vowels (namely, vowels that are not short, not long, and not r-controlled)

Considerations: Discuss the homophones *stake*, *leak*, and *peek* and their absent partners *steak*, *leek*, and *peak*. Students will also benefit from discussing the meanings of *dusk*, *fluke* and *pluck*. If possible, show students a picture of a whale's fluke and demonstrate a plucking action. If students wonder why such words as *music* and *comic* end with a c rather than a k, let them know that when words have more than one syllable, different principles for spelling sounds can apply. Walk students through this group of words as a pattern sort: ck, ke, and k. Then ask them to look for a way to subdivide the k category. The results should reflect Sort 42. Discuss what the words in each category have in common.

Sort 43. Complex Consonant Patterns: Triple-Letter Blends (k, qu, squ)

k	qu	squ	Oddball
kind	**quake**	**square**	**?**
key	queen	squash	knife
kick	quick	squat	quiche
king	quilt	squeeze	
	quit	squint	
	quite	squirt	
	quiz		
	quote		

What Is Known: Initial consonant k (at the letter name stage) and qu

What Is New: The three-letter cluster, squ, and a more in-depth look at qu

Considerations: Discuss the meanings of *quilt*, *quote*, and *quiche*, as well as any others that may be confusing. The meanings of *squat* and *squint* may be demonstrated. If students ask about the unusual pronunciation of q-u-i-c-h-e, call to their attention that English is a rich language with words borrowed from many languages. Because of this, the way words are pronounced is sometimes different from what we expect. For example, consider the foods *filet mignon* and *chow mein*. Students may also be intrigued by the pronunciation of *quay* (sounds like *key* or "K" and means wharf) and the spelling and pronunciation of *queue* (sounds like *cue* and means a line of waiting people or vehicles or a long braid). You may want to bring students' attention to the sound the *a* vowel makes when it follows *qu* or *squ*. The *qu* /kw/ + *a* has the same broad sound heard in many *wa* words: *swamp, swat, swan*, and so forth. This understanding can help students to correctly spell the vowel.

Introduce the sort by modeling with a pattern sort. After sorting a few examples, say to the students, "For the rest of the cards, I'm going to read the words, but I'm not going to show you the cards, so you will have to decide where the cards belong, based on sound." After the sorting is complete, discuss the categories. Because this sort is so highly visual, blind sorting activities should be incorporated.

Literature Links

Coerr, E. (1986). *The Josephina story quilt*. New York: HarperCollins.
Cronin, D. (2002). *Giggle, giggle, quack*. New York: Simon & Schuster Books for Young Readers.—Related word: *quack*. Extension word: *influence*.
Murphy, F. (2001). *Ben Franklin and the magic squares*. New York: Random House.

Sort 44. Complex Consonant Patterns: Triple-Letter Blends (*st, th, str, thr*)

st	*th*	*str*	*thr*
still	**thank**	**strike**	**three**
stale	there	strange	thread
steam	thick	stray	thrill
stood	thin	stream	throat
		street	throb
		string	
		strong	

What Is Known: Initial consonant blends *st* and *th*

What Is New: Triple-letter blends *str* and *thr*

Considerations: Discuss the meanings of *stale* and *throb*. Due to the highly visual nature of this sort, blind sorting should be incorporated into some of the activities. It may be used with the guided word walk (see Sort 43).

Integrating Idioms

"She can't sing tonight because she **has a frog in her throat**." (is hoarse)

Literature Link

London, J. (2003). *Giving thanks*. Cambridge, MA: Candlewick Press.

Sort 45. Complex Consonant Patterns: Triple-Letter Blends (sp, spl, spr)

sp	*spl*	*spr*	Oddball
spoon	**splash**	**spring**	**?**
spade	splint	sprain	sphere
spank	split	spray	
spear	splurge	spread	
spoil		sprig	
spike		sprout	
spur		spruce	
		spry	

What Is Known: Blend *sp* (at the letter name stage)

What Is New: Triple-letter blends *spl* and *spr*

Considerations: Discuss the meanings of *spur, splint, splurge, sprig,* and *spry. Sphere* may also need to be discussed. This is a good time to talk about words with the *ph* digraph. Students may be able to recall more *ph* words, such as *photo, phone, phrase,* and *phonics.* Once the words have been identified and their meanings discussed, involve competent students in a blind sort, being sure to model a few examples. This will encourage them to attend to sound, as well as pattern. If members of the group are more tentative in their understanding of triple-letter blends, you may want to guide them through a pattern sort instead and then discuss the results.

Integrating Idioms

"Let's not **split hairs** over this." (quibble over petty differences)

Sort 46. Complex Consonant Patterns: Triple-Letter Blends (sc, sh, scr, shr)

sc	*sh*	*scr*	*shr*	Oddball
scab	**shield**	**scrape**	**shrink**	**?**
scale	shall	scrap	shred	school
scalp	shark	scream	shriek	sure
		screen	shrill	
		scrub	shrimp	
			shrub	
			shrug	

What Is Known: Blend *sc* and digraph *sh* (at the letter name stage)

What Is New: Triple-letter blends *scr* and *shr*

Considerations: Discuss word meanings as necessary. The meanings of *scale, scalp, shriek, shrill,* and *shrug* may need to be clarified. Although *school* begins with *sc*, it is the *ch* that produces the /k/ sound. Introduce the patterns by asking students to complete a pattern sort: *sc, scr, sh,* and *shr*. When they have finished, ask them to read carefully through the categories, listening to the differences in sound between those words that begin with two consonants and those that begin with three. Then collect all of the word cards except for the key words, and engage students in a blind sort. Students need to pay close attention to the /r/ sound in each of the new categories.

Literature Link

Dubowski, C. E. (1998). *Shark attack.* New York: DK.

Sort 47. Complex Consonant Patterns: Final /ch/ (ch, tch)

ch	*tch*	**Oddball**
pinch	**pitch**	**?**
belch	catch	which
bench	crutch	
branch	ditch	
church	fetch	
lunch	hatch	
munch	itch	
march	sketch	
search	stitch	
	witch	

What Is Known: Final digraph *ch*

What Is New: Final digraph *tch*

Considerations: Discuss the homophones *which* and *witch*. The meanings of *fetch* and *sketch* may also be unclear to students. Walk students through a pattern sort with *ch* and *tch*. Help them to realize that short vowel words are spelled with final *tch*, unless a consonant sound is heard before the /ch/; then the spelling is *ch*. The latter *ch* principle holds true for *r*-controlled vowels as well. With this sort, and the two that follow, include blind sorting activities to call students' attention to sound clues that signal the spelling of the final /ch/ sound. *Which* (like *such*) is an exception that must simply be learned.

Integrating Idioms

"You're sure **out to lunch** a lot; what are you thinking about?" (not alert)

Sort 48. Complex Consonant Patterns: Final /ch/ (VVch, Cch, tch)

	ch		
VVch	**lch, nch, rch**	**tch**	**Oddball**
each	**porch**	**match**	**?**
bleach	bunch	hitch	rich
coach	drench	latch	(watch)
crouch	mulch	patch	
grouch	ranch	snatch	
pouch	starch	(watch)	
speech			

What Is Known: That *tch* is used with short vowel words unless a consonant is heard before the final /ch/; then *ch* is used. The same is true for *r*-controlled vowels.

What Is New: Long vowels and abstract vowels (vowels that are not short, not long, and not *r*-controlled) require *ch*.

Considerations: It may be necessary to discuss the meanings of *bleach*, *mulch*, *starch*, *hitch*, *latch*, and *snatch*. For *drench*, be sure that students understand it as not just to wet something, but to soak it. Due to its short *o* sound, *watch* may be sorted under the Oddball category. However, if students prefer to categorize it with the *tch* words, they may do so, since the word has a short vowel sound.

Sort 49. Complex Consonant Patterns: Final /j/ (Vge, Cge, dge)

	ge	
Vge	**lge, nge, rge**	**dge**
page	**large**	**edge**
cage	bulge	badge
rage	change	bridge
wage	charge	fudge
	plunge	hedge
	sponge	judge
	urge	lodge
		pledge
		smudge

What Is Known: Final ge, especially with VCe

What Is New: Final *dge*

Considerations: Although all of the Vge words in this sort include *age*, any long vowel pattern, as well as abstract vowel patterns, uses the ge spelling unless a consonant sound is heard before the final /j/. Other examples include *huge*, *stooge*, *gouge*, and *gauge*. The principle at work here parallels that discussed in the two previous sorts. Begin with a pattern sort: *dge* and *ge*. Then ask students to look the ge category over carefully in order to notice any way the list might be subdivided, or broken down into smaller groups. This should lead, with guidance as necessary, to the separation of Vge words from those with a consonant before the final /j/.

Integrating Idioms

"Try not to worry; we'll **cross that bridge when we come to it**." (deal with the problem when it happens)

Literature Link

Simon, S. (2005). *Bridges*. San Francisco: Chronicle Books.—Extension words: *arch*, *suspension*, and *span*.

Sort 50. Complex Consonant Patterns: Hard and Soft c

Hard c (a, o, u)	Soft c (e, i, y)	Oddball
call	**cent**	**?**
calf	cell	since
calm	center	sent
cast	cinch	
cool	city	
comb	cycle	
cope	scene	
core	scent	
count		
curve		

What Is Known: Consonant c with a /k/ sound

What Is New: Consonant c with a /s/ sound

Considerations: Discuss the meanings of the homophones in this sort—*cell, cent, scent,* and *sent*—as well as the meanings of *cope* and *cinch*. Students may notice that *cycle* and *city* are two-syllable words; their extra syllable is unlikely to present a spelling problem for students.

They will likely notice the final e after the v in *curve* and may recall that it is there to close off the v. Similarly, the final e in *since* ensures a soft c sound. Caution students to be aware of the silent letter at the end of *comb*.

Engage students in a sound sort: words that begin with /k/ versus those that start with /s/. Then help them to refine the sort so that it reflects pattern also: What vowel patterns indicate that the c will have a /k/ sound, and which a soft /s/ sound? Some students may wish to categorize *scene* and *scent* in the Oddball category, because they do not begin with c. This is fine. However, you might point out to them that the letter c may appear anywhere within the word, other than in the final position, and it will likely have an /s/ sound if followed by e, i, or y: *fence, voice,* and in the list word *since.* Contrariwise, when followed by a, o, or u, c has a hard or /k/ sound. This understanding will facilitate reading words with these patterns; however, students need to realize that when writing words, the sound of /s/ may be represented by either c or s.

Integrating Idioms

"Dad said not to **count my chickens before they hatch**." (plan on something until it happens)

Sort 51. Complex Consonant Patterns: Hard and Soft *g*

Hard *g* (*a, o, u*)	Soft *g* (*e, i, y*)	Oddball
game	**germ**	**?**
gang	gem	jingle
gas	gentle	gift
gasp	gerbil	
gawk	giant	
gold	gist	
good	gym	
guest		
gust		
guy		
gorge		

What Is Known: Consonant *g* with a /g/ sound

What Is New: Consonant *g* with a /j/ sound

Considerations: Students should come to realize that *g*, like *c* (see Sort 50), when followed by an *e, i,* or *y* has a soft sound /j/, and when followed by *a, o,* or *u* has a hard (or /g/) sound. Being aware of the letters that can signal a hard or soft *g* will facilitate reading words with these patterns; however, students need to realize that, when writing words, the sound of /j/ may be represented by either *g* or *j*, especially at the beginning of words; in other positions, such as at the end of words, the spelling will tend to be with *g*: *forge, George.* However, unlike *c, g* has numerous exceptions (*get, give, gift*), which tend to be words that were borrowed from Scandinavia. After word recognition and understanding of meanings have been checked, guide students through the words with a sound sort that focuses on the initial sound: /g/ or /j/. Refine the results by asking students to consider pattern and what letters seem to be common to one category but not the other. Due to its hard and soft *g*, *gorge* may be an Oddball.

Sort 52. Complex Consonant Patterns: Hard and Soft *c* and *g*

Hard (*a, o, u*)		Soft (*e, i, u*)	
c	*g*	*c*	*g*
call	**game**	**cent**	**germ**
candy	gather	certain	genius
color	gauge	cite	ginger
comic	goose	circle	giraffe
copy	guard	cyst	
	guilt		

What Is Known: Depending on whether this sort is completed after Sorts 50 and 51 or whether it is used in place of those two sorts, students may have prior knowledge of all four categories, or they may know only the hard sounds of *c* and *g*.

What Is New: Comparing and contrasting hard and soft *c* and *g* and, possibly, soft *c* and *g*.

Considerations: The key words for this sort were used in Sorts 50 and 51. This sort is intended as a more challenging substitute for those two sorts, as nearly all of the words are two-syllable words. If desired, additional words can be added from Sorts 50 and 51. Discuss the meanings of *gauge*, *cyst*, and *ginger*. In the last case, it may be helpful to bring in some of the spice or a piece of ginger root. To understand *cyst*, students might be able to relate to the bubble-like formation that can develop around a sliver or thorn under the skin.

Nearly the same approach that was used for Sorts 50 and 51 may be used here; however, begin by asking students to sort the words into two categories: initial consonants *c* and *g*. Then turn their attention to sound differences within each category and, last, to a consideration of the patterns that coincide with particular sounds of *c* and *g*. Some students may wish to categorize *gauge* and *circle* as Oddballs, because these two words contain both hard and soft sounds. Praise their excellent observations in noting that hard and soft *c* and *g* can occur at other places in the word besides the beginning, but maintain focus for this sort on the initial part of the word. With assistance, students should come to realize that when a *c* or a *g* is followed by an *e*, *i*, or *y*, it has a soft sound (/s/ or /j/), and when followed by *a*, *o*, or *u*, it has a hard sound (/k/ or /g/).

Sort 53. Complex Consonant Patterns: Silent Initial Consonants (*gn, kn, wr*)

gn	*kn*	*wr*	Oddball
gnat	**knee**	**wrote**	**?**
gnarl	knack	wreath	ring
gnash	knead	wren	
gnaw	knew	wrench	
	knight	wring	
	knit	wrist	
	knob		
	knoll		
	knot		

What Is Known: Sounded versions of the initial consonants *g, n, k*

What Is New: The silent nature of some consonants in certain contexts

Considerations: Discuss the meanings of the homophones *knew* (new and perhaps *gnu*), *knead* (need), *knot* (not), and *wring* (ring). *Gnarl, gnash, gnaw, knack, knoll,* and *wrench* may also need discussing. Maurice Sendak's *Where the Wild Things Are* provides good examples for *gnash* and *gnaw*. Reference to this book is likely to evoke fond memories for many students at this stage, as most will be familiar with the story. A few words with silent beginning consonants have been integrated into earlier sorts (*knife, knock, know, wrap, wreck, write, wrong*). You may want to bring these words to students' attention.

If students wonder just why the seemingly strange spellings of *gn*, *kn*, and *wr* exist, you can tell them that our language has a long and rich history and that many changes have occurred in it over time. Students may enjoy learning that people often speak of English as a "living" language. Just as we grow and change, so too has English. For some words, a lot of time has elapsed since they first became part of the language, making it difficult or even impossible to see the connection between the word as we know it today and the original word. People sometimes experience this same sort of disconnected feeling when they meet someone they haven't seen for years and have trouble recognizing them because they've changed so much. Imagine if we hadn't seen the person for 1,500 years, which could be how long ago the change occurred in English!

Over its long written history, many new words have been added to English through borrowings from other languages; unused words have been dropped; meanings have changed; and the original spelling and/or pronunciation of some of the words have also altered. For example, in the early days of English, *ice* and *house* were spelled *is* and *hus*, respectively. Similarly, the beginning letters of many of the words in this sort were at one time pronounced. Although pronunciation of the initial letter was lost over time, the spelling was maintained (except in the case of *kn*, which was originally *cn*). Some children might like to know what the original spellings looked like. The etymology of a word, usually shown in the dictionary in brackets after the word's pronunciation or at the end of all of the definitions, shows this. For example, *knee* and *gnaw* were once spelled *cneo* and *gnagan*, respectively. Students need to be on the alert for words with silent letters, as they can easily be misspelled.

Guide students through a sound sort; then, after discussing the results, ask them to re-sort the words by sound and pattern, as shown in Sort 53.

Integrating Idioms

"Does that **ring a bell**?" (remind you of anything)

Literature Link

Maynard, C. (1998). *Days of the knights: A tale of castles and battles.* New York: DK.—Extension word: *siege.*

Sort 54. Complex Consonant Patterns: Final /s/, /z/, and /v/ (ce, se, ve)

/s/ ce	/z/ se	/v/ ve	Oddball
chance	**please**	**twelve**	**?**
dance	cause	glove	false
once	choose	prove	freeze
peace	noise	shove	
piece	raise	solve	
prince	tease	starve	

What Is Known: The soft sound of *c* and the fact that numerous words include a final *e* for reasons other than magic *e*

What Is New: Careful attention to the sounds of *ce*, *se*, and *ve*.

Considerations: Discuss the meanings of the homophones *peace* and *piece*, as well as any other words that might be unfamiliar to students. This sort contrasts two confusing patterns: final *ce* and *se*. The /v/ category has been included as a relief to the other two more difficult categories and to review and emphasize what has been mentioned in several earlier sorts that included words with final /v/—*curve, leave, nerve, serve,* and *swerve*—namely, that words with final /v/ (excluding a few proper nouns) consistently require an *e* after the *v*. Besides teaching students to pay close attention to the pattern when learning to spell words with final /s/ and /z/, this sort can also be used to teach a "best guess" strategy: Final /s/ is usually spelled *ce* rather than *se*. Similarly, in most one-syllable words, the final /z/ is *se*, rather than *ze*. When it comes to reading words, *ce* is not likely to confuse readers, because it has a soft /s/

sound when followed by e; but se may be confusing due to its double identity, /s/ and /z/. context clues can often help, as in each of the following sentences: *How* close *is the park?* and *Please* close *the door.*

Guide students through a pattern sort and discuss.

Integrating Idioms

"**If push comes to shove,** we'll just have to go next week instead." (if things get really bad)

Sort 55. Complex Consonant Patterns: Final *th* and *the* (*th, the,* CC*th*)

th	*the*	(C)C*th*
bath	**bathe**	**depth**
broth	clothe	fourth
faith	soothe	health
froth	teethe	length
teeth		ninth
		strength
		twelfth
		warmth
		wealth
		width
		worth

What Is Known: Final *th* when preceded by a vowel, as in the first category

What Is New: The sound of *th* when followed by e, and the complex consonant unit that results when one or more consonants occur before the *th*, as in *depth*

Considerations: Discuss the meanings of *broth, froth,* the homophone *fourth,* and any other words with which students may be unfamiliar.

Th was studied in the initial and final positions of words at the letter name stage, and it was reviewed earlier at this stage when contrasted with the cluster *thr.* It is explored further here in the context of the final position of words. It is unusual to find three-consonant clusters ending words in English, and *th* is particularly remarkable in the number of different consonants that can precede it, including *dth, (l)fth, (n)gth, lth, mth, nth, pth, rth,* and *xth.* Final *th* often acts as a suffix to form ordinal numbers or abstract nouns (*six/sixth; grow/growth*). The change in sound from unvoiced to voiced /th/ with the addition of the final e adds further interest to this digraph. Students may recall *breath* and *breathe* from earlier sorts at this stage. You might ask them what they notice about the role (part of speech) of the words in the second category, as well as whether they know any other words of this type.

The letters themselves have an interesting history: Although *th* was used in the earliest English texts, before A.D. 700 a letter that looked like a lowercase *d* with a bar over it (ð) was used, and after that a letter that looked much like our uppercase P (þ). In early Scotland, even the letter Y was sometimes used to represent *th.* (Students might enjoy guessing the meaning of *Ye* on signs in colonial and other historical sights.) The digraph *th* returned to use in the mid-1500s.

Lead students through a pattern sort and discuss. Follow up another day with a blind sound sort, written if desired.

Complex Consonant Patterns: Final /k/ (*ck, ke*)

back	bake	tack
pack	wreck	pick
brick	sack	bike
think	neck	buck
dock	smoke	wake
take	snake	look
flake	click	?

sick	poke	silk
knock	jack	blank
honk	duke	black
mike	flick	bunk
stock	creek	stroke
disk	link	speck
took	ask	?

snack	hike	mark
book	stake	tick
stack	bank	leak
chunk	deck	dusk
slick	peek	fluke
drake	speak	shook
pluck	seek	

Complex Consonant Patterns: Triple-Letter Blends (*k, qu, squ*)

kind	quake	square
queen	squash	quote
squeeze	knife	quilt
quiz	key	squint
kick	squat	quite
quiche	quit	king
quick	squirt	?

still	thank	strike
three	there	strong
stream	stale	thread
thrill	thick	street
steam	string	thin
strange	throat	stood
throb	stray	

spoon	splash	spring
spear	spray	spike
sprain	spade	splint
sphere	spread	split
spoil	sprout	spank
spry	spruce	sprig
spur	splurge	?

scab	scrape	shield
shrink	shrill	scale
shall	scrub	shark
screen	shrub	scrap
shrug	school	shriek
scalp	shrimp	sure
shred	scream	?

Complex Consonant Patterns: Final /ch/ (*ch*, *tch*)

pinch	pitch	munch
lunch	witch	march
fetch	belch	ditch
church	sketch	stitch
catch	which	bench
hatch	search	crutch
branch	itch	?

SORT 48 Complex Consonant Patterns: Final /ch/ (VVch, Cch, tch)

each	porch	match
speech	ranch	coach
hitch	patch	bunch
mulch	pouch	latch
bleach	rich	crouch
snatch	drench	watch
grouch	starch	?

Complex Consonant Patterns: Final /j/ (Vge, Cge, *dge*)

page	large	edge
judge	change	wage
smudge	sponge	bridge
pledge	badge	plunge
rage	bulge	urge
hedge	cage	lodge
charge	fudge	

From *Word Sorts and More* by Kathy Ganske. Copyright 2006 by The Guilford Press. Permission to photocopy this form is granted to purchasers of this book for personal use only (see copyright page for details). Enlarge 135% to fill page.

Complex Consonant Patterns: Hard and Soft *c*

call	cent	curve
core	cool	cell
cast	since	cope
sent	calm	scent
cinch	calf	scene
count	comb	center
cycle	city	?

Complex Consonant Patterns: Hard and Soft *g*

game	germ	guy
gang	gasp	gas
gold	gist	gift
gym	gorge	guest
gust	gem	good
gentle	jingle	gerbil
gawk	giant	?

call	game	cent
germ	cite	gauge
color	guilt	giraffe
goose	candy	cyst
certain	genius	gather
copy	ginger	comic
circle	guard	

gnat	knee	wrote
knoll	ring	knight
knack	knot	gnarl
wrist	knew	wrench
gnash	wren	knead
wring	knob	wreath
gnaw	knit	?

Complex Consonant Patterns: Final /s/, /z/, and /v/ (ce, se, ve)

chance	please	twelve
freeze	starve	peace
false	glove	raise
prove	dance	shove
piece	choose	tease
once	solve	prince
noise	cause	?

bath	bathe	depth
fourth	wealth	teethe
strength	broth	length
teeth	soothe	worth
width	warmth	faith
clothe	ninth	health
twelfth	froth	

Abstract Vowels (DSA Feature J) (Words Only)

Many abstract vowels are dipthongs: vowel teams in which the sound of one vowel glides into the other, as in /oi/ or /ou/. These and other abstract vowels are presented in the sorts that follow.

Sort 56. Abstract Vowels: *oy, oi*

oy	oi	Oddball
boy	**coin**	**?**
employ	avoid	choir
enjoy	boil	
joy	choice	
soy	foil	
toy	hoist	
	join	
	joint	
	moist	
	point	
	soil	
	toil	
	voice	

What Is Known: The sounds of the individual vowels

What Is New: The patterns and sounds of *oi* and *oy*

Considerations: You will likely need to discuss the meanings of several of the following words: *soy, boil, foil, hoist, toil,* and *choir.*

After checking word recognition and understanding of word meaning, engage students in a sound and pattern sort. Due to the final e, some students may wish to classify *choice* and *voice* with the Oddball category, especially if they have not completed Sort 52 or 54 that include, tricky final consonants. Students should acquire the understanding that *oy* is used at the ends of words or syllables, whereas *oi* is used in the middle of them.

Sort 57. Abstract Vowels: *oo* and *ou* (*oo* /ū/, *oo* and *ou* with /o͝o/)

/ū/ oo	/o͝o/		Oddball
	oo	ou	
tooth	**cook**	**could**	**?**
fool	brook	should	threw
mood	foot	would	truth
roof	hood		
root	hook		
scoop	soot		
tool	wood		
	wool		

What Is Known: The long *u* sound of *oo* (*tooth*)

What Is New: An alternative sound for *oo*, /o͝o/, and an alternative pattern for that sound: *ou* (*could*)

Considerations: Some students may wonder if the slang word for an eccentric person, *kook*, is spelled *c-o-o-k*. Discuss the homophone *threw* (*through*) and the meanings of *mood*, *brook*, *soot*, and any other words with which students may be unfamiliar. Students may confuse *root* with its sometimes homophone, *route* (/ro͞ot/), so you may also want to talk about this word. Other students may think it best to classify the word with *cook* (/ro͝ot/). Both pronunciations are acceptable; if the group is divided in their perceptions, the word can always be placed in the Oddball category. The same issue may affect *roof*, which can be pronounced either way as well.

Ask students to first sort by sound, then by pattern, and lastly by sound and pattern with this set of words, because the *oo* pattern has multiple sounds and because there are multiple patterns for the /o͝o/ sound. The distinction between the *oo* in *tooth* and *cook* is a fine one. Some students may have difficulty discerning it. It may be helpful for them to hear the word pared down to the vowel, as *mood* → *ood* → o͞o versus *foot* → *oot* → o͝o. The most common pronunciation for the *oo* digraph is the long *u* sound as in *tooth*. There are a few words with this spelling that have neither sound: *flood* and *blood*, for example.

Sort 58. Abstract Vowels: *ow* and *ou* (*ow* /ō/, *ow* and *ou* /ou/)

| | /ou/ | | |
/ō/ ow	ow	ou	Oddball
crow	**town**	**shout**	**?**
bowl	brown	cloud	though
throw	crowd	found	touch
	down	ground	
	frown	loud	
	growl	mouth	
		noun	
		proud	
		south	

What Is Known: Long *o* spelled *ow*, and, to a slight extent, *ou* as a pattern

What Is New: The /ou/ sound for *ow* and *ou*

Considerations: Discuss any word meanings that may be unfamiliar to students. Although /ou/ at the end of a word is spelled *ow*, /ou/ in the middle of a word may be spelled either *ou* or *ow*, so students will need to pay careful attention when spelling words of this type. Remind them that awareness is important in spelling. Use of context and vocabulary knowledge can help students avoid potential pronunciation confusion during reading, as, for example, *After the play, the actor made a* **bow** *to the audience*, or *Several children got into trouble after the* **row** *on the playground*. Although context and vocabulary knowledge can also help in reading words with *ou*, this pattern is more difficult, because it can be pronounced in several different ways, as the following examples illustrate: *soul*, *soup*, *brought*, *rough*, and *should*. When there are multiple sounds for a particular pattern and multiple patterns for a particular sound, as in this sort, ask students to sort the words in multiple ways: by sound, by pattern, and finally by sound and pattern, as shown in the sort.

Integrating Idioms

"Keep in mind that **every cloud has a silver lining**: you lost your favorite glove, but now you'll be able to get a new one." (There's something good in everything.)

"She's been **down in the mouth** since her bike broke." (sad)

Sort 59. Abstract Vowels: *ow* and *ou* (*ow* and *ou* /ou/, *ou* /ô/)

/ou/			
ow	**ou**	**/ô/ ou**	**Oddball**
brow	**sound**	**bought**	**?**
clown	couch	cough	through
crown	count	fought	group
howl	doubt	ought	
owl	pound		
plow	pout		
scowl	scout		

What Is Known: /ou/ sound for *ow* and *ou*

What Is New: /ô/ sound of *ou*

Considerations: Discuss the meanings of *plow, scowl, pout,* and *ought,* as needed. You might ask students to demonstrate the looks of *scowl* and *pout*. Call students' attention to the spelling of the /f/ sound at the end of *cough*, and see if they can recall other words with this sound/pattern spelling (*rough, tough, enough,* and *laugh*). They might also notice that in some words the *gh* is silent. Students should take note of the silent *b* in *doubt* to aid recall of its spelling.

Ask students to first sort by pattern (*ow* and *ou*) and then by sound and pattern, as shown in the sort. Point out to students that usually the /ô/ sound is spelled with *au* or *aw*, a feature they will soon be exploring.

Integrating Idioms

"You're sure a **night owl**!" (someone who typically stays up late)

Literature Link

Duranat, P. (2005). *Sniffles, sneezes, hiccups, and coughs.* New York: DK.—Extension words: *marvelous, diaphragm,* and *mucus.*

Sort 60. Abstract Vowels: *au* and *aw*

/ô/

au	aw	Oddball
caught	**crawl**	**?**
fault	dawn	aunt
haunt	draw	laugh
gauze	jaw	
launch	law	
pause	lawn	
sauce	raw	
taught	straw	
	thaw	
	yawn	

What Is Known: /ô/ sound with *ou* pattern

What Is New: /ô/ sound of *au* and *aw*

Considerations: Discuss the meanings of words that may be unfamiliar to students, such as *gauze*, *launch*, *dawn*, and *thaw*. Call students' attention to the spelling of the /f/ sound at the end of *cough* and see if they can recall other words that end in *gh*, such as *rough*, *tough*, *enough*, and *laugh*.

Walk students through the words, using a sound and pattern sort. If students have not completed Sort 54 (tricky final consonants), they may think *pause*, *gauze*, and *sauce* should be placed in the Oddball category due to the final e. A few students may pronounce *aunt* as /ônt/ and, therefore, place it under *caught*, As with *ou* and *ow*, although /ô/ is spelled *aw* at the end of a word, /ô/ in the middle of a word may be spelled either *au* or *aw*, so students will need to pay careful attention when spelling words of this type. Hints about the correct spelling can sometimes be gained from thinking of families of words, for example, *jaw, law, paw* and *dawn, lawn, yawn*.

Integrating Idioms

"They say he was **caught red-handed**." (caught doing something wrong)

Sort 61. Abstract Vowels: Short *a* and *au, aw, al*

	/ô/		
Short *a*	*au*	*aw*	*al*
task	**haul**	**claw**	**salt**
grasp	taunt	bawl	chalk
tramp	vault	fawn	halt
		flaw	mall
		shawl	stalk
		sprawl	stall
		squawk	talk

What Is Known: Short *a*, the /ô/ sound of *au* and *aw*

What Is New: /ô/ sound spelled *al*

Considerations: This sort includes numerous words whose meanings you may need to discuss, including *grasp, tramp, taunt, vault, fawn, flaw,* and *sprawl,* and any others students may not understand. As with the previous sort, clues to the correct spelling of the /ô/ sound may be gained from thinking of word families: *claw/flaw, salt/halt,* and *chalk/talk.* However, as evident from the words above, /ôl/ is a sound that can be represented by several patterns, including *haul, sprawl,* and *stall.* Students will need to be attentive to the pattern when learning to spell words with this rhyming sound.

Literature Link

Prelutsky, J. (1984). Floradora Doe. In *The new kid on the block.* New York: Scholastic.—Related word: *talk,* as well as many synonyms: *chatted, recited, murmured, yammered, babbled, lectured, whispered, tittered, gossiped, prattled, regaled, moaned,* and *said.* Other extension words: *calamity, prose,* and a few flower names. You may want to revisit the poem during Sorts 62 or 63 to categorize the related words according to the sound of the *ed* ending.

boy	coin	moist
choir	joint	soy
toil	joy	choice
toy	point	boil
soil	join	voice
employ	foil	hoist
enjoy	avoid	?

tooth	cook	could
wool	hood	fool
scoop	would	brook
foot	mood	soot
tool	wood	roof
threw	root	hook
truth	should	?

Abstract Vowels: *ow* and *ou* (*ow* /ō/, *ow* and *ou* /ou/)

crow	town	shout
cloud	ground	throw
brown	proud	frown
though	bowl	south
down	found	growl
noun	loud	touch
mouth	crowd	?

From *Word Sorts and More* by Kathy Ganske. Copyright 2006 by The Guilford Press. Permission to photocopy this form is granted to purchasers of this book for personal use only (see copyright page for details). Enlarge 135% to fill page.

SORT 59 Abstract Vowels: *ow* and *ou* (*ow* and *ou* /ou/, *ou* /ô/)

brow	sound	bought
scout	clown	scowl
doubt	owl	cough
through	pout	ought
plow	count	howl
pound	group	couch
crown	fought	?

caught	crawl	taught
draw	straw	haunt
laugh	pause	jaw
thaw	lawn	gauze
yawn	aunt	raw
fault	dawn	sauce
law	launch	?

Abstract Vowels: Short *a* and *au, aw, al*

task	haul	claw
salt	squawk	mall
fawn	bawl	vault
stalk	grasp	stall
taunt	halt	shawl
sprawl	chalk	talk
tramp	flaw	?

Additional Sorts

(Possible Companion to Sort 63)

/id/	/d/	/t/
lasted	**showed**	**looked**
added	caused	asked
needed	climbed	helped
sounded	joined	missed
shouted	learned	passed
started	owned	reached
wanted	played	walked
	seemed	worked
	turned	

What Is Known: Students will likely be familiar with the *base words,* namely the words to which *ed* has been added, because most have been previously studied

What Is New: The concept that the *ed* spelling is generally used to show past tense, despite differences in sound (/t/, /d/, or /id/)

Considerations: This sort and the following sort are identified as "companion" sorts. They may be partnered or completed at different times and in different ways, as indicated. Words in this sort were selected because they occur frequently in text in their inflectional form, with *ed* or *ing.* The term *base word* is an important concept in this and the next three sorts; be sure students understand it.

Provided students are able to read the words, Sort 62 may be used at any time during the within word pattern stage. If used early or midstage, it should be with the purpose that students read and sort the words according to ending sound to gain an understanding of how to spell the past tense, but not with the expectation that they correctly spell the entire word; several of the vowel patterns are relatively difficult and are not explored until midstage to late in the stage. Sort 63 addresses the same feature but includes only short vowel words, so that sort may be substituted for Sort 62 or used as a companion to it, with the expectation that students be able to spell the words. You may wish to use both sorts, one early and one late. If Sort 62 is incorporated early or mid-stage, it can be returned to at the end of the stage with expectations for correct spellings, serving as a review of both the past tense ending and of various vowel patterns studied at this stage. Attention to this feature is appropriate when students are using and confusing the past tense spelling; for example; s-t-o-p-e-d and l-o-o-k-e-d but also *t-a-p-t* (tapped), *y-e-l-l-d* (yelled), or *s-p-o-t-i-d* (spotted). Whether or not the final consonant is doubled is not of concern at this time. Bear in mind that dialect differences may cause some children to have difficulty discerning the difference between the /d/ and /t/ pronunciations. Also, students should become aware that some words have an irregular past tense form: for example, *grew, kept, slept, felt.*

The sort should be completed as a closed sort with a high level of support and lots of modeling. You may wish to explicitly tell students before beginning to model that in English we show that an action has already happened by adding *ed* to a word and that the *ed* ending can be pronounced three ways—/id/, /d/, and /t/. Ask them to read the words with you and listen carefully as you begin to place the words in their appropriate categories. Invite volunteers to help.

Literature Link

The Jack Prelutsky poem listed in Sort 61 may also be used with Sorts 62–63.

Sort 63. Additional Sorts: Sounds of Past Tense *ed* (/id/, /d/, /t/)

(Companion to Sort 62)

/id/	/d/	/t/
printed	**spelled**	**jumped**
handed	dressed	blushed
landed	filled	cracked
planted	pressed	fished
slanted	spilled	locked
tilted	smelled	fixed
twisted	yelled	rushed
		shocked
		tricked
		wished

Sort 64. Additional Sorts: Looking Ahead to Past Tense with e-Drop (No Change, e-Drop)

No change	e-drop	Oddball
ended	**saved**	**?**
checked	blamed	built
dusted	lived	
parted	moved	
pulled	raised	
scolded	raked	
snowed	sliced	
sounded	smiled	
steamed	taped	
talked	whined	
toasted	used	

What Is Known: Adding *ed* to a word is how we typically show the past tense

What Is New: Some words require dropping of the final *e* before adding *ed* or *ing*

Considerations: Introduce the sort by reminding students that *ed* is an ending that is added to base words to show past tense. Then, as part of the process of identifying and discussing the words, ask students to underline the base word wherever possible, being sure to leave the *ed* untouched. Students should realize that this cannot be done for some of the words (the *e-drop* category). Let them speculate on why this is, then call their attention to what one or more of the words would be like if the *e* hadn't been dropped. "Imagine how strange words would look and sound if we didn't do this. For example, take *saved*; if we left both e's, we'd end up with *saveed* [writes the word on the board]." Emphasize the fact that we can't take the word *save* and just add *d* to it, because *d* is a letter and not a meaning unit that shows past tense. Also, point out to students that the final *e* must be dropped when adding *ing*. Thus it's *saving* and not *saveing*. Tell students that there are other changes that sometimes have to be made before adding *ed* or *ing*, but they will learn about these another day. Close the lesson by providing each student with a base word that involves no change or e-drop; ask them to spell the word with the *ed* or *ing* ending.

Integrating Idioms

"They sure **raked him over the coals** for being late." (scolded him severely)

Sort 65. Additional Sorts: Looking Ahead to Plurals (s, es)

Add *s*	Add *es*
words	**glasses**
boys	boxes
eyes	bushes
girls	classes
friends	dishes
hours	foxes
houses	guesses
months	inches
pieces	lunches
things	passes
years	patches
	riches
	wishes

What Is Known: The concept of a base word

What Is New: Adding s or es to make plurals

Considerations: Students are likely to be familiar with the meanings of these words, because many of the base words are part of the feature studies at this stage. In this sort, students learn two of the most common ways to form plurals—add *s* and add *es* (a third way is examined in the next sort)—so be sure they are thinking of the noun meaning of words such as *guess* and *pass*, which can also be verbs. Begin by asking students to identify the base word on each word card (for example, **thing**s and **glass**es). Complete this as a group, or, to save time, ask students to underline the base word before they come to the group meeting. Next, using the key words *things* and *glasses* as examples, explain to students that to make words *plural* (to mean more than one), we often add *s* or *es* to the base word. Ask them to find their key words and sort the rest of the words according to whether *s* or *es* was added to make the plural form. When finished, ask students to examine their lists to determine when to use *es* and when just *s*. After a minute or two of thinking time, tell them to pair up with a partner and discuss their thoughts. Allow time for an exchange of ideas, and then invite students to share their conjectures. List the hypotheses on chart paper or the board under the headings *Add s* and *Add es*. Prompt students as needed by providing additional examples. They should see that base words in the es category all end with *ch, sh, s,* or *x* (or *z*, not included but applicable). If there is time, provide students with an opportunity to apply their understanding by asking them to determine the appropriate plural ending for the following nonlist words: *kisses, nests, grasses, crafts, fishes, crashes, branches, sharks,* and *pitches.*

Sort 66. Additional Sorts: Looking Ahead to Plurals (s, es, *Change* y *to* i *and Add* es)

Add *s*	Add *es*	Change *y* to *I* and Add *es*
birds	**brushes**	**flies**
changes	benches	cries
groups	bosses	tries
hearts	crutches	spies
pies	ditches	
points	dresses	
shoes	flashes	
squares	glasses	
states	porches	
	taxes	
	watches	

What Is Known: The concept of a base word and the addition of *s* and *es* to form plurals

What Is New: Changing *y* to *i* before adding *es*

Considerations: Students should be familiar with the meanings of the words in this sort, but check to see if any need clarification. Pass out a note card to each student. Then as with the previous sort, ask them to underline each of the base words. Caution them that some of the words may not show the base word directly in the word. Tell them to record base words of this type on the note card, if they find any. Discuss the base words; congratulate students who were not caught off guard by *pie, fly, cry, try,* and *spy.* Ask students to locate the key words—*bird, brushes,* and *flies*—and to sort the remaining words under these three categories, thinking about the plural and how it was formed. Discuss the results, reviewing understandings gained from the previous sort about plural formation and adding on knowledge of a third way to form plurals: namely, change final *y* to *i* and add *es*. Let students know that few one-syllable words become plurals in this way but that many multisyllabic words do (for example, *copies, babies, cities, secretaries,* etc.).

Literature Link

Milton, J. (1992). *Wild, wild, wolves.* New York: Random House.—Contains many plural words, including some irregular plurals, such as *wolves,* which could be integrated into the study; *knives, calves, halves,* and *shelves* could also be added. Related words: *pack* and *survive.*

Sort 67. Additional Sorts: Looking Ahead to Compound Words
(*head, hand, foot, tooth, eye*)

head	hand	foot	tooth	eye
headlight	**handsome**	**football**	**toothbrush**	**eyelid**
headache	handcuff	footprint	toothache	eyebrow
headphone	handmade	footstep	toothpaste	eyesight
headway	handrail	footstool	toothpick	
	handshake			

Sort 68. Additional Sorts: Looking Ahead to Compound Words
(*every, some, any, no*)

every	some	any	no
everybody	**somebody**	**anybody**	**nobody**
everyone	someone	anyone	nothing
everything	somehow	anything	nowhere
everywhere	sometimes	anytime	
	something	anyway	
	somewhat	anywhere	
	somewhere		

What Is Known: For Sorts 67 and 68, the vowel patterns and even the spellings of some of the individual words that make up the compounds

What Is New: Putting words together to form compound words

Considerations: Ask students to sort the words according to meaning: in Sort 67, *head, hand, foot, tooth,* and *eye*; in Sort 68, *every, some, any,* and *no*. Then go over each category and discuss the word meanings. Ask students to brainstorm other body-related compounds for Sort 67 (such as *earache, earmuffs, earphone,* and *hairbrush*). For Sort 68, students might try to sort the words into groups according to the second part of the compound, for example: *thing, one, where,* and so forth. As a follow-up to this introduction to compound words, provide students with 16 to 20 word cards, such as *book, bed, fire, snow, place, room, shelf, storm,* and so forth. that can be combined to form compound words. Demonstrate how to play Concentration or Memory with the cards by creating a 4 × 4 or 5 × 4 array with the cards face down. Students alternate turning over two cards in an effort to create a compound word. When a match is made, the player provides a sentence for the word and keeps the cards; cards are returned to the array if there is no match. The player with the most cards wins. (Students will likely notice that the *no* in *nothing* is pronounced differently; if not, point this out.)

Literature Link

Clements, A. (1997). *Double trouble in Walla Walla.* Brookfield, CT: Millbrook Press.—Students will enjoy the innumerable hyphenated compounds in this tale about Lulu's topsy-turvy day at school.

Sort 69. Additional Sorts: Contractions

have	is	not	will	Oddball
you've	that's	aren't	we'll	?
could've	here's	doesn't	he'll	let's
should've	she's	don't	that'll	
they've	there's	haven't	they'll	
	what's	weren't	you'll	
	where's	wouldn't		
	who's			

What Is Known: Students should know how to spell the words that make up the contractions

What Is New: The idea of combining words and creating a shortened form by leaving letters out

Considerations: Prior to introducing this sort, cut out and tape together pages 1–2 of Sort 69. Then make copies for the students so that answers will appear on the back sides of cards when cut apart, or provide separate copies of the two pages. Then, because an understanding of the word meanings will come with knowledge of how contractions are made, begin by informing the students that they will be working with words called *contractions* and that all words of this type share something in common.

Start the investigation by asking students to sort their contractions according to ending pattern, under the following key words: *you've*, *that's*, *aren't*, and *we'll*. At this point, *let's* will be placed in the "*that's*" column. Point out to students that "Contractions, like compound words [students will probably be familiar with the term *compound* already, but if not provide a few examples, such as *fireman* and *cannot*], are made up of more than one word, but unlike compound words, in contractions writers take shortcuts. They leave out one or more letters and mark the place with an apostrophe."

Indicate *aren't* and ask if anyone knows what two words make up *aren't* and what letters are missing where the apostrophe is. Once the correct response is suggested, turn the card over, or place the card with *are not* next to it. Apply the word *not* to all of the words in this category to help students understand word meaning and to see if the delete-and-mark process is consistent. Check responses in the manner just described. You might also call attention to the fact that the compound *cannot* can be turned into a contraction of this type—*can't*—but that it involves deleting one of the *n*'s as well as the *o*. Then move on to either the *you've* or *we'll* category, because *that's* includes an exception. Draw students' attention to the fact that frequently more than one letter is omitted, as with the *ha* in *you've* and the *wi* in *we'll*.

Finally, address the column with *that's*. Putting the contraction into the context of a sentence can assist students who may have difficulty identifying what the contraction means. This technique can be especially helpful for determining that *let's* is an Oddball, because it actually stands for *let us*. To say *let is go to the movie* for *let's go to the movie* doesn't make sense. You might also caution students that although all of the remaining words in this category carry the meaning of *is*, *'s* sometimes has another meaning: For example, it makes little sense to think of *she's got a new dog* as meaning *she is got a new dog*. In this case, the *'s* stands for *has*, as it does sometimes in *he's*. Attention to the context will help readers to know which meaning to apply.

End the lesson by drawing students' attention to the way authors sometimes use apostrophes in special kinds of contractions to show differences in dialect or the way people talk. Students may enjoy deciphering the following: *I'm plannin' to 'ave a cup of tea* or *he's goin' to see who's fixin' supper*. Also, you may want to mention that another use of the apostrophe, for possessives, will be studied at the syllable juncture stage.

Note that page 2 of Sort 69 can also be used to initiate responses for a blind (written) sort.

Sort 70. Additional Sorts: Homophones Set 1, Vowel *a* (Long *a* and *R*-Controlled *a*)

Long *a*	*R*-Controlled *a*
break*/brake*	**fare*/fair**
plane*/plain	bare*/bear
sail/sale*	pair*/pare/pear
straight/strait	their/there*/they're
tail*/tale	
waist*/waste	
wait*/weight	

*Words previously studied.

Integrating Idioms

"I'm going to have to **set that straight** when I see her." (explain the situation)

Sort 71. Additional Sorts: Homophones Set 2, Vowel *i* (Short *i* and Long *i*)

Short *i*	Long *i*
which*/witch*	**right*/write***
its/it's	aisle/I'll/isle
gilt/guilt*	buy/by*bye
ring*/wring*	die/dye
	knight*/night*
	sight*/site
	time*/thyme

*Words previously studied.

Integrating Idioms

"I thought for sure she'd **die laughing**." (laugh so hard it would be the end of her)

Sort 72. Additional Sorts: Homophones Set 3, Vowel *u* (Short *u* and Long *u*)

Short *u*	Long *u*
some*/sum*	**blew*/blue***
one/won	chews/choose*
	chute/shoot
	crews/cruise*
	dew/do*/due*
	root*/route
	threw*/through*
	to/too/two
	who's*/whose

*Words previously studied.

Sort 73. Additional Sorts: Homophones Set 4, Vowel *o* (Short *o*, Long *o*, and *R*-Controlled *o*)

Short *o*	Long *o*	*R*-Controlled *o*
knot*/not*	road*/rode*	hoarse/horse*
	close*/clothes	coarse/course
	hole*/whole*	pore/pour
	groan*/grown	soar*/sore
	role/roll*	warn/worn
	rote/wrote*	

*Words previously studied.

Sort 74. Additional Sorts: Homophones Set 5, Vowel *e* (Short *e*, Long *e*, and *R*-Controlled *e*)

Short *e*	Long *e*	*R*-Controlled *e*
lead/led*	beat*/beet	dear*/deer*
	creak/creek*	peer*/pier
	feat/feet	
	flea/flee	
	heal/heel*	
	peace*/piece*	
	peal/peel	
	scene*/seen	
	weak/week*	

*Words previously studied.

What Is Known: (For Sorts 70–74) By the end of the within word pattern stage, students have studied short vowels, long vowels, *r*-controlled vowels, and abstract vowels. As a result, they should be quite familiar with vowel patterns in single-syllable words. They have also been exposed to numerous *homophones* (sound-alike words with different spellings). Homophones that have previously been studied, at this stage or the letter name stage, are asterisked.

What Is New: This is the first formal study of homophones, which are a source of confusion for spellers across the grades and a problem we cannot count on computers to solve, as the following poem (author unknown) suggests:

> Eye halve a spelling chequer;
> It came with my pea sea.
> It plainly marques four my revue
> Miss steaks eye kin knot sea.
>
> Eye strike a key and type a word
> And weight four it to say
> Weather eye am wrong oar write.
> It shows me strait a weigh.
>
> As soon as a mist ache is maid
> It nose bee fore two long,

And eye can put the error rite;
Its rare lea ever wrong.

Eye have run this poem threw it,
I am shore your pleased two no.
Its letter perfect awl the weigh;
My chequer tolled me sew.

Considerations: Each of the five homophone sets focuses on a different vowel and some of its short, long, or *r*-controlled patterns. You might ask students to pair (or trio) the words as a means of discussing their meanings and then to categorize the words according to type of vowel: short, long, or *r*-controlled. However, because misuse of a homophone partner is one of the key causes of spelling problems with homophones, meaning must play a critical role in their study. Therefore, the cards for these sorts are in a format that will encourage game-playing for reinforcement of word meaning, as well as spelling. The vertical layout makes the cards easy to hold; the large-size print of the centered word makes viewing by all players possible; and the smaller-print version in the upper left corner ensures that children can still read their words when holding several cards. Although a variety of card games may be used, Homophone Rummy is a favorite. Here are the basics for playing the game. A set of 24 cards will accommodate two to three players, and a set of 40, three to four players. The cards should be scrambled and distributed to players one at a time until each player has six cards. The remaining cards form a draw pile, with the top card turned over next to the pile. Before turn taking with the draw pile begins, players alternate in placing pairs (or trios) of homophones on the playing surface. In order for each pair or trio to remain on the table, players must demonstrate an understanding of the words' meanings by providing an appropriate meaning or sentence for each of the words. When all or part of the response is incorrect, the cards are returned to the player's hand. Turn taking with the draw pile then begins.

Player 1 may take the top card from the draw pile or opt to pick up the discarded card placed face up beside it. If the drawn card results in a pair, Player 1 places the cards on the table and follows the procedure described. If it does not, Player 1 must discard a card by placing the chosen card next to the one already face up. Play then passes to Player 2, who has the option of drawing from the pile, picking up the last discard, or choosing an earlier card from the discard line. In this last instance, every card that follows the one chosen in the line must also be picked up. Although every card picked up from the discard line does not need to be played, the chosen word must be playable. Rotations of play continue until someone runs out of cards. The player who has played the most cards wins.

Integrating Idioms

"You're **beating your head against the wall** trying to teach that dog to beg." (wasting time on something that is hopeless)

Sort 75. Additional Sorts: Be a Winner with High-Frequency Words (*be* and *a*)

be	*a*	**Oddball**
because	**across**	**?**
became	above	little
before	afraid	many
began	again	only
behind	ago	over
believe	ahead	people
belong	along	never
below	among	
beside	around	
between	asleep	
beware	away	
beyond	awhile	

What Is Known: Students have an understanding of numerous sight words with one syllable, and they should have studied nearly all of the vowel patterns represented in the second syllable of the words being studied.

What Is New: Attention to multisyllabic words

Considerations: Because some of the words in this sort are difficult to explain, to discuss the meanings of any unfamiliar words ask students to demonstrate the meaning or use the word in a sentence. Although this set of words may be sorted into categories, as shown above, the primary focus of the study is to reinforce various high-frequency words, especially those that begin with *a* and *be*, through game playing. Note that no "?" card is included in the template of words, so when sorting, students may place the Oddball words aside or use the label from the set of *header* cards included in Appendix E.

After explaining and demonstrating the guidelines for *Be a Winner*, build opportunities into the schedule for students to play the game.

Be a Winner Guidelines

Each pair of two players will need one *Be a* Winner Star Card (see Appendix E) for each player and a complete set of the 30 word cards.

1. Randomly place the word cards face down between the two players in a 5 × 6 array.
2. Play begins with Student 1, who chooses a word and reads it aloud to Student 2. Student 2 then attempts to spell the word by writing his or her response on the Star Card. Student 1 places the word card down on his or her side of the playing surface.
3. Student 2 then chooses and reads aloud a word for Student 1 to spell. This card is then placed face down next to Student 2.
4. Play alternates with the remaining cards until each student has responded to 15 words
5. Players then check the accuracy of their responses by comparing their answers with the words on the cards. Players with 10–12 words right are ☆ Winners, those with 13–14 correctly spelled words are ☆☆ Winners, and those with no errors are ☆☆☆ Winners. To play a second game, players scramble the cards and create a new 5 × 6 array.

lasted	showed	looked
seemed	missed	climbed
worked	turned	needed
wanted	passed	played
learned	added	helped
asked	walked	started
sounded	owned	reached
joined	shouted	caused

printed	spelled	jumped
dressed	locked	smelled
shocked	planted	tricked
yelled	fished	tilted
wished	pressed	rushed
slanted	fixed	cracked
spilled	twisted	filled
handed	blushed	landed

ended	saved	raised
moved	parted	snowed
taped	sounded	smiled
pulled	built	lived
used	talked	sliced
raked	blamed	dusted
scolded	steamed	toasted
checked	whined	?

words	glasses	years
hours	wishes	friends
dishes	boys	guesses
pieces	passes	bushes
lunches	foxes	things
eyes	girls	riches
inches	patches	months
houses	classes	boxes

birds	brushes	flies
shoes	watches	hearts
cries	ditches	points
flashes	squares	bosses
crutches	tries	glasses
porches	taxes	changes
pies	groups	dresses
benches	states	spies

headlight	handsome	football
toothbrush	eyelid	handmade
headache	handshake	toothpick
handcuff	headway	footprint
toothpaste	handrail	footstool
eyebrow	toothache	eyesight
footstep	headphone	

Additional Sorts: Looking Ahead to Compound Words
(every, some, any, no)

everybody	somebody	anybody
nobody	anywhere	everything
anyone	something	nothing
sometimes	everyone	somewhere
anyway	nowhere	somehow
everywhere	someone	anytime
somewhat	anything	

you've	that's	aren't
we'll	haven't	where's
doesn't	could've	she's
that'll	what's	you'll
here's	don't	they've
who's	he'll	there's
they'll	let's	wouldn't
should've	weren't	?

are not	that is	you have
where is	have not	we will
she is	could have	does not
you will	what is	that will
they have	do not	here is
there is	he will	who is
would not	let us	they will
?	were not	should have

break	fare	tail	there
break	**fare**	**tail**	**there**
weight	sale	pear	strait
weight	**sale**	**pear**	**strait**
brake	pair	fair	waste
brake	**pair**	**fair**	**waste**

bear	waist	plane	their
bear	waist	plane	their

they're	straight	tale	pare
they're	straight	tale	pare

sail	plain	bare	wait
sail	plain	bare	wait

which	right	time	buy
which	right	time	buy

its	gilt	wring	witch
its	gilt	wring	witch

write	aisle	night	ring
write	aisle	night	ring

dye	I'll	sight	bye
dye	**I'll**	**sight**	**bye**
guilt	thyme	it's	site
guilt	**thyme**	**it's**	**site**
by	knight	die	isle
by	**knight**	**die**	**isle**

some	blew	due	choose
some	**blew**	**due**	**choose**
blue	sum	route	one
blue	**sum**	**route**	**one**
through	to	crews	shoot
through	**to**	**crews**	**shoot**

whose **whose**	too **too**	won **won**	chews **chews**
threw **threw**	chute **chute**	who's **who's**	do **do**
dew **dew**	two **two**	cruise **cruise**	root **root**

knot	road	hoarse	whole
knot	road	hoarse	whole

close	coarse	roll	horse
close	coarse	roll	horse

rode	grown	not	sore
rode	grown	not	sore

pour	rote	soar	hole
pour	rote	soar	hole

role	pore	clothes	warn
role	pore	clothes	warn

course	worn	groan	wrote
course	worn	groan	wrote

lead	beat	dear	piece
lead	**beat**	**dear**	**piece**
flea	scene	feat	deer
flea	**scene**	**feat**	**deer**
beet	pier	heel	led
beet	**pier**	**heel**	**led**

From *Word Sorts and More* by Kathy Ganske. Copyright 2006 by The Guilford Press. Permission to photocopy this form is granted to purchasers of this book for personal use only (see copyright page for details). Enlarge 135% to fill page.

creak	peal	weak	peace
creak	peal	weak	peace
peer	flee	creek	seen
peer	flee	creek	seen
feet	week	peel	heal
feet	week	peel	heal

across	because	many
before	little	awhile
afraid	beside	below
beyond	away	never
among	began	above
people	ago	became
belong	over	around
again	between	believe
beware	along	only
asleep	behind	ahead

Appendix A

Emergent Literacy Assessments

Alphabet Recognition: Administration and Scoring

For each child being assessed, prepare a copy of the upper- and/or lowercase alphabet arrays. In addition, make one extra copy for the children to point to as they name the letters. As an alternative to the latter, some teachers prefer to cut apart the pointing copy so that the letters can be presented in flash-card style. If the latter approach is used, be sure to maintain the original order of presentation.

To begin the assessment, say to the child, "You're going to name letters of the alphabet for me as you point to them on this sheet [or if flash cards are used, "as I show them to you"]. If you don't know a letter, you can try a guess or just say, Don't know.' I'm going to write down what you say so that I can look back at your paper later and remember what you said. Ready?" Some teachers use a stopwatch to determine how long it takes a child to complete the task so that they can compare this aspect of letter recognition ability across time. If letter cards are used for the assessment, keep the pace moving so that any timing done reflects recognition rather than presentation. Award one point for each correctly named letter.

Phonemic Awareness—Beginning Sounds: Administration and Scoring

[Note: This activity may be completed in a small group if children are familiar with the task of sorting pictures according to beginning sounds.]

1. For each child, you will need a sorting mat and a set of the pictures to be sorted. Cut apart the pictures. Before modeling the process, check to be sure children know the names of all the pictures. Then use the starred row of pictures to demonstrate the sorting process. Explain to the children that they will be matching pictures to other pictures that start with the same sound. Begin modeling by identifying each of the key pictures on the sorting mat, stretching out its initial sound, as *dddog* or *fffish*. Next, randomly present one of the starred pictures. Name the picture, stretching out its sound, as *mmmug*. Then match it with each of the key pictures: "*Mmmug . . . mmman; mmmug . . . dddog; mmmug . . . fffish;* and *mmmug . . . kkkey. Mmmug* goes with *mmman* because they both begin with the /m/ sound. Watch me while I do some more." Continue modeling with the other three starred pictures.

2. Next, remove the pictures and say, "Now, I want you to do the same on your mat with each of the other pictures." Hand each child a scrambled stack of the 16 pictures. When finished, children may leave the pictures on their mats for teacher review, or they may be asked to use a glue stick to affix the pictures to the mat. In the former case, make a record of the assessment by writing the name of each picture on the mat before removing it.

Kindergarten Inventory of Developmental Spelling (KIDS; Ganske, 1995)

Administration

[Note: This assessment may be given individually or to two or three students at a time.]

1. Tell the children that you are going to ask them to write some words (on the KIDS Answer Sheet on page 345) so that you will know which letters and sounds to teach them.

2. Model spelling of the word *map* by demonstrating and thinking aloud on the chalkboard or on chart paper. Show the children how to stretch out the word so that you can better hear the sounds; a rubber band provides a useful visual of how this process works. Say, "We're going to write some words. Listen to me and watch what I do as I write a word. First, I'm going to say the word I want to spell, *map*. Now I'm going to say it again, but this time I'm going to say it slowly so that I can stretch it out, just like I can stretch out this rubber band. That way I can try to hear all of the sounds. *Mmmm-aaaa-ppp*. (*Stretches rubber band while saying the word.*) Now I need to think about all of the sounds I hear. Let's listen carefully. *Mmmm*. I hear an /m/ sound at the beginning, so I'm going to write down the letter m. *Mmmm-aaaa*. After the /m/, I hear an /ā/ sound, so I'm going to write the letter a. *Mmmm-aaaa-p . . . mmm-aaa-pppp*. At the end I hear a /p/ sound, so I'm going to write p. I think *map* is spelled m-a-p."

3. "Now I want you to write some words that I'm going to say. Stretch out the word and listen carefully. Then put down the sounds you hear. If you're not sure, just do the best you can. If you forget how to make a letter, you can use the alphabet strip at the top of your paper. Ready? Here's the first word."

4. Using one of the two forms of words below, dictate each of the words in order. It can be helpful for spellers to hear the word used in a short sentence, such as those provided. Don't assist with further modeling, but do prompt students with "What other sounds do you hear?" if they seem to stall in their writing.

5. When the spellings are finished, ask if children need clarification of any letters that are confusing before moving on to the next child or small group.

Form A Words

jam	*I had jam on my toast.*
rob	*He tried to rob the bank.*
fun	*She had a fun time at the fair.*
sip	*You can sip with a straw.*
let	*We let the dog in.*

Form B Words

sat	*He sat on the couch.*
mop	*I need to mop the floor.*
rug	*She bought a new rug.*
fin	*We saw the whale's fin.*
web	*The spider made a web.*

Scoring

1. Use the KIDS Scoring Guide on page 344 to score the spellings. Award points as follows:

   6 = Correct Spelling
   5 = Phonetically Correct Beginning, Middle, & Ending Sounds
   4 = Phonetically Correct Beginning & Ending Sounds
   3 = Phonetically Correct Beginning Sound
   2 = Phonetically Correct Ending Sound
   1 = Random Letters or Letters from Name: No Sound Connection
   0 = Scribbles, Waves, Letter-like Symbols

2. Locate the spelling that most closely matches the child's spelling; check off the word. Continue in like manner until the spelling of each word has been analyzed. Tally the total points. Record the total score and the point value that typifies the child's spellings: 6, 5, 4, 3, 2, 1, or 0.

Uppercase Letter Recognition

S   U   G   W   L

M   P   V   A   Q

I   C   B   Y   J

Z   K   E   H   D

N   X   R   O   F

T

Lowercase Letter Recognition

Name _____ Date _____ #Correct _____ Time _____

n   v   b   l   m

h   c   i   j   u

q   e   w   x   g

f   k   o   t   p

a   r   z   d   y

s

Phonemic Awareness: Beginning Sounds (Sorting Mat)

Name _____ Date _____ #Correct _____

Mm	Dd	Ff	Kk

Phonemic Awareness: Beginning Sounds (Pictures for Sorting)

★	★	★	★

KIDS Scoring Guide

Form A

6	**JAM**
5	GAM, JEM, GEM, JAME, GAME
4	JM, GM, JMA, GMA
3	J, G, or +(Random Letters)
2	M or +(Random Letters)
1	Random Letters
0	Scribbles, Waves, Letter-like Symbols

6	**ROB**
5	RIB, WIB, YIB, ROP, WOP, YOP, ROBE
4	RB, RP, WB, YB, RBA
3	R, W, Y, or +(Random Letters)
2	B, P, or +(Random Letters)
1	Random Letters
0	Scribbles, Waves, Letter-like Symbols

6	**FUN**
5	FON, VON, VUN, FONE, VONE
4	FN, VN, FNA, VNA
3	F, V, or +(Random Letters)
2	N, or +(Random Letters)
1	Random Letters
0	Scribbles, Waves, Letter-like Symbols

6	**SIP**
5	SEP, CEP, CIP, SIB, CIB, SIPA, SEPE
4	SP, CP, SB, CB, ZP, ZB, SPA, CPA, ZPA
3	S, C, Z or +(Random Letters)
2	P, B, or +(Random Letters)
1	Random Letters
0	Scribbles, Waves, Letter-like Symbols

6	**LET**
5	LAT, LAD, LED, LETE, LATE, LETA, LADA
4	LT, LD, LTA, LDA
3	L or +(Random Letters)
2	T, D, or +(Random Letters)
1	Random Letters
0	Scribbles, Waves, Letter-like Symbols

Form B

6	**SAT**
5	CAT, SET, CET, SATE, CATE, SATA
4	ST, CT, STA, CTA
3	S, C, or +(Random Letters)
2	T or +(Random Letters)
1	Random Letters
0	Scribbles, Waves, Letter-like Symbols

6	**MOP**
5	MIP, MIB, MOB, MIPA, MOBE
4	RB, RP, WB, YB, RBA,
3	R, W, Y, or +(Random Letters)
2	B, P, or +(Random Letters)
1	Random Letters
0	Scribbles, Waves, Letter-like Symbols

6	**RUG**
5	ROG, YUG, YOC, WUG, WOG, RUK
4	RG, RC, RK, YG, YKA,
3	R, Y, W, or +(Random Letters)
2	G, K, C or +(Random Letters)
1	Random Letters
0	Scribbles, Waves, Letter-like Symbols

6	**FIN**
5	FEN, FIN, VEN, FINE, FINA
4	FN, VN, FNA, VNA, FNE, VNE
3	F, V, or +(Random Letters)
2	N, or +(Random Letters)
1	Random Letters
0	Scribbles, Waves, Letter-like Symbols

6	**WEB**
5	WAB, RAB, YAB, REB, YEB, WEBE
4	WB, YB, RB, YB, WBE, WBA
3	W, Y, R, or +(Random Letters)
2	B, P, or +(Random Letters)
1	Random Letters
0	Scribbles, Waves, Letter-like Symbols

Note: For points 4 and 5 above, a string of letters may sometimes be added to the end of the word. Also, for points 2–5, a vowel may be placed in front of the consonant(s)—ELT for *let*.

KIDS Answer Sheet

Name _____ Date _____

Total Points _____/30_____ Representative Rating _____

A B C D E F G H I J K L M N O P Q R S T U V W X Y Z
a b c d e f g h i j k l m n o p q r s t u v w x y z

1.

2.

3.

4.

5.

Appendix B

Oh No! Card Game

To reinforce children's knowledge of alphabet letters and high-frequency words, engage them in a game of Oh No!*

    1. Determine whether to use the templates of letter cards or the bank of high-frequency words. The more children there are involved, the more letter or word cards you'll need, but keep in mind you don't want to overwhelm the players with too many unknowns. For example, the high-frequency-word bank includes two sets of 50 words each,** plus an additional 55 words "For Good Measure." (The 100 most frequently occurring words are included in the word bank.) Depending on the number of students playing, you may want to use only half of one set initially, then add more words as the children gain competence in recognizing the first set.

    2. Prepare the cards for the game. For longer use, copy the cards on card stock. Be sure to include two or three Oh No! cards.

    3. Scramble the word or letter cards and place the stack face down on the playing surface. Invite students to take turns drawing a card from the top of the pile and reading the word. If the word is correctly identified, they keep it. If not, the card is returned to the bottom of the pile. Whenever players draw an Oh No! card, they must return all of their word cards to the bottom of the stack, except for the Oh No! card, which is then laid aside and not reused for the rest of the game.

    4. The winner is the person with the most cards, Oh No! cards excepted, after the draw pile has been depleted. One point is awarded for each correctly read word.

---

*I have developed this game from a sight-word building activity that appeared in Strickland, Ganske, and Monroe (2002).

**The first set begins on page 350 and runs through the middle of page 352. The second set begins midpage of page 352 nad runs through page 354.

A	B	C
D	E	F
G	H	I
J	K	L
M	N	O
P	Q	R
S	T	U

V	W	X
Y	Z	
Oh No!	Oh No!	Oh No!
Oh No!	Oh No!	Oh No!
V	W	X
y	z	

a	b	c
d	e	f
g	h	i
j	k	l
m	n	o
p	q	r
s	t	u

a	all	and
are	as	at
be	but	came
for	from	go
got	had	have
he	her	him
his	I	if

in	is	it
me	my	of
on	one	out
said	saw	she
so	that	the
their	then	there
they	this	to

up	was	we
went	were	with
you	your	
OH NO!	OH NO!	OH NO!
about	after	an
because	been	by
come	could	day

did	do	down
find	get	going
has	house	how
into	it's	just
like	little	look
make	man	many
may	no	not

now	off	other
our	over	put
see	some	than
them	these	two
us	very	what
when	which	who
will	would	

am	back	best
big	boy	brother
call	can	children
drink	each	eat
family	father	first
friend	fun	give
good	here	jump

know	long	made
more	mother	name
new	nice	night
old	only	or
people	play	pretty
run	school	sister
small	stop	talk

teacher	tell	thank
they're	these	time
use	want	way
well	where	why
write		
OH NO!	OH NO!	OH NO!

Appendix C

Make-It, Break-It Letter Cards

Reproduce, enlarging if necessary, Set 1 of the Make-It, Break-It Letter Cards that follow. Depending on the capabilities of your students, select a variety of tiles for the students to work with. Be careful not to overwhelm those with more fragile understandings by giving them too many choices; usually 10–15 tiles work well. Limit the riming units to those studied. Model the process by combining an onset with a rime. Think aloud as you check to see if the result is a known word. Say the word (you may want to ask students to record their result) before returning the tile and trying a new beginning consonant. When no new words can be made with the riming unit, choose a new one and begin the process over. Tiles from Set 2 may be added, for children with some understanding of blends. Tiles from Set 3 may be used to reinforce children's knowledge of word families, short vowels, or digraphs and blends in the initial or final position of the word. Because the letters are centered, rather than offset, the onset and rime characteristics are de-emphasized.

Set 1. Initial Consonants and Word Families—Offset

b	c	d	f	g	h
j	k	l	m	n	p
r	s	t	v	w	y
z					
at	an	ap	ad	ag	am
ab	ig	in	ip	it	id
og	op	ot	ob	eg	en
et	ed	ug	un	ut	ub

Set 2. Initial Consonant Blends and Digraphs—Offset

sh	ch	th	wh		
st	sp	sk	sn	sm	sc
sw	sl	bl	cl	fl	gl
pl	br	cr	fr	gr	pr
dr	tr	qu	sw	tw	

Set 3. Vowels, Consonants, Digraphs, Blends, and Rimes—Centered
(p. 1 of 2)

a	e	i	o	u	
b	c	d	f	g	h
j	k	l	m	n	p
r	s	t	v	w	y
z	ch	sh	th	wh	sc
sk	sl	sm	sn	sp	st
sw	bl	cl	fl	gl	pl

br	cr	dr	fr	gr	pr
tr	qu	tw			
	ch	th	sh	sk	sp
lf	lk	pt	ft	lt	st
mp	nd	nt	ng	nk	
all	ell	ill			
ack	eck	ick	ock	uck	

Appendix D

Working with Spanish-Speaking English-Language Learners

In this section you will find a discussion of some of the issues that can arise when working with Spanish-speaking English-language learners. A few Spanish-language word sorts are also included. The words are grouped by their Spanish name according to the targeted sound and/or pattern, except in the case of the three initial consonant sorts, where the pictures chosen also begin with the same initial consonant sound in English, making it easier for students to transfer their Spanish letter–sound knowledge to English. To further assist teachers in their work with Spanish-speaking English-language learners, a complete listing of Spanish translations for the more than 500 pictures used throughout this book accompanies this section.

Initial Consonants with Similar Sounds in English and Spanish

English and Spanish share many of the same initial consonant sounds; however, spellings for some of the sounds may differ. Sounds common to both languages provide a good starting point for study.

Spanish–English Sort 1: *m, s, b*		
Mm	**Ss**	**Bb**
MÁSCARA (mask)	**SOL (sun)**	**BATE (bat)**
MAPA (map)	SEIS (six)	BARCA (boat)
MEZCLAR (mix)	SENTARSE (sit)	BICICLETA (bike)
MITÓN (mitten)	SIERRA (saw)	BOLLO (bun)
MONTAÑAS (mountains)	SIETE (seven)	BOTÓN (button)
	SOLLOZAR (sob)	BOLA (ball)
	SORBER (sip)	

Note. Information in this appendix is based on the work of Goldstein (2001), Helman (2004), and Nash (1977).

Spanish–English Sort 2: *t, n, p,* and *g*

As in English, in Spanish more than one sound is associated with the letter *g.* The /g/ sound is produced when the letter is followed by a consonant or the vowels *a, o,* or *u.* However, when *e* or *i* follows the consonant, a /h/ sound is produced: *gemelos (twins).* Words listed in Sort 2 with initial consonant *g* all have the /g/ sound.

Tt	**Nn**	**Pp**	**Gg**
TUBO (tube)	**NIDO (nest)**	**PERRITO (pup)**	**GUITARRA (guitar)**
TACHUELA (tack)	NARIZ (nose)	PASTEL (pie)	GAS (gas)
TINA (tub)	NETO (net)	PERA (pear)	
TORTUGA (turtle)	NÍQUEL (nickel)	PINGÜINO (penguin)	
TOSTADO (toast)	NOTA (note)		
	NUEVE (nine)		
	NUEZ (nut)		

Spanish–English Sort 3: *l, c, f,* and *d*

As in English, the sound of *c* in Spanish is influenced by the vowel that follows it. When followed by *a, o,* or *u,* the sound is /k/; when followed by *e* or *i,* the sound is /s/, as in *sing.* Words listed here with *c* all have the /k/ sound. *D* may cause some confusion because students may pronounce it as the *th* in *then,* especially in medial positions. Also, only single *l* is used in Sort 3; double *ll* results in the /y/ sound as in *llama;* it is discussed later.

Ll	**Cc**	**Ff**	**Dd**
LIMÓN (lemon)	**CARRO (car)**	**FUEGO (fire)**	**DADOS (dice)**
LAGO (lake)	CAÑA (cane)	FÚTBOL (football)	DESCARGAR (dump)
LÁMPARA (lamp)	CAPA (cape)		
LEÓN (lion)	CATRE (cot)		
LETRAS (letters)	CAVERNA (cave)		
LEVANTER (lift)	CONO (cone)		
LÍNEA (line)			

It should be noted that although the sound of *k* in Spanish is /k/, only foreign words, and none of the pictures provided in this book, begin with *K.* The sounds of other initial consonants differ between the two languages. A discussion of these consonants follows.

Consonants Whose Sounds May Cause Confusion to English-Language Learners Because They Differ in Spanish and English

H: Spanish *h* is silent, as it is in a few English words: *honor, honesty, honorable,* and *hour.* **Examples:** *hacha* (ax), *hendedura* (crack), *hierba* (grass), *hilar* (spin), *hoja* (leaf), *hombre* (man), *hormiga* (ant), *hornear* (bake), *hueso* (bone), *huevo* (egg), and *humo* (smoke).

J: Spanish *j* produces a sound similar to that typically associated with English *h,* /h/. **Examples:** *jabón* (soap), *jamón* (ham), *jarra* (mug), *jefe* (chief), *jirafa* (giraffe), *joroba* (hump), and *juego* (game).

Q: As in English, Spanish *q* is followed by *u;* however, the sound that results is not /kw/ but /k/, as in *bloque* [blō•kā] (block). **Examples:** *máquina* (engine), *níquel* (nickel), *queso* (cheese), *banquillo* (stool), *chaqueta* (jacket), *esquimal* (Eskimo), *esquís* (skis), and *etiqueta* (tag).

R: In Spanish, *r* is rolled or flapped on the palate; the sound for double *R* is even more pronounced, as in *arriba* (up), *carro* (car), and *gorro* (cap). **Examples:** *rana* (frog), *rasgar* (rip), *rastro* (rake), *rata* (rat), *ratones* (mice), *regalo* (present), *reina* (queen), *reloj* (watch/clock), *rey* (king), *rezar* (pray), *riel* (train track), and *robar* (rob).

W: There are no Spanish words with *w*; the /w/ sound often results from *ue*. **Examples:** *escuela* (school), *fuego* (fire), *huevo* (egg), *juego* (game), *nueve* (nine), *puerta* (door/gate), *sueño* (dream), *suéter* (sweater), and *tachuela* (tack).

V: Spanish *v* sounds very much like English /b/, as in *vaca* [bä•kä] (cow). **Examples:** *valentín* (valentine), *vaso* (glass), *veinte* (twenty), *veleta* (vane), *ventana* (window), *vestido* (dress), and *viña* (vine.)

X: This letter is rare in the initial position of words, including proper nouns. It is pronounced as /s/. In medial positions the pronunciation varies, as, for example, /h/ in *México*.

Y: Very few Spanish words begin with *y*—*yema* (yolk), *yoyo* (yoyo), and *yogur* (yogurt), but there are other words that begin with the /y/ sound, produced by double *l*: *llama* (flame), *llanta* (tire), *llave* (key), *llorar* (cry), and *lluvia* (rain). It should be noted that some dialects pronounce *ll* as /j/.

Z: Spanish *z* sounds like /s/, as in *zapatilla* (slipper), *zapato* (shoe), *zorillo* (skunk), and *zorro* (fox).

Initial Consonant Blends and Digraphs

English has many more blends than Spanish. Of the three main types, *s*-blends, *l*-blends, and *r*-blends, *l*-blends provide the greatest similarity. There are no *s*-blends in Spanish, and *r*-blends are pronounced differently due to the rolling of the *r*. In the former case, in Spanish the letter *e* precedes the consonants, creating a break in syllables between two consonants that would otherwise form an *s*-blend, as in *escalar* (climb), *escritorio* (desk), *escuela* (school), *espina* (thorn), *esponja* (sponge), *esquimal* (Eskimo), *esquís* (skis), *estampilla* (stamp), and *estornudar* (sneeze). Examples of *l*-blends include: *bloque* (block), *blusa* (blouse), *clavija* (peg), *clavo* (nail), *flauta* (flute), *flor* (flower), *flotar* (float), *globo* (balloon/globe), *planta* (plant), and *platos* (dishes).

Examples of *r*-blend include: *brazalete* (bracelet), *brincar* (skip), *cráneo* (skull), *crayón* (crayon), *dragón* (dragon), *frasco* (jar), *fruta* (fruit), *grande* (big), *grito* (yell), *pregunta* (question), *premio* (prize),, *tractor* (tractor), *trampolín* (trampoline), *trece* (thirteen), *treinta* (thirty), and *tronco* (trunk).

Because the digraphs *sh*, *th*, and *wh* do not exist in Spanish, students are likely to experience difficulty reading and writing words with these features. *Ch* does exist in Spanish and may be substituted for *sh*, as in CHEEP for *sheep*. *Th* may be represented by just the *t*, as in TINK for *think* and TIRTY for *thirty*. The latter substitution exists naturally in the translation of some words (*termo* for *thermos* and *termómetro* for *thermometer*).

Final Consonants: Single Consonants and Clusters

In English, nearly all consonants can appear in the final position; however, in Spanish only five consonants are found in this location: *d*, *l*, *n*, *r*, and *s*. The majority of words end in a vowel, as *carta* (letter), *mapa* (map), *leche* (milk), *llave* (key), *frasco* (jar), *cuerno* (horn), *mano* (hand), and *iglú* (igloo), none of which is silent. These differences may present difficulties for English-language learners in articulating some ending sounds during their reading or speaking, and in representing the ending sound during spelling. When reading or writing words with final consonants (whether single or as clusters) students may substitute or omit final consonants altogether, or they may attach a final vowel to the word where none is needed.

Vowel Differences and Similarities

Coming to terms with English vowel sounds presents a considerable challenge for Spanish-speaking English-language learners and may even seem overwhelming to them at times, because the Spanish system of vowels is much simpler. Each Spanish vowel has one basic sound. Of the English short vowel sounds, only one is found in Spanish: /ŏ/. The /ŏ/ sound is not represented with o, but—like the similar English broad a heard in father, and mama—is spelled with a, as in gato (cat), grande (big), and casa (house).

Long vowels also differ. The English sound of long a (bake and they) is similar to that produced by Spanish e, as in grande (big), golpe (hit), and peca (freckle). English long e (feet) is similar to the Spanish sound produced by the letter i, as in grito (yell) and limón [lē•mōn] (lemon). English and Spanish long o are very similar, as in cone (English) and cono (Spanish) or amigo (friend). Spanish long u also bears similarity to the English long u in flute and room: For example, cuchara (spoon), cuna (crib), and tubo (tube). Unlike vowel digraphs (such as beat, chief, coat, and so forth), which form a single sound, or the English silent final e, in Spanish each vowel produces a sound (compare pies in English to pies [pē′ās], the word for feet in Spanish).

The vowel differences described above may lead to numerous spelling confusions, such as spelling make as MEIK, shape CHEIP or even CHAP, kite as KAIT, and lock as LAK or LOK. Miscues during reading may also reflect the pronunciation differences, as pain [pä′ēn]. There are other vowel differences besides those that pertain to long and short vowels. R-controlled vowels in Spanish do not include the sounds typically associated with er and ir in English, as her, better, first, and girl. Nor do the abstract vowel sounds heard in taught and would occur in Spanish. Although not of relevance to the word studies in this book, the schwa vowel sound /ə/, a matter of considerable importance at the syllable juncture stage of spelling development, does not occur in Spanish either.

Awareness of the kinds of similarities and differences described in this section can help teachers to better understand and meet the needs of Spanish-speaking English-language learners. The more teachers know, the easier it is for them to intervene with the appropriate kind of support and scaffolding to enable English-language learners (of whatever first language) to build a solid foundation on which to become proficient users of English. As with English-speaking students, teachers should build on strengths (in the case just described, features that are common to both languages), while developing areas of weakness.

Spanish Translations for the English Names of Pictures Used

Spanish to English Translation

abajo	under	anillo	ring
abanico	fan	animales	animals
abeja	bee	anzuelo	hook
abrazo	hug	apagador	switch (light)
acariciar	pet	apartado postal	zipcode
aceitunas	olives	aplaudir	clap
afeitarse	shave	araña	spider
agitar la mano	wave	árbitro	umpire
aguja	needle	árbol	tree
agujero	hole	arca	chest (toy)
al revés	upside down	arpa	harp
ala	wing	arriba	up
aleta	fin	ascensor	elevator
alfabeto	alphabet	aspiradora	vacuum
alfiler	pin	autobús	bus
alfombra	rug	avión	jet, plane
alicates	pliers	ballena	whale
alto	stop, tall	bandeja	tray

bandera	flag	*carta*	letter
banquillo	stool	*casa*	house
barba	chin	*catre*	cot
barca	boat	*cavar*	dig
barco	ship	*caverna*	cave
barrer	sweep	*cebra*	zebra
báscula	scale	*cepillo*	brush
bate	bat (ball)	*cerca*	fence
bicicleta	bike	*cerdo*	pig
bigotes	whiskers	*cerezas*	cherries
bloc de papel	pad	*cero*	zero
bloque	block	*cerradura*	lock
blusa	blouse	*cerrar el cierre*	zip
bola	ball	*chaleco*	vest
bollo	bun	*chaqueta*	jacket
bolsa	purse	*chicle*	gum
bolsa (de papel)	bag (paper)	*chimenea*	chimney
bostezo	yawn	*choza*	hut
botiquín	kit	*cierre*	zipper
botón	button	*cinco*	five
brazalete	bracelet	*cinta*	tape
brincar	skip	*cinturón*	belt
bruja	witch	*ciruela*	plum
bucear	dive	*cisne*	swan
buey	ox	*clavija*	peg
bufanda	scarf	*clavo*	nail
caballero	knight	*cobertizo*	shed
caballo	horse	*cobija*	blanket
cabestrillo	sling	*cochino*	pig
cabra	goat	*cocina*	kitchen
cacerola	pan	*codo*	elbow
cadena	chain	*colina*	hill
caimán	alligator	*colmena*	hive
caja	box	*colmillo*	tusk
cajón	drawer	*columpio*	swing
calabaza	pumpkin	*comestibles*	groceries
calcetín	sock	*cometa*	kite
caliente	hot	*concha*	shell
callarse	quiet	*cono*	cone
cama	bed	*copo de nieve*	flake
camino	road	*corazón*	heart
camión	truck	*corbata*	tie
camisa	shirt	*corona*	crown
campana	bell	*corre (correr)*	run
caña	cane	*correr*	jog
cangrejo	crab	*corrió (correr)*	ran
canguro	kangaroo	*cortar*	chop
cantillos	jacks	*cortar*	cut
capa	cape	*cráneo*	skull
caracol	snail	*crayón*	crayon
carpa	tent	*crin*	mane
carreta	wagon	*cuarto*	quarter
carrete	spool	*cuatro*	four
carretilla	wheelbarrow	*cubierta*	deck
carro	car	*cubo*	cube, pail

cuchara	spoon	*flotar*	float
cuchillo	knife	*foca*	seal
cuello	neck	*fósforo*	match
cuenta	bead	*frasco*	jar
cuerda	jumprope, rope	*fregadero*	sink
cuerno	horn	*fruta*	fruit
culebra	snake	*fuego*	fire
cuna	crib	*furgoneta*	van
dados	dice	*furioso*	mad
dar golpecillos	pat	*fútbol*	football
dar vueltas al batón	twirl	*gallina*	hen
dedal	thimble	*ganar*	win
dedos del pie	toes	*garra*	claw
derramar	spill	*gas*	gas
derretir	melt	*gatito*	kitten
descargar	dump	*gato*	cat
dientes	teeth	*gemelos*	twins
diez	ten	*globo*	balloon, globe
doce	twelve	*golpe*	hit
dormir	sleep	*gordo*	fat
dos	two	*gorro*	cap
dragón	dragon	*gotear*	drip
duende	elf	*grande*	big
durazno	peach	*graznido*	quack
elefante	elephant	*grito*	yell
elote	cob (corn)	*guante*	glove
emparedado	sandwich	*guiño*	wink
enchufe	plug	*guisantes*	peas
enfermo	ill, sick	*guitarra*	guitar
escalar	climb	*gusano*	worm
escalera	stairs	*hacer compras*	shop
escoba	broom	*hacer malabarismos*	juggle
escocesa	plaid	*hacer pedazos*	smash
escritorio	desk	*hacha*	ax
escuela	school	*hendedura*	crack
espina	thorn	*heno*	hay
esponja	sponge	*hierba*	grass
esqueleto	skeleton	*hilar*	spin
esquimal	Eskimo	*hilo*	yarn
esquís	skis	*hoja*	leaf
estampilla	stamp	*hombre*	man
estante	shelf	*hombres*	men
estornudar	sneeze	*hormiga*	ant
estrella	star	*hornear*	bake
estufa	stove	*hueso*	bone
etiqueta	tag	*huevo*	egg
explorador	scout	*humo*	smoke
falda	skirt	*iglú*	igloo
fango	mud	*insecto*	bug
fantasma	ghost	*insectos*	insects
feliz	happy	*instrumentos*	instruments
flauta	flute	*jabón*	soap
flor	flower	*jalar*	tug
florero	vase	*jamón*	ham

jarra	mug	*mojado*	wet
jarro	jug	*moneda de a diez centavos*	dime
jeep	jeep		
jefe	chief	*mono de nieve*	snowman
jirafa	giraffe	*montañas*	mountains
joroba	hump	*mosca*	fly
juego	game	*motoneta*	scooter
labios	lips	*mover*	stir
ladrillo	brick	*muchacha*	girl
lago	lake	*muchacho*	boy
lámpara	lamp	*mula*	mule
lanza	spear	*muñeca*	doll
lanzar	flip	*murciélago*	bat (animal)
lata	can	*nadar*	swim
látigo	whip	*nariz*	nose
leche	milk	*neto*	net
lentes	glasses	*nevar*	snow
letras	letters	*nido*	nest
levantar	lift	*níquel*	nickel
león	lion	*nota*	note
libro	book	*novia*	bride
limón	lemon	*nubes*	clouds
línea	line	*nueve*	nine
linterna	flashlight	*nuez*	nut
llama	flame	*nutria*	otter
llanta	tire	*ocho*	eight
llave	key	*oler*	smell
llorar	cry	*olla*	pot
lluvia	rain	*oso*	bear
luna	moon	*oveja*	sheep
madriguera	den	*pájaro*	bird
maíz	corn	*palo*	stick
mancha	spot	*pan*	bread
manejar	drive	*pandear*	sag
manga	sleeve	*papá*	dad
manguera	hose	*papas francesas*	fries (French)
maní	peanuts	*papas fritas*	fries (French)
mano	hand	*paraguas*	umbrella
manto	robe	*pared*	wall
mantz	blanket	*parrilla*	grill
manzana	apple	*pastel*	pie
mapa	map	*patear*	kick
máquina	engine	*patinar*	skate
marco	frame	*patio*	yard
marrano	pig	*pato*	duck
más	plus	*payaso*	clown
máscara	mask	*peca*	freckle
mata	plant	*pegamento*	glue
mazorca	cob (corn)	*peine*	comb
menear	wag	*pelota*	ball
mermelada	jam	*peluca*	wig
mesa	table	*pensar*	think
mezclar	mix	*peonza*	top (toy)
mitón	mitten	*pera*	pear

perrito	pup	*saltamontes*	grasshopper
perro	dog	*saltar*	hop, jump
persiana	shade	*seis*	six
persona	person	*sentarse*	sit
pez	fish	*sierra*	saw
picar	sting	*siesta*	nap
picazón	itch	*siete*	seven
pico	beak, bill	*sigsag*	zigzag
piernas	legs	*silla*	chair
pies	feet	*sol*	sun
pingüino	penguin	*sollozar*	sob
pinzas	tweezers	*sombra*	shadow
pito	whistle	*sombrero*	hat
planta	plant	*sonrisa*	smile
plato	plate	*soplar*	blow
platos	dishes	*sorber*	sip
pluma	feather, pen	*sueño*	dream
pollito	chick	*sujetapapel*	clip
poste de luz	pole	*susurrar*	whisper
pozo	well	*suéter*	sweater
precio	price	*tachuela*	tack
pregunta	question	*taladro*	drill
premio	prize	*tallo*	stem
presa	dam	*talón*	heel
puente	bridge	*tambor*	drum
puerta	door, gate	*tapa*	lid
pulgada	inch	*tapete*	mat
pulgar	thumb	*taxi*	cab
pulpo	octopus	*taza*	cup
punto	dot	*techo*	roof
queso	cheese	*tela*	web
rana	frog	*tenedor*	fork
rasgar	rip	*termo*	thermos
rastro	rake	*termómetro*	thermometer
rata	rat	*tiburón*	shark
ratonera	trap (mouse)	*tijeras*	scissors
ratones	mice	*tina*	tub
regalo	present	*tinta*	ink
regazo	lap	*torcer*	twist
reina	queen	*torta*	cake
reloj	clock, watch	*tortuga*	turtle
resbaladero	slide	*tostada*	toast
resbalarse	slip	*tractor*	tractor
resultado	score	*trampolín*	trampoline
reventarse	pop	*trapeador*	mop
rey	king	*trece*	thirteen
rezar	pray	*treinta*	thirty
riel	track (train)	*tren*	train
robar	rob	*trenzas*	braids
roca	rock	*triángulo*	triangle
rogar	beg	*trineo*	sled, sleigh
rosa	rose	*triste*	sad
rueda	wheel	*trompo*	top (toy)
saco	coat	*tronco*	trunk

tronco de árbol	log, stump	*ventana*	window
tubo	pipe, tube	*verificar*	check
uva	grape	*vestido*	dress
vaca	cow	*viña*	vine
vaina	pod (pea)	*yelmo*	helmet
valentín	valentine	*yoyó*	yo-yo
varita	twig	*zapatilla*	slipper
vaso	glass	*zapato*	shoe
veinte	twenty	*ziper*	zipper
vela	candle, sail	*zoo*	zoológico
veleta	vane	*zoológico*	zoo
venado	deer	*zorrillo*	skunk
vendar los ojos	blindfold	*zorro*	fox

English to Spanish Translation

alligator	*caimán*	bride	*novia*
alphabet	*alfabeto*	bridge	*puente*
animals	*animales*	broom	*escoba*
ant	*hormiga*	brush	*cepillo*
apple	*manzana*	bug	*insecto*
ax	*hacha*	bun	*bollo*
bag (paper)	*bolsa (de papel)*	bus	*autobús*
bake	*hornear*	button	*botón*
ball	*bola, pelota*	cab	*taxi*
balloon	*globo*	cake	*torta*
bat (animal)	*murciélago*	can	*lata*
bat (ball)	*bate*	candle	*vela*
bead	*cuenta*	cane	*caña*
beak	*pico*	cap	*gorro*
bear	*oso*	cape	*capa*
bed	*cama*	car	*carro*
bee	*abeja*	cat	*gato*
beg	*rogar*	cave	*caverna*
bell	*campana*	chain	*cadena*
belt	*cinturón*	chair	*silla*
big	*grande*	check	*verificar*
bike	*bicicleta*	cheese	*queso*
bill	*pico*	cherries	*cerezas*
bird	*pájaro*	chest (toy)	*arca*
blanket	*cobija, manta*	chick	*pollito*
blindfold	*vendar los ojos*	chief	*jefe*
block	*bloque*	chimney	*chimenea*
blouse	*blusa*	chin	*barba*
blow	*soplar*	chop	*cortar*
boat	*barca*	clap	*aplaudir*
bone	*hueso*	claw	*garra*
book	*libro*	climb	*escalar*
box	*caja*	clip	*sujetapapel*
boy	*muchacho*	clock	*reloj*
bracelet	*brazalete*	clouds	*nubes*
braids	*trenzas*	clown	*payaso*
bread	*pan*	coat	*saco*
brick	*ladrillo*	cob (corn)	*elote, mazorca*

comb	*peine*	fish	*pez*
cone	*cono*	five	*cinco*
corn	*maíz*	flag	*bandera*
cot	*catre*	flake	*copo de nieve*
cow	*vaca*	flame	*llama*
crab	*cangrejo*	flashlight	*linterna*
crack	*hendedura*	flip	*lanzar*
crayon	*crayón, crayolas*	float	*flotar*
crib	*cuna*	flower	*flor*
crown	*corona*	flute	*flauta*
cry	*llorar*	fly	*mosca*
cube	*cubo*	football	*fútbol*
cup	*taza*	fork	*tenedor*
cut	*cortar*	four	*cuatro*
dad	*papá*	fox	*zorro*
dam	*presa*	frame	*marco*
deck	*cubierta*	freckle	*peca*
deer	*venado*	fries (French)	*papas fritas, papas francesas*
den	*madriguera*	frog	*rana*
desk	*escritorio*	fruit	*fruta*
dice	*dados*	game	*juego*
dig	*cavar*	gas	*gas*
dime	*moneda de a diez centavos*	gate	*puerta*
dishes	*platos*	ghost	*fantasma*
dive	*bucear*	giraffe	*jirafa*
dog	*perro*	girl	*muchacha*
doll	*muñeca*	glass	*vaso*
door	*puerta*	glasses	*lentes*
dot	*punto*	globe	*globo*
dragon	*dragón*	glove	*guante*
drawer	*cajón*	glue	*pegamento*
dream	*sueño*	goat	*cabra*
dress	*vestido*	grape	*uva*
drill	*taladro*	grass	*hierba*
drip	*gotear*	grasshopper	*saltamontes*
drive	*manejar*	grill	*parrilla*
drum	*tambor*	groceries	*comestibles*
duck	*pato*	guitar	*guitarra*
dump	*descargar*	gum	*chicle*
egg	*huevo*	ham	*jamón*
eight	*ocho*	hand	*mano*
elbow	*codo*	happy	*feliz*
elephant	*elefante*	harp	*arpa*
elevator	*ascensor*	hat	*sombrero*
elf	*duende*	hay	*heno*
engine	*máquina*	heart	*corazón*
Eskimo	*esquimal*	heel	*talón*
fan	*abanico*	helmet	*yelmo*
fat	*gordo*	hen	*gallina*
feather	*pluma*	hill	*colina*
feet	*pies*	hit	*golpe*
fence	*cerca*	hive	*colmena*
fin	*aleta*	hole	*agujero*
fire	*fuego*	hook	*anzuelo*

hop	*saltar*	mane	*crin*
horn	*cuerno*	map	*mapa*
horse	*caballo*	mask	*máscara*
hose	*manguera*	mat	*tapete*
hot	*caliente*	match	*fósforo*
house	*casa*	melt	*derretir*
hug	*abrazo*	men	*hombres*
hump	*joroba*	mice	*ratones*
hut	*choza*	milk	*leche*
igloo	*iglú*	mitten	*mitón*
ill	*enfermo*	mix	*mezclar*
inch	*pulgada*	moon	*luna*
ink	*tinta*	mop	*trapeador*
insects	*insectos*	mountains	*montañas*
instruments	*instrumentos*	mud	*fango*
itch	*picazón*	mug	*jarra*
jacket	*chaqueta*	mule	*mula*
jacks	*cantillos*	nail	*clavo*
jam	*mermelada*	nap	*siesta*
jar	*frasco*	neck	*cuello*
jeep	*jeep*	needle	*aguja*
jet	*avión*	nest	*nido*
jog	*correr*	net	*neto*
jug	*jarro*	nickel	*níquel*
juggle	*hacer malabarismos*	nine	*nueve*
jump	*saltar*	nose	*nariz*
jumprope	*cuerda*	note	*nota*
kangaroo	*canguro*	nut	*nuez*
key	*llave*	octopus	*pulpo*
kick	*patear*	olives	*aceitunas*
king	*rey*	otter	*nutria*
kit	*botiquín*	ox	*buey*
kitchen	*cocina*	pad	*bloc de papel*
kite	*cometa*	pail	*cubo*
kitten	*gatito*	pan	*cacerola*
knife	*cuchillo*	pat	*dar golpecillos*
knight	*caballero*	peach	*durazno*
lake	*lago*	peanuts	*maní*
lamp	*lámpara*	pear	*pera*
lap	*regazo*	peas	*guisantes*
leaf	*hoja*	peg	*clavija*
legs	*piernas*	pen	*pluma*
lemon	*limón*	penguin	*pingüino*
letter	*carta*	person	*persona*
letters	*letras*	pet	*acariciar*
lid	*tapa*	pie	*pastel*
lift	*levantar*	pig	*cerdo, cochino, marrano*
line	*línea*	pin	*alfiler*
lion	*león*	pipe	*tubo*
lips	*labios*	plaid	*escocesa*
lock	*cerradura*	plane	*avión*
log	*tronco de árbol*	plant	*planta, mata*
mad	*furioso*	plate	*plato*
man	*hombre*	pliers	*alicates*

plug	*enchufe*	sheep	*oveja*
plum	*ciruela*	shelf	*estante*
plus	*más*	shell	*concha*
pod (pea)	*vaina*	ship	*barco*
pole	*poste de luz*	shirt	*camisa*
pop	*reventarse*	shoe	*zapato*
pot	*olla*	shop	*hacer compras*
pray	*rezar*	sick	*enfermo*
present	*regalo*	sink	*fregadero*
pretzel	*(none available)*	sip	*sorber*
price	*precio*	sit	*sentarse*
prize	*premio*	six	*seis*
pumpkin	*calabaza*	skate	*patinar*
pup	*perrito*	skeleton	*esqueleto*
purse	*bolsa*	skip	*brincar*
quack	*graznido*	skirt	*falda*
quarter	*cuarto*	skis	*esquís*
queen	*reina*	skull	*cráneo*
question	*pregunta*	skunk	*zorrillo*
quiet	*callarse*	led	*trineo*
rain	*lluvia*	sleep	*dormir*
rake	*rastro*	sleeve	*manga*
ran	*corrió*	sleigh	*trineo*
rat	*rata*	slide	*resbaladero*
ring	*anillo*	sling	*cabestrillo*
rip	*rasgar*	slip	*resbalarse*
road	*camino*	slipper	*zapatilla*
rob	*robar*	smash	*hacer pedazos*
robe	*manto*	smell	*oler*
rock	*roca*	smile	*sonrisa*
roof	*techo*	smoke	*humo*
rope	*cuerda*	snail	*caracol*
rose	*rosa*	snake	*culebra*
rug	*alfombra*	sneeze	*estornudar*
run	*corre (correr)*	snow	*nevar*
sad	*triste*	snowman	*hombre de nieve*
sag	*pandear*	soap	*jabón*
sail	*vela*	sob	*sollozar*
sandwich	*emparedado*	sock	*calcetín*
saw	*sierra*	spear	*lanza*
scale	*báscula*	spider	*araña*
scarf	*bufanda*	spill	*derramar*
school	*escuela*	spin	*hilar*
scissors	*tijeras*	sponge	*esponja*
scooter	*motoneta*	spool	*carrete*
score	*resultado*	spoon	*cuchara*
scout	*explorador*	spot	*mancha*
seal	*foca*	stairs	*escalera*
seven	*siete*	stamp	*estampilla*
shade	*persiana*	star	*estrella*
shadow	*sombra*	stem	*tallo*
shark	*tiburón*	stick	*palo*
shave	*afeitarse*	sting	*picar*
shed	*cobertizo*	stir	*mover*

stool	*banquillo*	twig	*varita*
stop	*alto*	twins	*gemelos*
stove	*estufa*	twirl	*dar vueltas al batón*
stump	*tronco de árbol*	twist	*torcer*
sun	*sol*	two	*dos*
swan	*cisne*	umbrella	*paraguas*
sweater	*suéter*	umpire	*árbitro*
sweep	*barrer*	under	*abajo*
swim	*nadar*	up	*arriba*
swing	*columpio*	upside down	*al revés*
switch (light)	*apagador*	vacuum	*aspiradora*
table	*mesa*	valentine	*valentín*
tack	*tachuela*	van	*furgoneta*
tag	*etiqueta*	vane	*veleta*
tall	*alto*	vase	*florero*
tape	*cinta*	vest	*chaleco*
teeth	*dientes*	vine	*viña*
ten	*diez*	wag	*menear*
tent	*carpa*	wagon	*carreta*
thermometer	*termómetro*	wall	*pared*
thermos	*termo*	watch	*reloj*
thimble	*dedal*	wave	*agitar la mano*
think	*pensar*	web	*tela*
thirteen	*trece*	well	*pozo*
thirty	*treinta*	wet	*mojado*
thorn	*espina*	whale	*ballena*
thumb	*pulgar*	wheel	*rueda*
tie	*corbata*	wheelbarrow	*carretilla*
tire	*llanta*	whip	*látigo*
toast	*tostada*	whiskers	*bigotes*
toes	*dedos del pie*	whisper	*susurrar*
top (toy)	*peonza, trompo*	whistle	*pito*
track (train)	*riel*	wig	*peluca*
tractor	*tractor*	win	*ganar*
train	*tren*	window	*ventana*
trampoline	*trampolín*	wing	*ala*
trap (mouse)	*ratonera*	wink	*guiño*
tray	*bandeja*	witch	*bruja*
tree	*árbol*	worm	*gusano*
triangle	*triángulo*	yard	*patio*
truck	*camión*	yarn	*hilo*
trunk	*tronco*	yawn	*bostezo*
tub	*tina*	yell	*grito*
tube	*tubo*	yo-yo	*yoyó*
tug	*jalar*	zebra	*cebra*
turtle	*tortuga*	zero	*cero*
tusk	*colmillo*	zigzag	*sigsag*
tweezers	*pinzas*	zip	*cerrar el cierre*
twelve	*doce*	zipcode	*apartado postal*
twenty	*veinte*	zipper	*cierre, zíper*

Spanish–English Sort 1: Initial Consonants (*m, s, b*)

Mm	Ss	Bb

Spanish–English Sort 2: Initial Consonants (*t*, *n*, *p*, and *g*)

Tt	Nn	Pp
Gg		
9		

Spanish–English Sort 3: Initial Consonants (*l*, *c*, *f*, and *d*)

Ll	**Cc**	**Ff**
Dd		
† G E s R c e Y w v k N A o		

Appendix E

Templates and Other Materials

Be a Winner Star Card

Be a Winner Star Card	
1.	1.
2.	2.
3.	3.
4.	4.
5.	5.
6.	6.
7.	7.
8.	8.
9.	9.
10.	10.
11.	11.
12.	12.
13.	13.
14.	14.
15.	15.
Game 1: ☆ Winner _____ Points ☆ ☆ Winner _____ Points ☆ ☆ ☆ Winner _____ Points	**Game 2:** ☆ Winner _____ Points ☆ ☆ Winner _____ Points ☆ ☆ ☆ Winner _____ Points

Additional Pictures for Use with Letter Name Sorts 66 and 68–72
(p. 1 of 2)

Sort 66 Extras: Final *ll*   Sort 68 Extras: Blends with *t*   Sort 69 Extras: Final *mp, nd, nt*

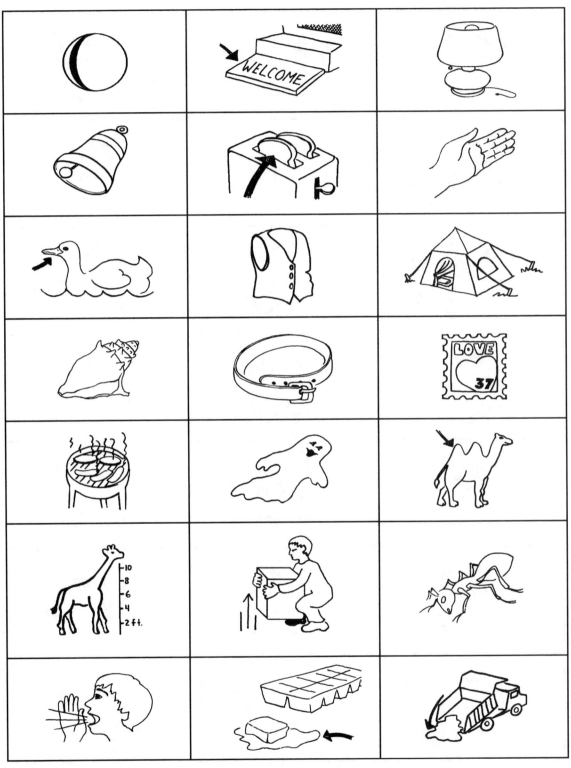

Additional Pictures for Use with Letter Name Sorts 66 and 68–72
(p. 2 of 2)

Sort 70 Extras: Final *n*, *g*, *ng*, and *nk*   Sort 71 Extras: Short Vowels   Sort 72 Extras: Short Vowels

Category Labels

Short ă	Long ā	R-controlled
Short ĕ	Long ē	Hard g
Short ĭ	Long ī	Soft g
Short ŏ	Long ō	Hard c
Short ŭ	Long ū	Soft c
Short	Long	Other
No change	E-drop	

Oddball Category Labels

Oddballs	What's up with that?	Out of Sorts
Miscellaneous	Puzzlers	Think about It
The Great Dismal Swamp	Tricksters	Just Plain Different
Cuckoos	Birds of a Different Feather	Misfits
Eccentrics	Mavericks	Wait and See
Different	Nonconformists	Odds and Ends
Other	Sooner or Later	Curiosities

Blank Spello Card

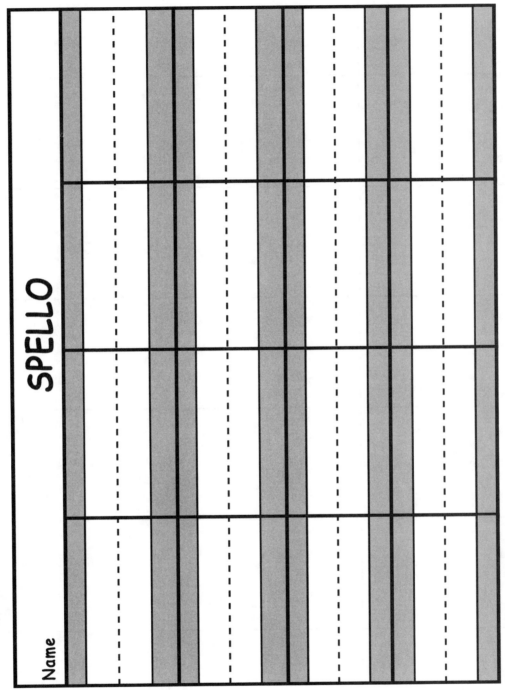

Name

SPELLO

Blank Word Card Template for 21 Words

Blank Word Card Template for 24 Words

Homophone Rummy Card Template

References

Beck, I., McKeown, M., & Kucan, L. (2002). *Bringing words to life: Robust vocabulary instructions.* New York: Guilford Press.

Block, C. C. & Mangieri, J. N. (2003). *Exemplary literacy teachers: Promoting success for all children in grades K–5.* New York: Guilford Press.

Cary, S. (2000). *Working with second language learners: Answers to teachers' top ten questions.* Portsmouth, NH: Heinemann.

Coles, G. (1998). *Reading lessons: The debate over literacy.* New York: Hill & Wang.

Ganske, K. (1995). *Kindergarten inventory of developmental spelling—KIDS.* Unpublished manuscript.

Ganske, K. (2000). *Word journeys: Assessment-guided phonics, spelling, and vocabulary instruction.* New York: Guilford Press.

Ganske, K., Monroe, J. K., & Strickland, D. S. (2003). Questions teachers ask about struggling readers and writers. *The Reading Teacher, 57*(2), 118–128.

Goldstein, B. (2001). Transcription of Spanish and Spanish-influenced English. *Communication Disorders Quarterly, 23*(1), 54–60.

Helman, L. A. (2004). Building on the sound system of Spanish: Insights from the alphabetic spellings of English-language learners. *Reading Teacher, 57,* 452–460.

Krashen, S. (1994). The pleasure hypothesis. In J. Alatis (Ed.), *Georgetown University round table on languages and linguistics* (pp. 299–322). Washington, DC: Georgetown University Press.

McCarrier, A., Pinnell, G. S., & Fountas, I. C. (2000). *Interactive writing: How language & literacy come together, K–2.* Portsmouth, NH: Heinemann.

McDermott, P. C., & Rothenberg, J. J. (1999, April 19–23). *Teaching in high poverty, urban schools: Learning from practitioners and students.* Paper presented at the Annual Meeting of the American Educational Research Association, Montreal, Quebec.

Nash, R. (1977). *Comparing English and Spanish phonology and orthography.* New York: Regents.

National Reading Panel. (2000). *Teaching children to read.* Washington, DC: National Institute of Child Health and Human Development.

Rasinski, T. V., & Zimmerman, B. S. (2001). *Phonics poetry: Teaching word families.* Boston: Allyn & Bacon.

Ruddell, R. B., & Unrau, N. J. (2004). Reading as a meaning construction process: The reader, the text, and the teacher. In R. B. Ruddell & N. J. Unrau (Eds.), *Theoretical models and processes of reading* (pp. 1462–1521). Newark, DE: International Reading Association.

Snow, C. E., Burns, S., & Griffin, P. (1998). *Preventing reading difficulties in young children.* Washington, DC: National Academy Press.

Strickland, D. S., Ganske, K., & Monroe, J. K. (2002). *Supporting struggling readers and writers: Strategies for classroom intervention 3–6.* Portland, ME: Stenhouse, Newark, DE: International Reading Association.

Vygotsky, L. (1978). *Mind in society.* Cambridge, MA: Harvard University Press.

Children's Literature

Ada, A. F. (1997). *Gathering the sun: An alphabet in Spanish and English*. New York: Lothrop, Lee & Shepard.

Adams, P. (1988). *There was an old lady who swallowed a fly*. China: Child's Play International.

Ahlberg, J., & Ahlberg, A. (1978). *Each peach pear plum*. New York: Viking.

Andersen, H. C. (1999). In J. Pinkney (Illustrator), *The ugly duckling*. New York: HarperCollins.

Angelou, M. (2003). Life doesn't frighten me. In G. Hale (Ed.), *An illustrated treasury of read-aloud poems for young people*. New York: Black Dog & Leventhal.

Arnold, T. (1997). *Parts*. New York: Puffin.

Asch, F. (1988). Sunflakes. In B. S. de Regniers (Ed.), *Sing a song of popcorn: Every child's book of poems*. New York: Scholastic.

Aylesworth, J. (1991). *Old black fly*. New York: Holt.

Bang, M. (1999). *When Sophie gets angry-Really, really angry*. New York: Blue Sky Press.

Bayer, J. (1984). *A: My name is Alice*. New York: Trumpet Club.

Bell, R. (2000). *Farm animals*. Portsmouth, NH: Heinemann.

Belloc, H. (2003). The lion. In G. Hale (Ed.), *An illustrated treasury of read-aloud poems for young people*. New York: Black Dog & Leventhal.

Bennett, R. (1988). From *The witch of Willowby Wood*. In B. S. de Regniers (Ed.), *Sing a song of popcorn: Every child's book of poems*. New York: Scholastic.

Bennett, R. (1988). Necks. In B. S. de Regniers (Ed.), *Sing a song of popcorn: Every child's book of poems*. New York: Scholastic.

Black, S. (1999). *Plenty of penguins*. New York: Scholastic.

Boiko, C. (1998). The seal. In R. Alexander (Ed.), *Poetry place anthology*. New York: Scholastic.

Brett, J. (1989). *The mitten*. New York: Putnam.

Brown, M. W. (2003). *The fierce yellow pumpkin*. New York: HarperCollins.

Buzzeo, T. (2003). *Dawdle duckling*. New York: Dial Books for Young Readers.

Cannon, J. (1993). *Stellaluna*. San Diego: Harcourt, Brace.

Cannon, J. (1997). *Verdi*. San Diego: Harcourt Brace.

Carle, E. (2000). *Does a kangaroo have a mother, too?* New York: HarperCollins.

Christelow, E. (1999). *Five little monkeys jumping on a bed*. Boston: Clarion.

Chute, M. (1988). Dogs. In B. S. de Regniers (Ed.), *Sing a song of popcorn: Every child's book of poems*. New York: Scholastic.

Ciardi, J. (1991). The early bird. In B. Lansky (Ed.), *Kids pick the funniest poems: Poems that make kids laugh*. New York: Meadowbrook Press.

Clements, A. (1997). *Double trouble in Walla Walla*. Brookfield, CT: Millbrook Press.

Coatsworth, E. (1995). Swift things are beautiful. In E. H. Sword (Ed.), *A child's anthology of poetry*. Hopewell, NJ: Ecco Press.

Coerr, E. (1986). *The Josephina story quilt.* New York: HarperCollins.

Cowley, J. (2003). *Mrs. Wishy-Washy's farm.* New York: Philomel.

Crandell, R. (2002). *The hands of the Maya: Villagers at work and play.* New York: Henry Holt.

Cronin, D. (2000). *Click, clack, and moo: Cows that type.* New York: Scholastic.

Cronin, D. (2002). *Giggle, giggle, quack.* New York: Simon & Schuster Books for Young Readers.

Davis, A. (1997). *The enormous potato.* Tonawanda, NY: Kids Can Press.

Day, E. (2003). *I'm good at . . . .* Portsmouth, NH: Heinemann.

Degan, B. (1983). *Jamberry.* New York: Harper.

dePaola, T. (1985). *Tomie dePaola's Mother Goose.* New York: Putnam's Sons.

Dodds, B. (1989). *Jamberry.* New York: Harper.

Douglas, L. A. (2003). The hen. In G. Hale (Ed.), *An illustrated treasury of read-aloud poems for young people.* New York: Black Dog & Leventhal.

Driscoll, L. (1997). *The bravest cat! The true story of Scarlett.* New York: Scholastic.

Dubowski, C. E. (1998). *Shark attack.* New York: DK.

Duranat, P. (2005). *Sniffles, sneezes, hiccups, and coughs.* New York: DK.

Durston, G. R. (1998). The hippopotamus. In R. Alexander (Ed.), *Poetry place anthology.* New York: Scholastic.

Dyer, J. (2002). *Little Brown Bear won't take a nap!* Boston: Little, Brown.

Editors of *Time for Kids.* (2005). *Planets! Discover our solar system.* New York: HarperTrophy.

Editors of *Time for Kids.* (2005). *Snakes!* New York: HarperTrophy.

Egan, B. (1996). *"Pop" pops the popcorn* [Ready Readers series]. Parsippany, NJ: Modern Curriculum Press.

Ehlert, L. (1989). *Eating the alphabet: Fruits and vegetables from A to Z.* San Diego: Harcourt.

Ehlert, L. (1993). *Nuts to you.* San Diego: Harcourt Children's.

Ellingwood, L. B. (1998). At the zoo. In R. Alexander (Ed.), *Poetry place anthology.* New York: Scholastic.

Fleming, D. (2002). *Alphabet under construction.* New York: Henry Holt.

Fredericks, A. D. (2000). *Slugs.* Minneapolis: Learner.

Funk, A. L. (1998). My dream. In R. Alexander (Ed.), *Poetry place anthology.* New York: Scholastic.

Fyleman, R. (1988). Mice. In B. S. de Regniers (Ed.), *Sing a song of popcorn: Every child's book of poems.* New York: Scholastic.

Galdone, P. (1985). *The little red hen.* Boston: Clarion.

Glaser, S. (2005). *The big race.* New York: Hyperion.

Gordon, J. R. (1991). *Six sleepy sheep.* New York: Puffin.

Gregorich, B. (1996). *Jog, Frog, jog* [Start to Read series]. Grand Haven, MI: School Zone.

Grover, E. O. (Ed.). (1997). *Mother Goose* (The Original Volland Edition). New York: Derrydale.

Guarino, D. (1989). *Is your mamma a llama?* New York: Scholastic.

Hall, K. (1995). *A bad, bad day.* New York: Scholastic.

Hall, K. (2005). *Turkey riddles.* New York: Puffin

Hartung, S. K. (2002). *One leaf rides the wind.* New York: Viking.

Hays, A. J. (2004). *Here comes silent e!* New York: Random House.

Henkes, K. (1996). *Lilly's purple purse.* New York: Greenwillow.

Hobby, H. (1997). *Toot and Puddle.* Boston: Little Brown.

Holub, J. (2004). *Why do snakes hiss?* New York: Puffin.

Howland, N. (2000). *ABC drive!* Boston: Clarion.

Hubbell, P. (1998). Our washing machine. In R. Alexander (Ed.), *Poetry place anthology.* New York: Scholastic.

Hughes, L. (1994). Dreams. In *The dream keeper and other poems.* New York: Scholastic.

Hurwitz, J. (1997). *Helen Keller: Courage in the dark.* New York: Random House.

Inkpen, M. (2000). *Kipper's A to Z: An alphabet adventure.* San Diego, CA: Harcourt.

Jacobson, E. (1998). The spider. In R. Alexander (Ed.). *Poetry place anthology.* New York: Scholastic.

Johnson, S. (1995). *Alphabet city.* New York: Viking.

Jorgensen, G. (1988). *Crocodile beat.* New York: Scholastic.

Kenah, K. (2004). *Destruction earth.* Columbus, OH: Children's.

Kennedy, X. J. (1992). Paperclips. In B. S. Goldstein (Ed.), *Inner chimes: Poems on poetry.* Honesdale, PA: Boyds Mills Press.

Killon, B. (1998). Think of it. In R. Alexander (Ed.), *Poetry place anthology.* New York: Scholastic.

Kirk, D. (1998). *Miss Spider's ABC.* New York: Scholastic Press.

Krosoczka, J. J. (2002). *Baghead.* New York: Knopf.

Kulling, M. (2000). *Escape north!: The story of Harriet Tubman.* New York: Random House.

Kuskin, K. (1990). *Road and more.* New York: Harper.

Lane, L. (2003). *Snuggle mountain.* New York: Clarion.

Lansky, B. (1991). How I quit sucking my thumb. In B. Lansky (Ed.), *Kids pick the funniest poems: Poems that make kids laugh.* New York: Meadowbrook Press.

Lansky, B. (1993). *The new adventures of Mother Goose: Gentle rhymes for happy times.* New York: New Meadowbrook Press.

Larson, B. (2001). *Itchy's alphabet book.* Kelowna, BC: ABB Creations.

Lawson, J. (2002). *Audrey and Barbara.* New York: Atheneum Books for Young Readers.

London, J. (2003). *Giving thanks.* Cambridge, MA: Candlewick Press.

Martin, B., Jr. (1971). *"Fire! Fire!" said Mrs. McGuire.* San Diego, CA: Harcourt.

Mauchan, W. L. (1998). Quiet. In R. Alexander (Ed.), *Poetry place anthology.* New York: Scholastic.

Maynard, C. (1998). *Days of the knights: A tale of castles and battles.* New York: DK.

Meisel, P. (2003). *Zara's hats.* New York: Dutton's Children's.

McCord, D. (1969). I want you to meet. In B. S. de Regniers (Ed.), *Poems children will sit still for: A selection for the primary grades.* New York: Macmillan.

McCord, D. (1996). Every time I climb a tree. In B. E. Cullinan (Ed.), *A jar of tiny stars: Poems by NCTE award-winning poets.* Honesdale, PA: Boyds Mills Press.

Merriam, E. (1969). Weather. In B. S. de Regniers (Ed.), *Poems children will sit still for: A selection for the primary grades.* New York: Macmillan.

McKinney, J. B. (1998). Twins. In R. Alexander (Ed.), *Poetry place anthology.* New York: Scholastic.

Merriam, E. (1998). A cliché. In R. Alexander (Ed.), *Poetry place anthology.* New York: Scholastic.

Metropolitan Museum of Art. (2002). *Museum ABC.* New York: Little, Brown.

Miles, E. (2003). *Animal parts.* Portsmouth, NH: Heinemann.

Miles, E. (2003). *Legs and feet.* Portsmouth, NH: Heinemann.

Miles, E. (2003). *Tales.* Portsmouth, NH: Heinemann.

Milne, A. A. (1988). The more it snows. In B. S. de Regniers (Ed.), *Sing a song of popcorn: Every child's book of poems.* New York: Scholastic.

Milton, J. (1992). *Wild, wild, wolves.* New York: Random House.

Monks, L. (2004). *Aaaarrgghh! Spider!* Boston: Houghton Mifflin.

Morgan, M. (2000). *I looked through my window* Barrington, IL: Rigby.

Murphy, F. (2001). *Ben Franklin and the magic squares.* New York: Random House.

Nash, O. (1988). The camel. In B. S. de Regniers (Ed.), *Sing a song of popcorn: Every child's book of poems.* New York: Scholastic.

Palmer, T. H. (1995). Try, try again. In E. H. Sword (Ed.), *A child's anthology of poetry.* Hopewell, NJ: Ecco Press.

Parks, R. (1997). *I am Rosa Parks.* New York: Penguin.

Peck, J. (1998). *The giant carrot.* New York: Dial.

Penner, F. (2005). *The cat came back.* New Milford, CT: Roaring Book Press.

Peterson, J. (1993). *The Littles*. New York: Scholastic.

Pfeffer, W. (1997). *Wiggling worms at work*. New York: HarperTrophy.

Plath, S. (1995). From *The bed book*. In E. H. Sword (Ed.), *A child's anthology of poetry*. Hopewell, NJ: Ecco Press.

Prelutsky, J. (1982). *The baby uggs are hatching*. New York: Mulberry.

Prelutsky, J. (1984). Drumpp the grump. In *The new kid on the block*. New York: Scholastic.

Prelutsky, J. (1984). Floradora Doe. In *The new kid on the block*. New York: Scholastic.

Prelutsky, J. (1984). I wonder why Dad is so thoroughly mad. In *The new kid on the block*. New York: Scholastic.

Prelutsky, J. (1984). Jellyfish stew. In *The new kid on the block*. New York: Scholastic.

Prelutsky, J. (1984). Louder than a clap of thunder! In *The new kid on the block*. New York: Scholastic.

Prelutsky, J. (1984). My mother says I'm sickening. In *The new kid on the block*. New York: Scholastic.

Prelutsky, J. (1984). Nine mice. In *The new kid on the block*. New York: Scholastic.

Prelutsky, J. (1984). We heard Wally wail. In *The new kid on the block*. New York: Scholastic.

Prelutsky, J. (1984). What nerve you've got, Minerva Mott! In *The new kid on the block*. New York: Scholastic.

Prelutsky, J. (1984). When Tillie ate the chili. In *The new kid on the block*. New York: Scholastic.

Prelutsky, J. (1990). Last night I dreamed of chickens. In *Something big has been here*. New York: Scholastic.

Prelutsky, J. (1990). Something big has been here. In *Something big has been here*. New York: Scholastic.

Reeves, J. (1969). W. In B. S. de Regniers (Ed.), *Poems children will sit still for: A selection for the primary grades*. New York: Macmillan.

Richstone, M. (1998). Tug-of-war. In R. Alexander (Ed.), *Poetry place anthology*. New York: Scholastic.

Rockwell, A. (2005). *Honey in a hive*. New York: HarperTrophy.

Roop, P., & Roop, C. (1987). *Keep the lights burning, Abbie*. Minneapolis: Lerner.

Rosenbloom, J. (1976). *Biggest riddle book in the world*. Sterling, CO: Sterling.

Rossetti, C. (1988). Clouds. In B. S. de Regniers (Ed.), *Sing a song of popcorn: Every child's book of poems*. New York: Scholastic.

Rossetti, C. (2003) Caterpillar. In G. Hale (Ed.), *An illustrated treasury of read-aloud poems for young people*. New York: Black Dog & Leventhal.

Rossetti, C. (2003). What is pink? In G. Hale (Ed.), *An illustrated treasury of read-aloud poems for young people*. New York: Black Dog & Leventhal.

Sandburg, C. (1995). Fog. In E. H. Sword (Ed.), *A child's anthology or poetry*. Hopewell, NJ: Ecco Press.

Schaefer, L. M. (2003). *It's my body*. Portsmouth, NH: Heinemann.

Seuss, Dr. (1963). *Hop on pop*. New York: Random House.

Seuss, Dr. (1985). *The cat in the hat*. New York: Random House.

Shannon, D. (2002). *Duck on a bike*. New York: Blue Sky Press.

Sharmat, M. (1989). *Gregory, the terrible eater*. New York: Scholastic.

Shulman, L. (2002). *Old MacDonald had a woodshop*. New York: Putnam's Sons.

Sierra, J. (1998). Penguins' first swim. In *Antarctic antics: A book of penguin poems*. San Diego, CA: Harcourt Brace.

Silverstein, S. (1964). *The giving tree*. New York: HarperCollins.

Silverstein, S. (1995). Sick. In E. H. Sword (Ed.), *A child's anthology of poetry*. Hopewell, NJ: Ecco Press.

Silverstein, S. (2005). *Runny Babbit*. New York: HarperCollins.

Simmie, L. (1991). Bug. In B. Lansky (Ed.), *Kids pick the funniest poems: Poems that make kids laugh*. New York: Meadowbrook Press.

Simon, S. (2005). *Bridges*. San Francisco: Chronicle Books.

Slate, J. (1996). *Miss Bindergarten gets ready for kindergarten*. New York: Dutton Children's Books.

Slepian, J., & Seidler, A. (2001). *The hungry thing.* New York: Scholastic.

Smith, D. J. (2002). *If the world were a village: A book about the world's people.* Tonawanda, NY: Kids Can Press.

Smith, W. J. (1998). The toaster. In R. Alexander (Ed.), *Poetry place anthology.* New York: Scholastic.

Spence, R., & Spence, A. (1999). *Clickety clack.* New York: Puffin.

Stanford, N. *The bravest dog ever: The true story of Balto.* New York: Random House.

Stevenson, R. L. (2003). My shadow. In G. Hale (Ed.), *An illustrated treasury of read-aloud poems for young people.* New York: Black Dog & Leventhal.

Stevenson, R. L. (1995). The swing. In E. H. Sword (Ed.), *A child's anthology of poetry.* Hopewell, NJ: Ecco Press.

Tarpley, N. A. (2002). *Bippity bop barbershop.* Boston: Little Brown & Company.

Taylor, J. (2003). The star. In G. Hale (Ed.), *An illustrated treasury of read-aloud poems for young people.* New York: Black Dog & Leventhal.

Taback, S. (2000). *Joseph had a little overcoat.* New York: Viking.

Terban, M. (1998). *Scholastic dictionary of idioms.* New York: Scholastic.

Thomas, I., & Whitehouse, P. (2005). *The colors we eat.* Portsmouth, NH: Heinemann.

Thompson, L. (2003). *Little Quack.* New York: Simon & Schuster Books for Young Readers.

Tolstoy, A., & Goto, S. (Illustrator). (2003). *The enormous turnip.* San Diego, CA: Harcourt.

Uegaki, C. (2003). *Suki's kimono.* Tonawanda, NY: Kids Can Press.

U'Ren, A. (2003). *Mary Smith.* New York: Farrar, Straus, and Giroux.

Van Dusen, C. (2003). *A camping spree with Mr. Magee.* San Francisco: Chronicle Books.

Viorst, J. (1987). *The tenth good thing about Barney.* New York: Aladdin.

Watts, M. (1998). Freckles. In R. Alexander (Ed.), *Poetry place anthology.* New York: Scholastic.

Welte, L. A. (1998). Start of a storm. In R. Alexander (Ed.), *Poetry place anthology.* New York: Scholastic

West, C. (1991). Norman Norton's nostril's. In B. Lansky (Ed.), *Kids pick the funniest poems: Poems that make kids laugh.* New York: Meadowbrook Press.

Whitehouse, P. (2002). *Plants.* Portsmouth, NH: Heinemann.

Whitehouse, P. (2003). *Zoo animals.* Portsmouth, NH: Heinemann.

Wilson, K. (2002). *Bears snores on.* New York: Margaret K. McElderry Books.

Wood, A. (1984). *The napping house.* Orlando, FL: Harcourt Brace.

Wood, A. (2001). *The little penguin.* New York: Dutton Children's.

Wulffson, D. L. (2003). *Abracadabra to zombie: More than 300 wacky word origins.* New York: Dutton Juvenile.

Index of Words and Pictures Used in the Sorts

Note. Italics for page numbers indicate that the entry appears on a sort template; *p* = the word appears as a picture only; *pl* = the word appears as a picture and one or more letters (but no word); *pw* = both a picture and the word appear.